SHIFTING LANGUAGES

INTERACTION AND IDENTITY IN JAVANESE INDONESIA

Indonesian is the national language of a vast, plural nation-state, the world's fourth-largest country with a population of more than 200 million people. Local minority languages are rapidly being displaced by Indonesian, and it is predicted that by 2020 roughly 70 percent of the projected population of 260 million will be Indonesian-speaking. This growth, unprecedented in the developing world, is largely due to the forceful presence of state institutions which use, promote, and disseminate a language first introduced by the Dutch colonial rulers. Joseph Errington's third book on language in Indonesia is a detailed analysis of "shifting languages" in two small Javanese communities. A key figure in this area of research, he examines changing conversational practices in relation to questions of ethnicity, nationalism, and political culture. The theoretical observations have implications beyond the two villages for other parts of Indonesia, Southeast Asia, and for the developing world in general.

JOSEPH ERRINGTON is the author of two books on language and social change in Java, and numerous articles. He is Professor of Anthropology and East Asian Languages and Literatures at Yale University.

STUDIES IN THE SOCIAL AND
CULTURAL FOUNDATIONS OF LANGUAGE NO. 19

This series represents the concerns of scholars in the anthropology and sociology of language, sociolinguistics, and socially and culturally informed psycholinguistics. Its aim is to develop theoretical perspectives on the social and cultural character of language by methodological and empirical emphasis on the occurrence of language in its communicative and interactional settings, on the socio-culturally grounded "meanings" and "functions" of linguistic forms, and on the social scientific study of language use across cultures. Exploring the essentially ethnographic nature of linguistic data and language practices, the approaches may be synchronic or diachronic, normative or variational, spontaneously occurring or induced by an investigator. The books in the series make substantive and theoretical contributions to debates over the nature of language's embeddedness in social and cultural life, and over the role of language in sociocultural systems.

Editors

Judith Irvine   *Brandeis University*
Bambi Schieffelin   *New York University*

Editorial board

Marjorie Harness Goodwin   *University of South Carolina*
Joel Kuipers   *George Washington University*
Don Kulick   *Stockholms Universitet*
John Lucy   *University of Chicago*
Elinor Ochs   *University of California, Los Angeles*
Michael Silverstein   *University of Chicago*

A list of books in the series can be found after the index.

SHIFTING LANGUAGES

INTERACTION AND IDENTITY IN JAVANESE INDONESIA

J. JOSEPH ERRINGTON

PUBLISHED BY THE PRESS SYNDICATE OF THE UNIVERSITY OF CAMBRIDGE
The Pitt Building, Trumpington Street, Cambridge CB2 1RP, United Kingdom

CAMBRIDGE UNIVERSITY PRESS
The Edinburgh Building, Cambridge, CB2 2RU, United Kingdom
http://www.cup.cam.ac.uk
40 West 20th Street, New York, NY 10011–4211, USA   http://www.cup.org
10 Stamford Road, Oakleigh, Melbourne 3166, Australia

© J. Joseph Errington 1998

This book is in copyright. Subject to statutory exception and to the provisions of relevant collective licensing agreements, no reproduction of any part may take place without the written permission of Cambridge University Press.

First published 1998

Printed in the United Kingdom at the University Press, Cambridge

Typeset in 10/12pt Times   CE

A catalogue record for this book is available from the British Library

Library of Congress Cataloging in Publication data
Errington, James Joseph, 1951–
Shifting languages : interaction and identity in Javanese Indonesia / J. Joseph Errington;
[editors, Judith Irvine, Bambi Schieffelin].
p. cm. – (Studies in the social and cultural foundations of language)
ISBN 0 521 63267 6 (hardbound). – ISBN 0 521 63448 2 (pbk.)
1. Javanese language – Social aspects.   2. Speech and social status – Indonesia – Java.
3. Java (Indonesia) – Social life and customs.   4. Linguistic change.
I. Irvine, Judith T.   II. Schieffelin, Bambi B.   III. Title.   IV. Series.
PL5161.E778   1998
499'.222 – dc21   98–20577   CIP

ISBN 0 521 63267 6 hardback
ISBN 0 521 63448 2 paperback

CONTENTS

List of figures, maps, and tables	*page*	viii
Acknowledgements		ix
Preface: suggestions for use		xi
Note on orthography and transcription		xiii
1 Introduction		1
2 A city, two hamlets, and the state		16
3 Speech styles, hierarchy, and community		35
4 National development, national language		51
5 Public language and authority		65
6 Interactional and referential identities		82
7 Language contact and language salad		98
8 Speech modeling		117
9 Shifting styles and modeling thought		139
10 Javanese–Indonesian code switching		155
11 Shifting perspectives		184
Notes		195
Works cited		202
Index of Javanese and Indonesian words		210
General index		213

FIGURES, MAPS, AND TABLES

Figures

3.1	Generic markedness relations between speech styles	*page* 39
3.2	Structural relations between styles of *básá*	40
3.3	Traditional exemplary repertoire/use	41
3.4	Contemporary conservative elite Javanese use	44
3.5	Contemporary urban/village usage	46

Maps

1	The Indonesian archipelago	xvi
2	Eastern Central Java	xvii

Tables

3.1	Examples of Javanese address styles	37
3.2	Changing uses of polite second-person pronouns	49
6.1	Changing patterns of kin term use	84
6.2	Indonesian personal pronoun paradigms	93
6.3	Javanese vs. Indonesian personal pronoun usage	97
7.1	Complementary Javanese/Indonesian usage	113
7.2	List of elements in text 7.1	114

ACKNOWLEDGEMENTS

Research on which this book is primarily based was carried out in 1985 and 1986 with intellectual, financial, and institutional support from numerous organizations and people. For financial support I am grateful to the National Science Foundation, the Social Science Research Council, and the Wenner–Gren Foundation; I also owe thanks for a Junior Faculty Fellowship from Yale University for the 1985–86 academic year. The Indonesian Academy of Sciences (Lembaga Ilmu Pengetahuan Indonesia) and Sanata Dharma University also gave me crucial institutional support. To all these organizations, and especially to Rama Danu, my sincere gratitude. None is responsible for this book's contents.

If there has been any benefit to the slowness with which this work has gestated, it has been the chance to interact with other scholars in ways which have shaped it directly and indirectly over ten years or so. I cannot refrain from mentioning some of these. In 1988, support from a Yale Senior Faculty Fellowship made possible a six-month residence at the Center for Psychosocial Studies in Chicago. Then and since, I have continually benefited from animated discussions involving members of several of the Center's working groups. I hope the influence of those contacts is as apparent to them as it is to me; I owe thanks to Barney Weissbourd, Ben Lee, and Greg Urban.

Thanks for inspiration and supportive criticism are due to members of the Center's working group on language ideologies, including Dick Bauman, Sue Gal, Jane Hill, Judy Irvine, Ben Lee, Bambi Schieffelin, Jacquie Urla, and Kit Woolard. I am grateful also to persons who responded to material which I presented first in a variety of venues, en route to this writing: at the University of Pennsylvania, the University of Wisconsin, the University of Arizona, Yale University, and Harvard University, various conference panels, and the 1995 meeting of the Southeast Asian Linguistics Society. In addition, I owe sincere thanks to Alton Becker, Joel Kuipers, and Kit Woolard, as well as anonymous reviewers who made the heroic effort of reading all or parts of previous drafts.

Some things never seem to end, including (it seems) my engagement with people in south-central Java. So my debt of thanks to them shows no signs of diminishing. I did not know when I met her in 1986 that I would have Mbak Tinuk as a companion now, as then; her help with the drudgery of research then was invaluable, and her gracious presence over the years since has helped me to feel that my writing has not become totally remote from the Javanese language or people. I owe no less to the persons who worked and consulted with me during the research. I cannot help but extend thanks specifically to Mas Dib, Pak Hari, Mas Poino, Pak Wanda, and Mbak Endhang for their interest and help.

My village hosts, who never made me feel like the encumbrance I surely often was, showed a graciousness and patience which I remember fondly and with gratitude. Their willingness to accept me as a visitor made it possible; my memory of that acceptance has sometimes been an impetus for seeing it through as best I can. So too I owe much to people in Java I was unable to meet, but whose voices have lingered in my memory as their words have entered this text. For better or worse, all of these people deserve credit for whatever value this book has, and certainly none of the blame for its inadequacies. *Nyuwun pangapunten saderengipun.*

PREFACE: SUGGESTIONS FOR USE

As this book has developed, I have found myself addressing two different audiences: "area specialists" on one hand, and anthropological linguists on the other. Each imagined readership was focal for one of two earlier works which I wrote about Javanese, and both together have shaped this work. One way to provide a sense of what might be in this book for both, then, is to sketch its relation to its two predecessors.

Those two previous works were much more narrowly focused: on Javanese to the exclusion of Indonesian, and on use in tightly knit elite circles to the exclusion of the vast majority of Javanese. One could leave either book with little sense that the elites described in them are bilingual, as are millions of their coethnics; that they speak in ways significantly different from those found in other Javanese communities; that the Javanese part of Indonesia is being massively transformed by national development and a saturating, authoritarian state. This book represents an effort to redress these points of neglect comprehensively but also fairly concisely.

I wrote one monograph (*Language and social change in Java: linguistic reflexes of modernization in a traditional royal polity*, Ohio University Monographs in International Studies, 1985) for area specialists, aiming to diagnose some fairly broad dimensions of social change from some fairly narrow aspects of Javanese usage since the turn of the century. Chapters 2 through 5 of this book are aimed at much the same audience, but deal more broadly with dimensions of Javanese and Indonesian usage alike. My goal there is to develop a multifaceted overview of Javanese and Indonesian as mediators of shifting forms of political authority, and thus as linguistic grounds for shifting understandings of ethnic and national hierarchy. I hope that readers interested in social change will find that their willingness to deal with a few linguistic particulars is rewarded with some sense of Indonesian development's most intimate engagements with everyday life, as it enters and is mediated in bilingual interaction.

My second book (*Structure and style in Javanese: a semiotic view of linguistic etiquette*, University of Pennsylvania Press, 1988) was a more abstract, model-driven account of systemic change in Javanese elite usage, and was organized around descriptive particulars and comparative/theoretical concerns of primary interest to anthropological linguists. In its latter part, this book deals with similar details under a broader social purview. Descriptive material in chapters 6 through 10, framed with an eye to the politics and culture of bilingualism in south-central Java, is intended to subserve an account of talk as social praxis: structurally shaped, interactionally emergent, but also tacitly informed by shifting senses of both languages' broader values.

Although this book's two parts are thus framed with an eye to institutional and interactional dimensions of language use, I have tried to link them in thematically explicit, reciprocally revealing ways. If I have succeeded, then "macro" social forces can be considered in relation to "micro" social processes of everyday life; transient textures of talk can be considered interpretively as ripples on the surface of larger, shifting social tides. If I have failed to create such links, I hope that each part can nonetheless stand on its own as a more modest but useful sketch of aspects of a complex dynamic of sociolinguistic change.

NOTE ON ORTHOGRAPHY AND TRANSCRIPTION

For the sake of convenience, I transcribe Javanese and Indonesian with orthographies as similar as possible to their standard spelling systems, introducing diacritics for just a few salient instances of allophonic variation. Provenances of words and talk in Javanese and Indonesian are marked as J and I respectively. In the following charts I note phonetic values of some allophones otherwise not transcribed.

INDONESIAN
Vowels

	Front unrounded	Central unrounded	Back rounded
High	i~(I)		u~(U)
Mid	e	e	o
Low		a	

Following ordinary spelling rules, I do not distinguish orthographically between front-mid /é/ and mid-central shwa. Low, tense allophones of /i/ and /u/ are not orthographically distinguished.

Consonants

	Labial	Apico-dental	Palatal	Dorso-velar	Glottal
Voiceless stop	p	t	c	k	
Voiced stop	b	d	j	g	
Fricatives	f	s	sy	kh	h
Nasal	m	n	ny	ng	
Liquid		r, l			
Glides	w		y		

/k/ ordinarily alternates with glottal stop in word final position and intervocalically in Javanese dialects.

JAVANESE

Standard Javanese orthography (Subalidinata and Nartoatmojo 1975) is adapted here.

Vowels

	Front unrounded	Central unrounded	Back rounded
High	i~(I)		u~(U)
Mid	é~è	e	o
Low		a~	á

Back rounded á, a regular allophone of low central unrounded a, appears in final, open syllables and penultimate open syllables preceding such a syllable. Differences between front-mid, front-low, and central shwa, not ordinarily transcribed, are distinguished in this book.

Consonants

	Labial	Apico-dental	Apico-alveolar	Palatal	Velar	Glottal
Voiceless stop	p	t	th	c	k	
Voiced stop	b	d	dh	j	g	h
Fricatives	(f)	s				
Nasal	m	n		ny	ng	
Liquid		r, l				
Glides	w			y		

In the standard dialect, /k/ is realized as glottal stop in word final and intervocalic positions. I transcribe it here in all environments as /k/. /f/ is non-native and appears only in foreign words. Voiced stops are generally articulated with breathy voice in non-final positions.

OTHER CONVENTIONS

Conversational texts are set out in columns, such that transcriptions of original verbiage are on the left with translations on the right. I have tried to match original verbiage with its translation on a line-by-line basis; much detail not directly relevant to expository concerns has been omitted in the interests of accessibility.

Line numbers, provided for convenience of reference, appear in multiples of five.

Conversational latchings are marked as follows:

        ending segment==

                ==latching segment.

Conversational overlaps are marked as follows:

preceding | segment
| beginning of overlap.

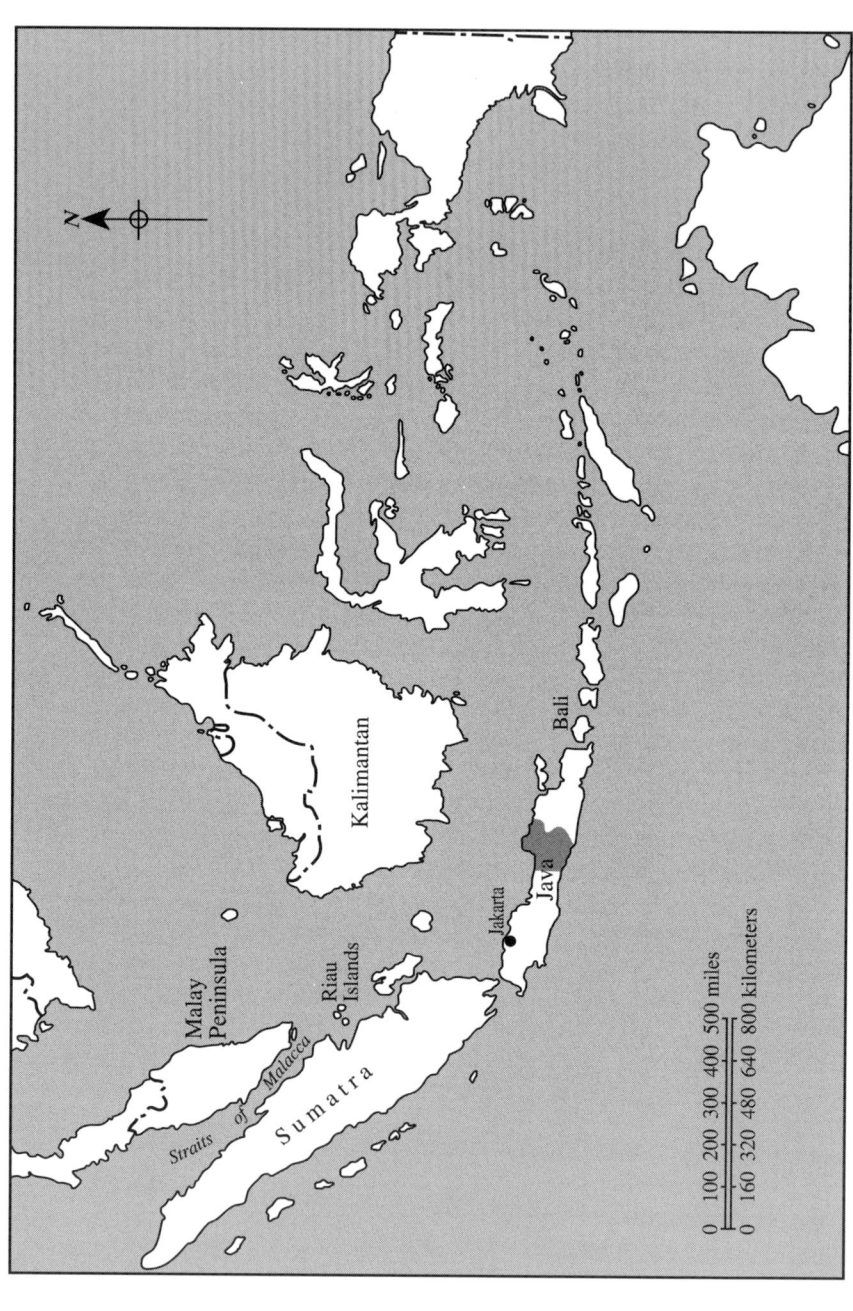

Map 1 *The Indonesian archipelago*

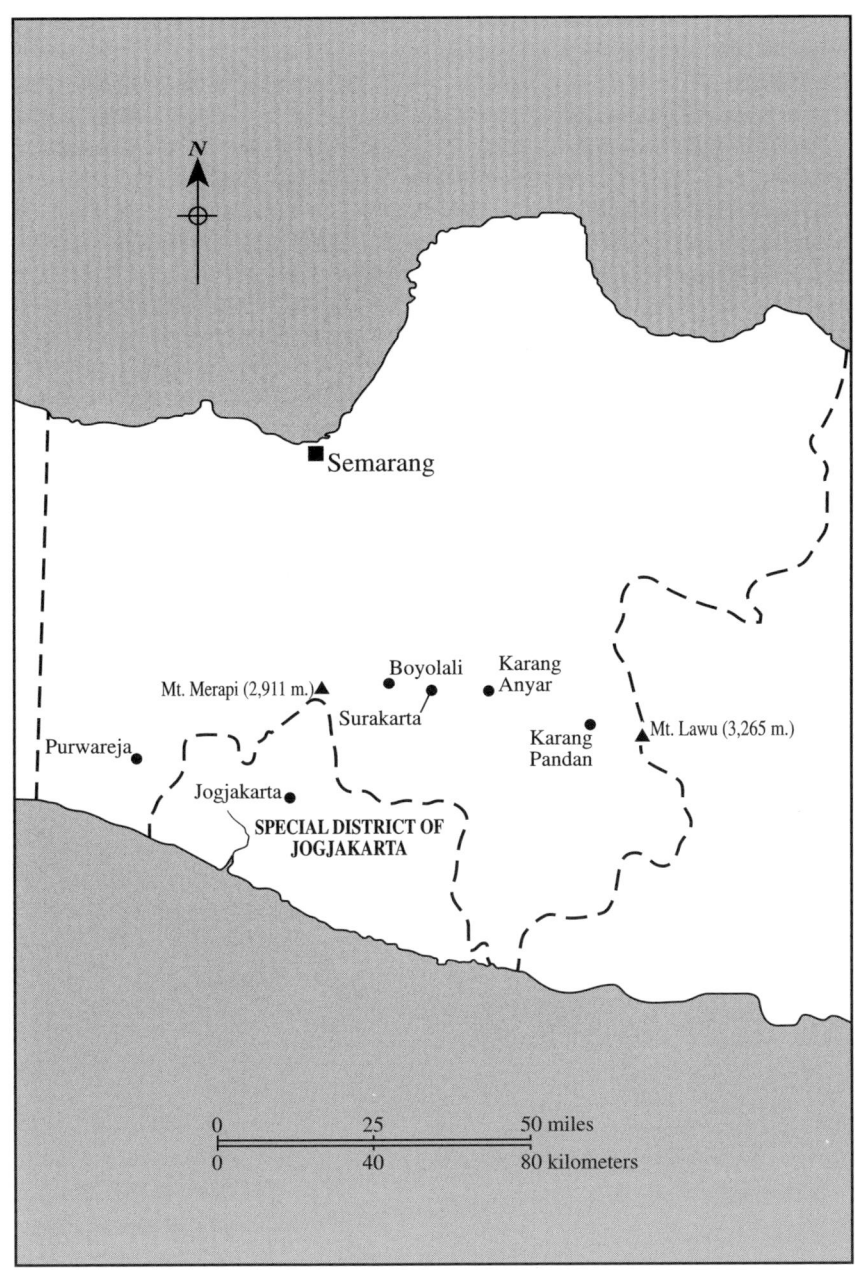

Map 2 *Eastern Central Java*

I
INTRODUCTION

In 1995, in the afterglow of the Asia Pacific Economic Conference (APEC) which it had hosted the previous year, Indonesia celebrated its fiftieth anniversary as a newly visible power on the international scene. Some believed Indonesia came of age twice then, at a doubly vindicating moment for the regime which had overseen its conspicuously successful thirty-year project of nation-building. Since 1965, the quasi-military New Order state had progressively centralized its political control and implemented an uncontested, long-term project of national development. Under its supervision a Western-educated, technocratic elite had successfully engineered the macrodevelopment which has gained Indonesia newfound stature on the world scene.

From Jakarta, the national capital and nexus of political and economic power, the New Order had progressively spread and deepened its oversight across the Indonesian archipelago. Communities once at the peripheries of the state's jurisdiction, and hardly touched by state institutions, are increasingly engaged with the ideology of nationalism and modernity which it propagates. As state institutions increasingly impinge on everyday life, ideas of modernity, national identities, and obligations of citizenship are increasingly salient in communities which only recently were loosely integrated into the national polity.

The New Order can be seen as fostering a native sense of Indonesian-ness by "ethnicizing" the Indonesian polity, yet simultaneously working to avoid overtly effacing antecedent ethnolinguistic diversity, or promoting the ascendance of any "native" subnational group. But in fact there is one ethnic group, the Javanese, which looms very large on the national landscape. Javanese dominate demographically in the nation as a whole; sixty million or so live in the ethnic "heartland" of Central and East Java – two of Indonesia's twenty-seven provinces but home to almost a third of its population – and a century of migration has led to the growth of large, distinctively Javanese ethnic communities elsewhere in Indonesia and the world.

Officials of Javanese descent likewise predominate in the state apparatus, and in urban elite circles a new version of "high" Javanese cultural tradition is being actively reinvented. Upwardly mobile Indonesians, not all of whom are Javanese, are adopting modern versions of a refined "hothouse" culture which flourished during the Dutch colonial era. This new urban elite tradition refers back to a Javanese golden age, and so to the two royal cities of south-central Java: Jogjakarta and Surakarta. Both were once famous primarily for their courtly elites, and as the political and cultural centers of the prenational Javanese heartland. Both cities now count as the originary homes of traditions of the *priyayi* community, which the New Order elite had taken for its cultural if not genetic precursor. (For more on this connection see Anderson 1966; Pemberton 1994; Florida 1987; J. Errington 1986, 1998.)

Through a dynamic which Djajadiningrat-Nieuwenhuis (1987) appropriately calls priyayization, this small bit of south-central Javanese territory has become a cultural epicenter for the nation at large. It does not seem coincidental in this respect that the national motto, *Bhinneka tunggal ika*, "Unity in diversity," likewise acknowledges the nation's ethnic diversity in a Javanese idiom: its Old Javanese form and nationalistic content together suggest a modern version of ethnic Javanese tradition, which is helping to elide or straddle received distinctions between modern and traditional forms of governmentality (see, e.g., Tsing 1993).

In 1998 the New Order found itself grappling with social upheaval and economic uncertainty in troubled times, which recall for some the circumstances of its emergence more than thirty years ago. International praise for successful New Order development has suddenly begun to ring hollow, and Indonesia's progress toward "national modernity" seems more illusory than real. But these troubled conditions and uncertain successes throw into relief what may prove to be among the New Order's most enduring effects on the Indonesian landscape: its success in propagating Indonesian-ness with and through the Indonesian language.

Every aspect of the New Order's "development" of Indonesia has been subserved by the Indonesian language. As the language of state, Indonesian is infrastructural for institutional development; as the language of the nation, it effaces differences between citizens who live in antecedent, ethnolinguistically distinct communities. At the end of World War II, the artificial administrative Malay which counts as Indonesian's immediate precursor was just one of several dialects of that language, spoken natively by a few million residents of the Dutch East Indies' colonial empire. Now Indonesian is a fully viable, universally acknowledged national language, non-native but also clearly ascendant over hundreds of languages spoken natively among more than two hundred million Indonesians. Notwithstanding difficulties in evaluating the results of censuses which include questions about knowledge and use of Indonesian (see Steinhauer 1994), such censuses provide grounds for broad consensus that Indonesia is well on its way to solving "the national language problem," and enhancing its status as what Fishman (1978:333) has called a "miraculous" language in the developing world.[1] The slogan "language indicates nationality" (I: *bahasa menunjukkan bangsa*), which once expressed a nationalist hope, seems more and more to describe a national condition (Geertz 1973:315).

But in ethnically homogeneous areas, like south-central Java, Indonesian is little used across self-evident lines of ethnolinguistic difference. Speakers there have no native models to emulate because, as ethnic Javanese, they are not in contact with a native-speaking Indonesian community. They are learning to speak Indonesian not by emulating the concrete verbal "practice[s] of . . . specific group[s] of [Indonesian] speakers" but instead by assimilating an underdetermined, "vague ideal norm" to local, native ways of dealing with coethnics (DeVries 1988:125).

So in Central Java, at least, Indonesian is not so much a non-native language learned from or used with members of some linguistically distinct group. It is more an *un-native* language, whose forms and uses are being acquired and used in interaction with otherwise native (-speaking) Javanese. As an outgroup language without an outgroup, Indonesian carries no immediate sense of social "otherness"; it can be said – with apologies to Gertrude Stein, and prior to discussion in chapter 10 – that for Indonesian there is no native (-speaking) "they" there.

Indonesian's modernity

Indonesian's un-nativeness crucially enables and informs its place in the Indonesian national project. As Benedict Anderson recognized in the 1960s, it makes Indonesian a "*project* for the assumption of 'modernity' within the modalities of an autonomous and autochthonous socialpolitical tradition" (1966:89). Anderson wrote these words on the eve of the fall of President Sukarno, in 1965, but they are still apposite for considering here Indonesian's broadest political cultural saliences in the 1990s, and in communities well beyond the elite circles which he discussed.

As New Order development has been superposed ("from above") on communities which were recently peripheral to state control, Indonesian territory has become the scene of many such "projects of modernity." These can be thought of as emerging situations of "contact" – between local community and national polity, between citizen and authoritarian state – which are mediated and shaped by the Indonesian language. At the same time, Indonesian is an increasingly common way of talking in the "ordinary" interactional engagements which make up much of the fabric of everyday interactional experience. Among the many institutions which subserve New Order power and oversight over Indonesians' lives, Indonesian is uniquely available for appropriation to the most self-interested purposes, which can be entirely at a remove from state interests or venues. For this reason, Indonesian can be considered a state-fostered institution which is subject to situated appropriation "from below."

On one hand, then, the Indonesian language is quite transparently part of a state system, that is, a "palpable nexus of practice and institutional structure, extensive, unified and dominant" (Abrams 1988:58). On the other hand, Indonesian talk, situated in conversational contingencies of everyday life, can mediate a "state idea" of Indonesian-ness as it is "projected, purveyed, and variously believed" (ibid.). Indonesian can figure in such interactional self/other relations as the intimate vehicle for a *doxa* – "diffuse, full, complete, and 'natural'" (Barthes 1989:121) – of modernity and nationalism. This point of convergence has been recognized by observers other than Anderson who see Indonesian as "perhaps the most important single ingredient in the shaping of the modern [Indonesian] culture" (Liddle 1988:1).

This book frames bilingual Javanese and Indonesian usage as mediating this divide between nation-state and everyday life, the "realm of institutional politics" and "order[s] of [verbal] signs and [conversational] practices" (Comaroff and Comaroff 1991:23). It describes ongoing "contact" between the Indonesian and Javanese languages on a shifting, south-central Javanese landscape; in it I seek to read language use as a point of dynamic convergence between institutional hierarchy and the "individualized, familiar, habitual, micro-climactic of daily life" (Jelin 1987:11, translated in Escobar 1992:29).

My expository strategy for sketching this scene of "contact" between Javanese and Indonesian is two-sided in ways signaled by the book's systematically ambiguous title. On one hand, the phrase "shifting languages" resembles "language shift," the sociolinguistic term of art used for patterns of historical change in the knowledge and use of two languages within communities. Typically, language shift occurs as a community's native language (usually minority or "ethnic") is progressively displaced by or relinquished for another (usually majority or "national"). These are cumulative, "long-term" processes which occur among collectivities of speakers, and as such can sometimes be read as mediating the effects of "large-scale" forces – political, cultural, economic – which shape broader senses of collective identity. As a rubric for collective phenomena, more sociohistorical happenings than intentful doings, "language shift" corresponds to a grammatically intransitive reading of "shifting languages."

On the other hand, "shifting languages" is a phrase which can be used to describe what happens in interactional process when bi- or multilingual speakers juxtapose elements (minimally phrase-long) of two languages. Such transient bits of conduct, more commonly called instances of code switching, are particulars of talk in the "real time" of social life, concrete enough to leave traces (in recordings and transcriptions) for retrospective scrutiny. This is the sphere of language as immediate, situated, other-oriented self-conduct. As other-directed social practice in which speakership presents at least the guise of communicative agency, code switching corresponds to a transitive reading of "shifting languages."

Even if the pun is clumsy, it helps here to thematize the expository counterpoint I try to develop in the following chapters between institutional and interactional aspects of Javanese and Indonesian language in change and use. It provides a way of framing distinct issues while avoiding either a prejudicially unitary metatheoretical profile, or juxtaposed, disjoint sketches. I try instead to develop a dynamic tension between these institutional and interactional perspectives, a tension which is a bit like the one linking yet separating these two readings of "shifting languages." To read the phrase in one sense does not cancel the other possibility; instead it binds them in an asymmetric, "both/and" relation of foregrounded and backgrounded element. I can outline this double strategy here by showing how it helps me to work against the grain of accounts which are predominantly weighted to the side of macro institutional forces, and residualize micro interactional processes.

Certainly the figures on language use cited earlier are easily mobilized for predictions of massive social and language change which will lead to a shift from Javanese to Indonesian. Here is one such vision of Java's linguistic future, taken from the writings of Yoshimichi Someya (1992:61–62):

Indonesian will spread ... like a tide to rural areas ... eventually replacing Javanese [which] is gradually becoming incompatible with such values as directness, clarity, effectiveness, and speed of communication – necessary conditions for the national unity, the "blending" of Indonesian ethnic groups, democracy, modernization, and rationalization required by today's Indonesian government, industries, education, arts, and sciences.

However much some New Order officials would deny it, this allusion to Indonesian "values" resonates strongly with the state's own ideology of development. Because he emphasizes the homogenizing effects of "large-scale" institutional forces, operating uniformly across Javanese territory and communities, Someya likewise echoes writings on "language engineering" dating from the heyday of development (see, e.g., Fishman et al. 1968). Predictions like these center Indonesian among the various state-fostered institutions which will presumably become social grounds and taken-for-granted frames of reference in everyday life.

Before critiquing this politically fraught position and its ideological grounds in chapter 4, I can quickly consider it here in terms of the complicating factors which it elides and which I address in the following chapters. Each point of criticism can be thought of as an upshot of tacit assumptions about the autonomy of the Indonesian language: as a structured linguistic system, as a social institution shared within and across communities, and as a verbal instrument mobilized for situated communicative ends. So too each of these issues can be broached preliminarily here with an eye to its correlates in Javanese language structure, political culture, and interactional dynamics.

Language, territoriality, and ideology

Someya tacitly dissociates Indonesian's "values" from its role as an instrument of New Order oversight; he similarly brackets any relevance which Javanese might have for contemporary, national political culture. I seek to avoid such simplifying assumptions in this book's first chapters, where I foreground aspects of language use which mediate and legitimize authority. To this end I contrast Javanese and Indonesian with an eye to recent work at the juncture of human geography and critical theory (see, e.g., Peet and Thrift [1989]), which provides a way to consider each language as integrally bound up with a distinct mode or strategy of *territoriality*. In this way, each language can be considered as institutionally and ideologically bound up with one of two distinct strategies to "affect, influence, or control people, phenomena, and relationships, by delimiting and asserting control over geographic area" (Sack 1986:19).

Chapter 2 provides a territorially framed, language-centered sketch of ongoing change in upland village communities of south-central Java where I spent time. It juxtaposes Javanese and Indonesian as extensions and symbols of two distinct modes of lowland territorial power, and in shifting perceptions of the modes of territoriality which bind these rural peripheries to cities, where prenational Javanese and national Indonesian authority have both been centered.

Someya's top-down picture of Indonesian's spread likewise ignores any possible salience which antecedent, ethnic, social, and linguistic conditions might have for a national future. It presupposes, rather, that Indonesian language and culture are autonomous with respect to "local" language and traditions, and so together will effect a quantum leap which leaves the prenational era to recede on the rear horizon of history. It matters little from this broadly epochalist point of view that prenational south-central Java has for centuries been far from a social or linguistic *tabula rasa* onto which New Order institutions and language are now being straightforwardly superposed.

This politically fraught assumption is thrown into question in chapters 2 and 3 alike, which center on some enduring political and cultural saliences of Javanese as a mediator and symbol of authority. I sketch there the Javanese language's role in the territoriality or geosocial control which was exercised by the colonial-era kingdoms based in Jogjakarta and Surakarta. Language and social hierarchy were then linked in obvious and complex ways through Javanese linguistic etiquette, best known as the "speech levels."[2]

These speech styles, as I prefer to call them, are still hallmarks of elite Javanese tradition, and still famous for their extensive vocabularies of "crude" and "refined" elements. In use, these styles serve as interactionally nuanced and very conspicuous mediators of status and intimacy between people. But in chapter 3 I focus less on their overt interactional saliences than on their broader institutionally grounded roles as naturalizers of sociolinguistic inequality, within and across lines of territorial hierarchy. In this way they can be considered as the idiom of non-national imagined communities of persons, linked in asymmetric "nets of kinship and clientship" (Anderson 1991:6) which were centered on south-central Java's "exemplary centers" (Geertz 1980) or "galactic polities" (Tambiah 1976). (See in this regard also Cohn and Dirks' discussion [1988:224] of "theater[s] of power.")

Finally, Someya's prediction of language shift is overtly teleological, like New Order development rhetoric. It promotes a secular, ameliorative vision of profound social change, framed as a broad transition from *Gemeinschaft* to *Gesellschaft*, or from mechanical to organic divisions of social labor. This developmentalist ideology accords to language a special place in social change, which I consider in chapter 4 with an eye to the striking fit between New Order development ideology on one hand, and Ernest Gellner's (1983) functionalist account of nationalism on the other. Because of the privileged place of standard languages in his account of nationalism, Gellner helps to explicate the consequences of un-native Indonesian's curious social history, and what Someya calls its value for "directness, clarity, effectiveness, and speed of communication" (Someya 1992:61). Someya's specific assertion, together with Gellner's general account, speaks to the broadest, tacit assumptions of New Order development ideology regarding the "meanings" which accrue to Indonesian, over and against ethnic pasts and languages. In this way the ideological correlates of Indonesian's institutional grounds can be explicated, and its perceived privilege as the vehicle of abstract, rational thought can be foregrounded.

Syncretic usage

Over and against such sweeping pictures of sociohistorical change stand the modest particulars of everyday life, including talk: the fabric of situated, face-to-face relations cocreated among persons who are each others' consociates, and share the social biography of "a community of space and a community of time" (Schutz 1967a:163).

Even statements as broad as Someya's carry implicit predictions about such situated transiencies of Indonesian and Javanese usage. By imputing autonomy or separateness to Indonesian in relation to Javanese, he makes it easy to figure particulars of "mixed" Javanese–Indonesian usage as historically transitional in an epochal shift between languages and eras, as socially residual in everyday life, and as structurally interstitial with respect to two distinct, autonomous language systems.

This book's middle chapters speak to this position through descriptive particulars which reflect indirectly, narrowly, but (I hope) revealingly on considerably more complex shapes of sociolinguistic change. In chapters 5 through 8 I rebut such epochalist positions with sketches of usage, ranging from authoritative public discourse to everyday conversation, in which Javanese and Indonesian intimately shape each other in discourse. These can be read as syncretic in two broad senses of that term.

"Syncretism" recurs in writings about Javanese culture as a notion which has proven malleable enough for self-conscious framings of ethnicity in the nation (e.g., former minister of education, Professor Priyono 1964:23), for ethnographic description (e.g., Geertz 1960), for analysis of political culture (e.g., Anderson 1972), and for quasi-prescriptive social criticism (e.g., Mulder 1978). In such contexts, "syncretism" can intimate a sense of Javanese tradition as being mutable but coherent, accommodative yet resilient, perduring in the distinctive manner in which it incorporates "outside" influences. But in this way "syncretism" can also license essentialist understandings of Javanese culture's unity and autonomy in the face of variation across geosocial space, and change across historical eras.

In chapter 5 I try to read "syncretic" dimensions of Javanese *cum* Indonesian political culture from a few transcribed specifics of authoritative public talk. Framed with an eye to the preceding chapters' sketches of shifting territoriality, a few tiny texts of official Indonesian and formal Javanese speech are considered as more or less efficaciously representing Indonesian authority to peripheral Javanese publics. This is an account of public speech, speakers, and audiences which locates such talk in triadic relations created and presupposed between sources of territorial authority, the speakers who im-person-ate it, and the collective addressees who count as an audience. The ways public Indonesian business is sometimes done in Javanese, and in which Indonesian sometimes figures in otherwise markedly Javanese ceremonial occasions, show such "mixed usage" to be constitutive of emergent, syncretic understandings of authority.

In structural linguistic description, "syncretism" has a distinct technical sense which was introduced to the study of bilingualism in Jane Hill and Kenneth Hill's work on "mixed" language use in upland communities of central Mexico (1986). In chapters 6 and 7 I broach similar particulars of bilingual usage with an eye to their adaptation of Kurylowicz's structurally grounded definition of syncretism as the "suppression of [system internal] relevant opposition[s] under certain determined conditions" (1964:40). My interest, like theirs, is in "mixed" usage which suppresses the social relevance of oppositions *between* systems, and in which the provenances of talk's elements – native Javanese, or un-native Indonesian – are interactionally muted.

Chapter 6 deals with personal pronouns and kin terms, resources for speaking of the speech partners, interactional selves and others, who cocreate the intersubjective grounds for conversation. Javanese Indonesians have common recourse for such acts of reference to kin terms, which are interactionally focal and broadly syncretic. That such usage represents a point of convergence between interactional and institutional identities is obvious enough, but has unobvious social implications. Formerly Javanese kin terms have been subjected to institutional treatment in Indonesian venues; they have been assimilated to new hierarchies and understandings of status. In use, then, they count as "small-scale" transiencies of talk which reflect "large-scale" shifts in status, class, and territoriality; they mediate face-to-face relations in ways which are tacitly shifting along with understandings of collective identity on an ethnic yet national landscape.

Personal pronouns, on the other hand, are indexically grounded in the interactional identities assumed by persons, speaker ("I") and addressee ("you"), to whom they refer. In chapter 6 I also focus on unobvious but interactionally salient patterns of *non-use* of Indonesian pronominal resources. Javanese speakers tacitly but consistently avoid using a full stylistic range of (prescribed) Indonesian pronominal reference, and so seem to create rather than merely accept a sense of interactional "flatness" in their national language. This interactionally keyed "anti-syncretism" makes Indonesian relatively de-situated in comparison with stylistically nuanced Javanese; it is part of the reason why Indonesian can be counted over and against Javanese as a "third person" or im-personal language which is relatively uninflected for self/other relations.

I believe that these narrow but revealing aspects of usage represent points of purchase in everyday life for the developmentalist ideology of language, explicated in chapter 4. If such otherwise negligible patterns of (non-)use mark a point of entry for national modernity into everyday conversational life, then it shows that conversational practice can, as Woolard and Schieffelin put it (1994:70), "distort . . . [Indonesian] in the name of making it more like itself."

Chapter 7 deals with two other, more disparate patterns of syncretic language use involving discourse particles on one hand, and lexical items on the other. Extensive repertoires of discourse particles serve Javanese Indonesians as means for marking feelings about and stances toward conversational topics, contexts, and participants. Their non-referential, crucially situated significances appear to make them peripheral for speakers' awarenesses relative not just to their encoded linguistic functions (Silverstein 1976, 1981), but also with respect to their various provenances as well. For this reason their use takes on an osmotic quality across categorical, prescriptive boundaries between the codes of Javanese and Indonesian.

Lexical borrowings from Indonesian into Javanese, on the other hand, are conspicuous in what Javanese themselves sometimes call "salad language." But I suggest in chapter 7 that grammatical and phonological homologies between the two languages enable intimate borrowing from Indonesian to Javanese which recalls stylistically "mixed" Javanese usage sketched in chapter 3. Considered in light of antecedent patterns of Javanese usage, even these conspicuously bilingual ways of talking can be seen as tacitly syncretizing un-native lexical resources into otherwise native interactional dynamics.

Chapters 6 and 7 together frame particulars of everyday Javanese Indonesian bilingual usage to elude broadly epochalist visions of language shift like that quoted earlier. Such syncretic aspects of usage, considered to be "sedimentation[s] of practices that incorporate extralinguistic social . . . factors" (Hanks 1996:195), provide clues to broader, partial accommodations between native and un-native languages. As points of interactionally situated language "contact," they provide structural insights into interactional dynamics of the bilingual usage I sketch in chapters 8, 9, and 10. They are oriented to talk as it is shaped by native senses of Javanese conversational practice on one hand, and an un-native Indonesian language ideology on the other.

Javanese conversation and Javanese–Indonesian code switching

Code switching is a central topic in sociolinguistics, but deserves broader attention among students of social change as a point of convergence between social life and social history. On one hand, code switching emerges in the transient, interactionally situated micro-phenomena of talk which mediate social biographies of relationships among consociates. On the other hand, acts of code switching involve languages which have distinct institutional grounds, yet come together in situations of sustained "contact" between social collectivities of speakers. In this respect code switchings can be read as transient, interactional figurings of "self" and "other" shaped within broader political and economic contexts (cf. Gal 1988:247).

Code switchings' significances, situated in microinteractional processes but informed by macrohistorical change, can have a double meaningfulness which makes them daunting for descriptive and interpretive projects. Socially relevant studies of code switching must draw a few drops of water from oceans of talk, and make them speak to the nature of shifting social tides.

Two major, socially relevant factors obtrude in such an effort for "the Javanese–Indonesian case." On the macrosocial side is Indonesian's unnativeness, which raises obvious questions about the social "otherness" it might serve to figure in interaction among Javanese. Under received comparative approaches like the one I discuss in chapter 10, it seems problematic that Indonesian lacks a native speaking outgroup (or "they") over and against which Javanese counts as the language of an ingroup ("we"). In south-central Java, at least, "they" (with apologies to Walter Kelly) can only be "us." Indonesian's un-nativeness in this way throws expository weight onto its institutional groundings in the nation-state and the "project of modernity" it symbolizes and subserves. For this reason the ways Indonesian figures in otherwise Javanese interaction invite interpretation relative to the modernist language ideology discussed in chapters 4 and 6.

The other unusual aspect of Javanese–Indonesian code switching involves the Javanese speech styles: speakers commonly shift between them in ways which, Suzanne Romaine has suggested, are "tantamount to code switching between different languages" (1995:321). But these monolingual, multistylistic patterns of usage turn out to be related to broader, less obvious interactional dynamics in which style shiftings sometimes, but not always, figure. I discuss this broader aspect of Javanese interactional process in chapter 8, under a broad rubric of "speech modeling" (which also covers "thought modeling"). There I develop a context for considering shiftings between Javanese styles as broader shiftings in interactional self/other relations, what Erving Goffman (1981) famously dubbed "footing."

These speech modelings involve rapid, minimally cued, transient shifts in modes of conversational engagement; they have close analogs (as far as I can tell) neither in Javanese uses of Indonesian, nor in native speakers' use of English. Because of their language- and culture-specific character, particularly when they serve to exteriorize internal states, I can deal with speech modelings only illustratively, through selected transcriptions of recordings of talk in which they occurred. One reason for relativizing style shifting to this broader practice of speech modeling is to show how style shifting and code switching fit together, and so to speak to Goffman's concerns (1981:155) about descriptions of (sub)code switching which are "too mechanical and too easy." In chapter 9 I show multistylistic usage to be more than a matter of switching between distinct communicative vehicles; it is bound up with shifts in interactional *cum* intersubjective engagement which, like changes in glance or stance, can be more or less intentful, strategic, or shifty.

These joined discussions of speech modeling and style shifting serve as grounds for sketching bilingual code switching in chapter 10 as shaped by Javanese conversational practice on one hand, and an Indonesian language ideology on the other. Together, chapters 8 and 9 inform an interpretive approach to Javanese–Indonesian code switching, one which attends to both languages as shapers of interactional relations. On one hand, I provide examples of usage which show Indonesian's assimilation to the distinctively Javanese conversational practices of modeling speech and thought. On the other hand, I foreground Indonesian's use in situatedly impersonal, "third-person" guises, which serve to transform social relations.

These three chapters center on transcriptions of talk, and so involve expository strategies which are fraught with operational and interpretive problems. Because I seek to present these transcriptions as traces of conduct – informed by shared senses of native practice and un-native ideology – it is difficult for me to treat them as transparent records of categorically intentful conduct. To read "through" them to the taken-for-granted, "large-scale" grounds of "small-scale" interactional transiencies, I must treat them instead as highly mediated re-presentations of Javanese–Indonesian bilingualism. So I work in this exposition to avoid presenting transcriptions of talk as im-mediate windows on or im-mutable records of social reality.

From talk to transcription to text

The transcriptions of everyday talk set out in this book's later chapters may seem overnumerous and overlong. But they are just a tiny fraction of the thirty-one hours of usage which I and my collaborators recorded and transcribed at different times, in different communities, and on different occasions. A few are drawn from recordings made by a colleague, David Howe, during his research project in 1980 and 1981 in Surakarta, where I was also working (see Howe 1980). But many more were made during research focused on bilingualism in rural Java, between January and August of 1986. Some were recorded by me, but most were made by five consultants/collaborators who lived in various of the peripheral communities of Surakarta and, in one case, of Jogjakarta (shown on map 2).

Earlier research had already made me familiar with what William Labov (1971:113) dubbed the "observer's paradox": wishing to observe how people talk when one is not there to observe that talk. Only after gaining adequate facility in a range of spoken Javanese styles could I feel that my own talk was not too obtrusive in casual conversation; only among people I knew fairly well could I feel that my tall, white foreignness might not fundamentally shape interactional dynamics.

So I had strong practical reasons for enlisting help from Javanese collaborators who used the inexpensive tape recorders I provided. At the outset I asked each to record casual talk in his or her home, neighborhood, and workplace, suggesting that bilingual usage in everyday contexts might be most interesting. I asked each to carry the tape recorder for a while before using it, so as to acclimatize people they saw regularly to its presence. I also asked them to explain my efforts to study the ways Javanese is spoken on an everyday basis, and to request permission before turning the tape recorder on, while also minimizing its visual presence by using small omnidirectional clip-on microphones.

All five of my collaborators had at least high-school educations; three (two women, one man) were in their late twenties and teaching in high schools (Sekolah Menengah Atas) while living in their respective home villages. This may have had a skewing effect on the material which they recorded and which I present here. Still, as some of these rural communities' first bilinguals, "locals who have made good," they may likewise represent the first wave of bilingual community which will come of age with youngsters like those they are teaching. My other two consultants, a man and a woman, both in their forties, were a farmer and housewife respectively; though they lived in rural communities, they had lived outside rural Java for some time, and so were slightly unusual as older, bilingual village residents.

When the first recorded cassettes were returned to me by consultants, I listened to them with the idea of selecting particular segments for transcription. But it did not take long to realize that this strategy was leading me away from interesting aspects of usage. Thereafter I asked consultants to transcribe as much of the recordings they made as was audible. Though I paid for transcribing on an hourly basis, this intensive, time-consuming work was onerous enough to cost me early on the services of three other consultants, who were unwilling to listen repeatedly to tapes to pick up fast speech, tease apart voices in overlapping conversation, or catch repetitions of words or interspersed, back-channel comments.

All transcriptions were written in standard Javanese spelling or some approximation of it which I have normalized here (see the note on orthography). I did not ask my collaborators to try to transcribe details of talk's sequencing – the gaps and overlaps in turns taken by speech partners – nor much other fine-grained information which is often included in transcriptions intended for conversation-analytic purposes. These original transcriptions are highly partial but, with suitable emendation, adequate for my purposes here. (For discussion of the theory- and interest-laden nature of transcription see Ochs 1979, Urban 1996, and Haviland 1996a.)

I was fortunate to be able to have these transcriptions keyed into the laptop computer I had brought with me to the field, which made it easy to revise and emend transcriptions after reviewing them. I did this on my own and with consultants on a recurring, usually weekly basis. This slow, painstaking process yielded rich, specific contextual information – about the social surround of talk, the people involved, the prior and following dynamics of interaction, etc. – as well as background on the aspects of usage taken up in this book.

Just as significantly, these sessions made me forcibly aware of speakers' common lack of verbalizable "insight" into many of the aspects of monolingual and bilingual usage which attracted my attention, and which I repeatedly queried. I discuss in later chapters their seeming indifference, if not resistance, to my attempts to elicit focused interpretations of particular aspects of usage with recourse either to "forced choice" strategies of interpretation, or to collaborative interpretation in some "native" metalinguistic vocabulary. This practical aspect of the research has in turn shaped my discussion here of expository and theoretical problems of comparison. I am recurringly concerned with the "potential circularity" which, as Romaine (1995:175) observes, is a real danger for analyses of code switchings (or speech modelings, or style shiftings) which lack fit with or confirmability from native speakers' points of view.

Before returning to the United States, I intended to visit and introduce myself to all the persons whose voices had been recorded, and personally to ask their permission to use transcriptions of those recordings in my writing. This proved to be impossible due to a serious illness which left me bedridden during four of my last six weeks in Java. When I asked consultants to request permission on my behalf, they reported back to me that none of the persons they had recorded objected.

It is important to make clear here that I did not witness or participate in all of this talk, and so cannot license all these transcriptions "in the first person." They came to me as recordings and transcriptions: physical traces which speakers' actions left on magnetic tape, and their orthographic surrogates. Those recordings and transcriptions, in turn, required extensive supplement in the form of contextualizing narratives by the persons who recorded them. These descriptions, like their objects, can be only partly reproduced here, and in "the third person." So these transcriptions are neither transparent windows on concrete social realities, nor empirical bedrock for general social description: their intelligibility rests on situated paraphrase, explication, and interpretation.

These mediating operations are in the first place practically motivated by the need to select very small portions of indefinitely long transcriptions for re-presentation here. This operation presupposes their separability and self-contained character as records of conduct; it requires me to assume my ability to supplement them with adequate narrative descriptions of their originary, verbal, and non-verbal surround. These excising operations are in turn grounded in the thematic purposes of an expository "here and now," which confer salience to records of conduct in an originary "there and then."

To keep in mind the mediated character which these expository operations confer on usage in the last three chapters, I refer to them as *texts* of usage. This helps to maintain an expositorily keyed sense of variation in the kinds of explications I make of them, and the motivations or intentfulness I impute to the conduct of which I present textualized traces. A notion of "weakly" intentful conduct helps to adduce recurring patterns from use on which native speakers had little *post hoc* interpretive purchase. I contrast these with other, fewer, "strongly" strategic or intentful instances of usage which offered themselves to speakers, and sometimes to me, as parts of larger social and conversational projects, as transparently verbal means to identifiable, extrinsic social ends.

This distinction helps me to avoid conflating distinct analytic and interactional perspectives under an overbroad rubric of "function" or "strategy." It also helps me to work toward a dynamic sense of relation between the shared, tacit grounds for use of language systems, and the to-handedness of language in the "small-scale" immediacies of social life. By developing a productive, "both/and" tension and simultaneity between both faces of language, I try to avoid reducing one to the other, and develop a double, shifting picture of Javanese and Indonesian in use and change.

2
A CITY, TWO HAMLETS, AND THE STATE

As lowland New Order authority and language have entered upland Javanese territory, villagers' senses of community have been shaped by their dealings with the nation-state's saturating presence. Antecedent understandings of community and relations between communities are shifting under social pressures for change which are linguistically mediated by Javanese and Indonesian alike. So too village images of Surakarta, which have long been politically salient on this landscape, are shifting with that city's new relevances for those living at its peripheries. Village ambivalence about the city and city-based institutions were striking to me partly because I was a semi-regular traveler between city and village. But I believe that villagers' shifting perceptions of the city were very much bound up with changing understandings of the territorial authority located there, and of the languages which subserve it.

A convenient way to broach language-related modes of territoriality and village–city relations is the bit of conversation between Javanese villagers – old and young, bilingual and monolingual – set out below as text 2.1. I is Pak Iman, a sixtyish upland villager who remembers the halcyon days of the last "real" king (*ratu*) of Surakarta (Pakubuwana X, 1893–1939). He refers to the city by its less formal, commoner name, Solo, which I also use in the following discussion.

Text 2.1

I: Solo ki yá kuná, ora tá yásá Solo ki, ora nèng wong ngusung *ndhuk*. [1]	I: The Solo of old wasn't built, it wasn't done by humans, *ndhuk*.
E: Thik mboten piyé tá lik, nggih ènten wong arak-arakan nggáwá wit ringin loro. Ditandur kok. [5]	E: What do you mean, *lik*, there were long lines of people who brought the banyan trees. They were planted.
I: Lha iyá, yásá kraton Solo kuwi ki butuh watu ésuk-ésuk yá wis munthuk-munthuk ngono. Yá jaman yásáné kuwi, butuh kayu, kayu yá wis teká dhéwé, ora menungsá sing [10] nekakké, nèk butuh wedhi watu yá Merapi kuwi sing ngeteri, ésuk-ésuk yá wis bak ngalun-alun.	I: At the time of the building of the palace in Solo, when stones were needed, early in the morning they were already all piled up. Then, when wood was needed, it came by itself, it wasn't brought in by humans. When sand and stone was needed, [the volcano] Merapi brought it, the next morning the field [by the palace] was all full.

E: Kok kalah kalih Yogjá.
I: Nèk Yogjá ki rak ora ratu.
E: Mboten?
O: Lha ápá nèk ra ratu?
I: Sultan, ratu ki saklumahing bumi kuwi gur siji.

E: Then how did [Solo] lose out to Jogja?
[15] I: In Jogja there's no king [*ratu*].
E: No?
O: Well, what is [the king in Jogja] if not a *ratu*?
I: A *sultan*. A *ratu*, in the entire world, is only one.

Pak Iman's remark invokes a mythic chronotope of the city's founding, one which resonates broadly with scholarly descriptions of the political culture of traditional *exemplary centers*. Surakarta, as a locus of supramundane power – a *kraton*, "place of a king" – is the residence of a singular ruler (*ratu*) supernaturally sanctioned by the spiritual powers which helped build it. Pak Iman's description recalls Surakarta's name, which can be glossed as "made by the gods," and its status on the prenational landscape not as capital but as defining center of a realm. In 1986 older villagers like Pak Iman still used the Javanese term *nagari* for the city, although that term traditionally served to refer to royal city and larger polity alike (see J. Errington 1988:25–28).

The other main party, Endhang, recorded this conversation.[1] Mbak Endhang (as I called her) was born in 1955, ten years after the declaration of Indonesian independence. For her Solo is the city nearest her upland village, where she went to university. For her and Omar – marked as O at line 17, her age-mate and companion – it is one *urban center* among others, hardly unique and in fact politically subordinate to the provincial and national capitals of Semarang and Jakarta (see maps 1 and 2). As a local nexus for state institutions, Surakarta is likewise less prominent on the national scene than its nearby traditional rival, Jogjakarta. Omar can voice friendly skepticism about the reality and relevance of Surakarta's supernatural origins by emphasizing its current, subordinate status as a subprovincial district of the nation.

This conversation reflects broad intergenerational differences in perceptions of the city and, by implication, of the territorial relations in which it counts as a center for such peripheral communities. In the next two chapters I elaborate these views of territorial authority from a linguistic angle; here I juxtapose them as contrasting frames for construing upland relations to the wider, lowland world. Insofar as Solo is both an exemplary and urban center, and partakes of different understandings of polity and authority, each of its images can serve here to sketch the intergenerational difference which briefly surfaced in text 2.1.

Even a bare sketch of upland–lowland difference needs also to include mention of senses of local difference between neighboring upland villages, which were in place long before the advent of the New Order state. Important here is how the state's assimilating, homogenizing presence has in fact exacerbated antecedent inequalities, while its institutions have licensed local, religiously inflected expressions of collective autonomy. These may be negligible on the supralocal scene, but reflect some of the broader hegemonic qualities of the state's presence in rural communities, and the quality of oversight it can exercise. I draw attention here to this centralizing presence of the New Order as a way of sketching villagers' perceptions of its national language.

Between city and village

The Surakarta my wife and I left in 1980 after eighteen months of residence was already showing signs of accelerating modernization. When we returned with our infant daughter in 1985 that process was in full swing. The city's fringes had by then sprawled so far as to blur its boundaries with the neighboring towns of Kartasura and Palur, and to occupy considerable amounts of what had formerly been farmland. New capital, industry, and workers were entering it in a major way. Although my purpose in returning was to spend time with villagers, health concerns for our infant daughter made Solo important for us nonetheless; we elected to set up house there instead of in the fairly distant village where I hoped to live and work.

By dividing my time between city and mountain hamlets, I put myself in a doubly marginal position as not just foreigner but semi-commuter. My oscillations between city and village periphery have doubtless shaped this description of a shifting rural Javanese landscape. But the semi-commuter status I adopted was becoming increasingly common at that time, as Solo's attraction as a place of employment grew for residents of the surrounding areas. Recent statistics indicate, for instance, that the city's official population now stands at about 537,000, but at mid-day it has as many as two million people within its precincts (Kompas Online 1996).

Not long after setting up house I was fortunate to find a village some distance away in which to spend time. Acquaintances with an interest in my project took me to a village on the slopes of Mt. Lawu, a dormant volcano some forty kilometers east of the city, and quite visible on a clear day. Mt. Lawu, still known as the realm of the mythico-historical Sunan Lawu, has an important place in local traditions of cosmic geography. Heavily populated by supernatural powers, and widely regarded as home to many of Java's most powerful, autochthonous spiritual forces, Mt. Lawu also marks the westernmost edge of the "sea of mountains" (J: *segárá gunung*) which spans the provincial border between Central and East Java.

Though this area is now in new proximity with the sprawling city below, this did not much affect my initial impression of cool, quiet isolation, which made the area seem more distant from the lowlands. Our trip took one and a half hours in my friend's car; fifteen years earlier, before the paving of the steep, winding road which was the last leg of our trip, it would have taken more than a day; by public transportation, which was to become my usual way of traveling, it took three or four hours. In the following months I fell into a weekly routine of travel between my Solo household and the homes of my hosts in two neighboring hamlets in this area. This made me very familiar with the cheap, relatively rapid transportation infrastructure which began to link this upland area with the lowlands in the late 1970s.

My trips from Solo began on double-decker city buses which lumbered past the businesses, stores, gas stations, and offices stretching along roads from the city center well beyond the Brantas River to the east. Many of my fellow passengers were university students who disembarked at the huge new university campus on the city's fringe, where rice fields were giving way to housing complexes, factories, and the accoutrements of urban life. I disembarked not long after at Palur, a major transit point for people moving between the city and rural areas to the east and north. This growing industrial region has been drawing labor from much of the surrounding rural area, including my destination. I rarely had a long wait there for one of the buses which ferried country people between the region's villages, market centers, its subregional administrative center of Karang Anyar, and Solo itself. In their newer days, the buses we shared had probably plied more lucrative routes between Solo and large cities like Jogjakarta and Semarang. Though these have since been taken over by larger, newer, more comfortable buses, older vehicles still did good business on the more minor routes: traffic during the day was rarely light, and buses were usually full.

I got off this bus some twenty kilometers further north and east at Karang Pandan, a town small enough to offer everywhere glimpses of the carefully tended rice terraces which dominate the rural landscape. From there buses took the road forking south- and eastward up the steep road to Tawamangun, high on the slopes of Mt. Lawu. Others, like me, would ride further to the mountain's more northerly slopes on one of the thirty or so jitneys shuttling back and forth along the less heavily traveled route into the hills. The first few times I disembarked in Karang Pandan, I was approached by enterprising drivers as a tourist who might want to charter a trip up the road to Candhi Cetha, the spectacular, remote remnant of a temple from pre-Islamic Java (on which more below). But as I became a regular I began to run fairly often into acquaintances from further up the slopes who had business downslope and in the lowlands: going to and from high school, visiting relatives, going to a market, or traveling for any number of other reasons.

This last leg of my trip ended a half hour or so later twenty kilometers north of Karang Pandan, just below the jitney's northern terminus. Sharp turns on this steep upland road gave on to striking panoramas of well-tended rice fields, terraces, and gardens. But this aesthetic pleasingness was an indirect side effect of the same population pressure which led not just to highly intensive cultivation, but also to considerable out-migration.

At least since the 1970s, villagers too unfortunate to have inherited land, too poor to buy it, or too poorly connected to gain access to it have found themselves economically marginal in the area, and have been increasingly likely to leave. As seasonal or permanent out-migrants, they have recourse to the same transportation infrastructure I used to find their way to lowland cities and, in some cases, off the island of Java entirely. Many upland families now have close kin living in the lowlands, as became apparent from my informal survey in Gudhangan, the hamlet I describe further below.

By 1986, roughly half of the villagers who were born between 1960 and 1970 in the thirty-seven households I visited there (out of 110) had moved at least semi-permanently to the lowlands.[2] In this respect they represent a small part of the much larger trend evident in the rapid growth of Solo's population. Permanent and temporary migration away from the village is probably nothing new, but has changed in scale in large part due to the same infrastructure which enabled my own oscillating pattern of travel between uplands and lowlands. The same infrastructure which allows family ties to be maintained at larger distances is also the avenue for lowland influence in village life. I sketch here just the most obvious institutional forces which are rising from the lowlands to permeate local communities.

Two hamlets

This sketch is organized to contrast modernization's unequal effects on everyday life in two neighboring hamlets, which I call Gudhangan and Mulih. I mention here three major forces for change – economic, technological, and educational – which are directly shaping and exacerbating long-standing inequalities between these communities, and which are grounded in longstanding ecological differences. Though Gudhangan is poor by most lowland standards, it is relatively well off in comparison with hamlets like Mulih which are on the other side of the ecological threshold where intensive irrigated rice agriculture gives way to nonirrigated cultivation on steeper, less fertile slopes.

Gudhangan farmers grow the Javanese dietary staple, rice, but the region's cool climate is unkind to the hybrid high-yield rice varieties (HYVs) widely used in the lowlands. One effect is that villagers there have been less inclined or obliged to participate in the state-sponsored, capital-intensive agricultural systems – involving pesticides, artificial fertilizers, concomitant credit relations, etc. – which have transformed lowland rural society. The local, distinctively red-tinged varieties of rice they cultivate provide relatively lower yields, but are judged locally by the same token to be more pest-resistant and less fertilizer-dependent. Local rice farming in the area remains a somewhat old-fashioned affair that provides little marketable surplus for the lowlands.

Prior to the Japanese invasion, Gudhangan had a small tea plantation of some slight economic significance in the larger, lowland scheme of things, but which was a significant source of local employment despite its small, mediocre crops. After the Communist uprising of 1965 it fell into desuetude, along with a few neighboring groves of mace trees. The untended tea plants, together with stumps of the teak trees which once shaded them, testify to the area's decline from its former position of modest economic importance.

I first visited Mulih, the other hamlet described here, a few weeks after my first visit to Gudhangan. It lies a half-hour walk up the paved road which begins to deteriorate past the local jitney terminal. A smaller, poorer cluster of two dozen houses perched on a ridge, Mulih is home to farmers who depend on rainwater for their subsistence crops of corn. There and further up the mountain, sheaves of corn hang from rafters in every kitchen. Ground and steamed as "corn rice" (J: *segá jagung*), it serves villagers as the thrice-daily substitute, as its name implies, for real rice (*segá*). Rice may be the dietary staple in the lowlands and hamlets like Gudhangan, but can be had in Mulih only through purchase with scarce money.

This local dietary *cum* social distinction maps onto broader, analogous understandings of urban/rural social difference. The upslope/downslope corn/rice distinction parallels widespread associations of village life with the "low-class" snack cassava (J: *puhung*), over and against the daintier baked goods and cookies city dwellers can afford. Most city dwellers would hardly distinguish between the "village people" (*wong désá*) or "mountain people" (*wong gunung*) who live in Gudhangan and Mulih, but, in the upland scheme of things, the corn/rice divide is central to a constellation of locally salient social differences.

Gudhangan people seemed sometimes amused and sometimes incredulous at my proffered denials that two days and six meals of "rice corn" made me ill; it was, after all, too "rough" (*kasar*) even for their own stomachs. In Mulih, on the other hand, a chance remark on the place of corn in the American diet led to a line of inquiry in which I was obliged to engage often, and which clearly was ammunition for local discussion of attitudes to dietary difference. Even if this distinction took on artificial salience in the presence of a high-status foreigner, it clearly antedated my presence.

The phrase *wong gunung* commonly entered my conversations in Gudhangan when they turned to my visits to upslope Mulih, and in Mulih when villagers living there used it in half-defensive, half-humorous allusions to their way of life. More than one Gudhangan resident jokingly asked how I had slept after returning from a night on a dirt floor in Mulih. So too the Mulih custom of stabling livestock (goats and cows) in fenced off parts of residences was sometimes a point of some amusement further down the slope. Even the gait of some upland "mountain people" is seemingly distinctive. While walking past some children on their way to school one morning, my host in Gudhangan remarked that "The way mountain people [*wong gunung*] walk is very apparent. It's different because they're always carrying loads up and down the hill." Several Gudhangan residents told me that uplanders were clannish and distrustful, which was one reason they were, in the words of a visiting, lowland college student working in the area, "still ignorant and backward" (I: *masih bodoh, masih terbelakang*).

It is unlikely that people in Mulih are able to ignore or entirely gainsay their perceivedly subordinate, backward status. But recent years have seen a heightening of their sense of collective deprivation relative to their downslope neighbors, who are enjoying greater access to the benefits of state-backed development (*pembangunan*). I quickly review here three ways in which national "modernity" has differentially benefited villagers in settlements like Gudhangan, and so augmented local senses of inequality.

The new transportation infrastructure has enabled farmers in Gudhangan to enter the regional economy in ways those in Mulih cannot. In the late 1970s enterprising Gudhangan farmers discovered that trucks could carry cash crops cheaply and quickly to the lowlands, so that they could reap notable profits by turning their rich, well-drained hilltops over to carefully tended rows of onion and garlic. As the area has become increasingly integrated with lowland markets, local plots are being leased by wealthy city-dwelling brokers (mostly ethnic Chinese) who pay landowners to tend crops they do not own. These brokers often bring in their own manpower and trucks, thus injecting cash into the village economy while displacing traditional labor relationships. In this way Gudhangan is being brought into a much more widespread pattern of capital-intensive agriculture, and into closer economic relations with the lowlands as its residents increasingly produce for and consume in a cash-based economy.

In the early 1970s one of Gudhangan's leading citizens (introduced below) planted an experimental grove of clove trees which proved so lucrative that by the mid-1980s one or two of the fragrant, shiny-leaved trees could be seen in virtually every yard in the area, including

Gudhangan and Mulih. As harvest time approached in March, villagers kept close track of offering prices in Karang Pandan by word of mouth, and of wholesale prices in Semarang by radio broadcast. Although Mulih people participate marginally in this market, they are at a disadvantage both because of their late entry into the market, and because of the relatively small harvests they are able to gather.

Gudhangan presents a picturesque appearance: its neat houses, in well-tended gardens, are protected by sturdy retaining walls of stone and cement. This neat appearance, it turned out, was directly related to the village's access to electric power, discussed below, which at night makes it something of an island of brightness on the area's otherwise dark slopes. In the late 1970s Gudhangan won a "village competition" (I: *lomba desa*, discussed below) as Central Java's "most developed village." It was rewarded by the government with a diesel electric generator which clatters to life each evening in time to amplify the call to prayer from the local mosque. In roughly half the village's households which can afford to pay for a connection, 200 watts or so of electricity power a few lights and a radio through the night. In at least four houses, televisions came to life with the generator and stayed on until signoff at eleven, bringing government-controlled broadcasts into the village from the provincial capital of Semarang, or directly from Jakarta.

As it happened, Gudhangan was nominated to participate in the village competition again in 1986, and so I had a chance to get a sense of the regional government's public dealings with residents of candidate villages. I spent two days accompanying delegates of the local village office – an inspection team of five women, dressed in Western-style dresses, each carrying a checklist – as they prepared villagers for the impending visit of the evaluating team from the provincial capital. I followed this team into virtually every household in the village, and virtually every room in every household. Moving and acting as a group, these women would invite themselves (and me) into each household in a superficially polite, hurried manner, issuing a running list of requests for improvements to health and appearance: adding glass tiles to a roof to give more light to a room, removing damp laundry from indoor clothes lines, planting flowers in the yard, repairing stone pathways, white-washing woven bamboo walls, and so on.

It became clear that these officials were working to bring each household into conformance with an extrinsic set of standards developed by and in accordance with the sensibilities of a distant, urban administration. In style and substance, their supervisory project bespeaks a custodial vision of village life, and the right which state agents assume to oversee the most domestic spheres of social life. By phrasing questions and requests in polite Javanese, officials could simultaneously mitigate the imposing character of their presence, and put their nonplused hosts at a disadvantage. Because these uneducated villagers did not control these polite varieties of speech, they were unable to respond in the style of speech being spoken to them, and so were led, somewhat abashedly, to say as little as possible. I discuss antecedents of this mode of sociolinguistic inequality in the next chapter.

At other times, as conversation turned to the upcoming *lomba desa*, it could be difficult for me to evaluate villagers' bland characterizations of what struck me as a highly intrusive process. I was likewise unable to elicit many strong comments about how little motorized traffic used the roads which the villagers had worked so hard to grade and widen. Certainly villagers were quite aware of the personal costs of such competitions, which extend beyond money and labor to collateral environmental impact. As one villager pointed out, since stones had been taken from nearby streams to build retaining walls and cobble alleys, their banks had become much steeper, making fishing less productive and more dangerous.

The *lomba desa* competition is significant here as a local instance of the New Order's mode of territorial control, which makes all aspects of village life homogeneously available for evaluation and supervision by its agents, and in accordance with its own, superposed criteria. This vision of uniformity, in many ways indifferent to distinctions between private and collective life, does not accept that any part of Indonesian space is beyond its purview. It is a broadly centripetal project aimed at fostering homogeneity within and across locales. As such, the *lomba desa* is of a piece with the state's broader project of national development, in which language development has a special place (discussed in chapters 4 and 5). More directly relevant here, though, are immediate effects of the advent of electricity in Gudhangan, especially as an enabling factor for the entry of mass media into village households.

This opened a larger, local window on the lowland, conspicuously Indonesian-speaking world in Gudhangan. Households with televisions, like my host's, often had young, uninvited guests in the evening. Sitting quietly to watch music videos, sententious reports on development, bland news programs, and Indonesian dramas and comedies, young visitors passively witnessed and participated in the national language in a context different from but complementary to that in state-sponsored schools. Undubbed, unsubtitled American shows ranging from *Mr. Ed* to *Star Trek* may have been opaque, but commanded careful attention as parts of and clues to a different, modern world.

Mulih and its neighboring upland hamlets, on the other hand, had not been able to participate in this event and so had no chance to gain access to electrical power. Mulih residents were likewise too poor to buy car batteries of the sort used in some villages to power televisions or radios. Still, one or two cheap transistor radios could be heard there at night, carrying a variety of Indonesian- and Javanese-language programming, and so offering a more modest entree to the city-based world and the national language which Mulih children were also learning in school.

By facilitating the mass media's entry into domestic Javanese space, electricity has indirectly augmented intergenerational social and linguistic differences being created elsewhere. In the many households where older members know only Javanese, but their juniors know Indonesian, mass media broadcasts in Indonesian can be ubiquitous background source of reminders of change understood better by young people than their elders. A tiny, unremarkable conversational symptom of the mass media's presence is worth providing here.

Text 2.2 transcribes a bit of conversation recorded by Mbak Endhang in her own house one rainy afternoon as she chatted with her 22-year-old younger brother (Y), and her sixtyish, monolingual father (B) and mother (S). During a lull in the conversation, all happen to hear a radio advertisement for a unicycle race starring radio celebrities in the stadium in Solo. The text begins as E answers her mother's question about the advertisement. (The entire passage is in the low, familiar, *ngoko* style of Javanese save for the Indonesian particle *kan*, italicized, at line 13.)

Text 2.2

E: Balapan roda siji niku lho.
Y: Bal-balan ora anu, Semarang karo Solo.
Bal-balan nganggo pit roda siji.
S: Pit roda siji?
E: Kuwi nganggo uthik pá ora tá?
Y: Ra, yá sikilé no.
S: Lha lé népang piyé?
Y: Yá, sikil no.
S: Lha dinggo médhal ngono.
Y: Médhal yá gur siji tá.
E: Gayeng anggeré . . .
B: Nèk pacuan kudhá aku ndhélok.
Y: Nèk ènèng, lha Manahan mbiyèk *kan* áná.
S: Opahé pirá?
Y: Ora mbayar nèk nèng Manahan.
S: Nèng anu, nèng Sunggingan.
Y: Telung atus sèket.
S: Ning telung atus, ning telung atus "bediri bediri" [*sic*] ngono kaé?
Y: Kuwi rak Sriwedari, *berdiri* ki ngadeg, ngerti ora?
S: Ngerti, lha nèk lé bayarané séwu limang atus karo yangé pira ngono kaé?
Y: Kuwi rak nèng nggon iyub-iyuban.

[1] E: It's for that unicycle race.
Y: Soccer not, uh, Semarang and Solo. Soccer with unicycles.
S: Unicycles?
[5] E: Do they use a stick to hit the ball or not?
Y: No, they use their feet.
S: Well then, how do they pedal?
Y: Yeah, with their feet.
S: They use it to pedal.
[10] Y: They pedal with just one.
E: It's fun, as long as . . .
B: I've seen horse races.
Y: If there were, they were in Manahan, long ago, right?
[15] S: How much is admission?
Y: You don't pay in Manahan.
S: In, uh, in Sunggingan.
Y: Three hundred fifty.
S: But three hundred, but three hundred is
[20] "standing, standing," like that?
Y: That's Sriwedari, *berdiri* means "stand," understand or not?
S: I understand, so if you pay fifteen hundred with your girlfriend, how much is it?
[25] Y: That's if you sit under the pavilion.

At line 19, elderly S asks (with distinctly Javanese pronunciation) about the Indonesian language advertisement's phrase *berdiri, berdiri* – Indonesian for "standing, standing" – which she has guessed means that one may stand for the admission price of three hundred rupiah. Her son – who has already impatiently told her that she has misunderstood the venue, a park in Solo called Sriwedari rather than Sunggingan – glosses *berdiri* into Javanese at line 21, punctuating his remark with a rhetorical question (*ngerti ora?*) "understand or not?," intoned in a way clearly expressive of impatience with her. Notwithstanding her defensive retort, it seems in fact she does not.

This interactional ripple reflects generational differences arising in knowledge of and engagement with city and nation, as Indonesia and Indonesian enter Javanese domestic space. Younger school-educated villagers have greater access to and (often) interest in the images and language emanating from cities: pop songs on the radio, television shows they can occasionally see, movies shown every month or so in the auditorium of the local government office. All are windows on an urban space of modernity, with Solo as its proximate instance, and Jakarta as its paradigm. Older villagers understand little of the urban pop youth culture which is entering their children's and grandchildren's imaginings of modern urban life. I suspect they would have been dumbfounded by the impromptu break-dance performance I saw a boy of fifteen put on one night for friends at a local youth gathering.

Related to the mass media is the sphere of formal state-sponsored education, a third major mode of Indonesia(n)'s entry into these peripheral areas. Between the opening of Gudhangan's first elementary school in 1968, and a middle school in a neighboring town in 1980, formal education became an increasingly ubiquitous, important aspect of the Indonesian state's presence in the area. All but one or two of Gudhangan's fifty-odd children between the ages of six and twelve were enrolled in the hamlet's elementary school; school days there, as elsewhere in Indonesia, are punctuated by the sound and sight of groups of uniformed, chattering schoolchildren going to and from school.

School gives children access to Indonesian and literacy as a secular, exoteric technology. But among their elders, at least, literacy has powerful residual associations with traditional Javanese elitehood and esoteric knowledge. In chapter 3 I touch on prenational understandings of Javanese literacy as the vehicle of what Anderson (1991:22) would call the "truth language" of literary Javanese (known as *kawi*). For older villagers, literacy's broadly symbolic values endure, as is evident in the care taken by some illiterate Mulih farmers to carry pens in their shirt pockets when they attended biweekly Hindu religious gatherings, which I discuss below. If literacy's traditional values still exert a pull on older villagers' imaginations, the state has conversely figured illiteracy in Indonesian as dysfunctional and abnormal, a condition of being "blind to letters" (I: *buta huruf*). Villagers who know little other Indonesian know this phrase, and the no less condescending description closely allied with it: *masih bodoh* (I: "still stupid/ignorant").

So parents in Mulih and Gudhangan alike have strong impetus to see that their children attend at least the local elementary school, notwithstanding the necessary sacrifices which some were quick to point out to me. Even the relatively small amounts of cash needed for children attending subsidized government schools are non-negligible in village households; some parents grumbled even to me, a paradigm of modernity, not just about cost in money but the unavailability of extra hands around the house and in the fields. But most see that their children go to school at least four or five years, and so gain at least rudimentary, perhaps passive proficiency in spoken and written Indonesian. Low school absentee figures reported by the local office of the Department of Education likewise suggest that those children are concerned to acquire at least a minimal Indonesian-language education.

But parents' general concerns for their children's education and access to an Indonesian-speaking world were complemented by a curiously studied disinterest in opportunities which the government made available to them to take adult education classes. Mulih villagers evinced a tacit, common disinclination to attend basic literacy classes at the elementary schools, and thus declined to acquire advantages they seek for their children. So they willingly leave unredressed the differences which emerge of an evening when they gossip in one corner of a room in Javanese, while youngsters sit in another, working on homework and whispering together in Indonesian and Javanese.

In this way too, then, villagers must countenance the nation-state's presence in domestic life. Nor would they deny that benefits accrue to their lives from that presence. But they did evince ambivalence, distrust, and sometimes fear of change to me in suitably indirect ways: they projected them onto images of the city of Solo as a proximate, concrete sourcepoint for these threatening, disruptive effects. In this way the darker side of modernization and development came to be realized in images of an urban way of life which were less neutral and knowledgeable than that Endhang invoked in the talk transcribed in text 2.1. The villagers' version of Solo the urban center emerged gradually and mutedly in talk with me, the part-time Solo dweller.

Solo the urban center was the scene for cautionary tales about unwary neighbors who had been cheated when visiting there; it was invoked by villagers who advised me to bring my family to live in the village where it wasn't so noisy and dirty, where people helped instead of cheating each other, where you don't need money for everything. Of a piece with such images of the city are stories of morally suspect city spendthrifts. One evening in Mulih I unexpectedly earned approval from the men I was sitting with when I tried to roll a cigarette of the sort they commonly smoked, made with coarsely cut tobacco, local cloves, and thick cigarette paper. Their common approval of my efforts to economize conveyed to me a sense of the moral propriety of my fumbling efforts to do without the expensive factory-made clove cigarettes smoked in the city.

Less exotic outsiders have become personal examples and extensions of city life in the village, and likewise been targets for local anxieties for the future of family and friends. Mulih and neighboring "backward" hamlets have been for some time destinations for university students required to work in a kind of outreach program called in Indonesian *kuliah kerja nyata* (*KKN*), roughly, "working real(-life) classes." Knowingly or not, some of these visitors have fueled and confirmed local suspicions about city people's bad habits. I heard three separate renditions of a cautionary tale about two students from Solo (it was recurringly emphasized) who had brought a bottle of beer into a neighboring uphill hamlet for an evening's entertainment, an act almost as appalling for the beer's astounding cost as for their raucous behavior.

One Mulih resident's vigilance against lowland influence took quite specific, gendered form. One of his daughters, something of a beauty and at fifteen quite marriageable by local standards, had attracted the interest of a lowland student staying down the hill in Gudhangan. The student's visits to the house became frequent enough to make her father worried that he intended to carry her off to the lowlands. So the father abruptly arranged for her to marry the sixteen-year-old son of his neighbor, thus ensuring her continuing presence, and her safety from the unknowns of city life.

Upland suspicions of lowland modernity resonate with older, monolingual Mulih villagers' habit of referring to Indonesian (*bahasa Indonesia*) as *básá Mlayu*. This term, glossable as "Malay language," permits them to project emergent generational and territorial distinctions – older/younger, but also upland/lowland – onto a now spurious ethnolinguistic difference (discussed in chapter 4). It allows them to disidentify with Indonesia(n) as a non-Javanese ethnic language, imputing to it the status of what Gumperz (1982) calls a "they code," which I discuss in chapter 10. But this distinction flies in the face of state ideology and emerging social realities. Indonesian's rapid entry into village life was quite evident in Mulih's teenagers' self-conscious enjoyment in speaking Indonesian with me, and the ways they ostentatiously contrasted it as *bahasa nasional* (I: "national language") with Javanese as *bahasa daerah* (I: "regional language").

The New Order's ubiquitous, multifaceted presence in this area has the broad purpose of integrating upland communities into a larger lowland economy, and its residents into a national citizenry. But its assimilative, homogenizing presence has not eradicated antecedent lines of social and ecological difference. It has rather extended and reproduced inequalities in access to a range of new economic, technological, and educational benefits. Accommodation and resistance to its influence have centered on new versions of Javanese ethnic tradition, and so on shifting understandings of the authority of the Javanese language.

Exemplary speech and speakers

If Solo the urban center looms on the horizon, Solo the exemplary center has not entirely disappeared. Prior to national independence, Gudhangan and Mulih were among the most peripheral domains under the suzerainty of Prince Mangkunegara of Surakarta. In 1986, descendants of that royal house, and representatives of its exemplary *priyayi* tradition, still lived in Gudhangan. I had come to the area in the first place thanks to extended kin connections between my friends, who were connected with that princedom in Solo, and my host-to-be in Gudhangan. This was Pak Mulya, a *priyayi* of some local distinction even if, by traditional standards, he lived rather far "down" the traditional hierarchy, and "away" from the courtly exemplary center.

Pak Mulya was one of two traditional elites in Gudhangan with real if comparatively restricted influence in village life, and each was still regarded as a source of moral authority and an exemplar of a traditional *priyayi* ethos. Though Pak Mulya held no office, and acted with no official authority, he was nonetheless prominent throughout the area as a distant princely descendant, and the son of the Mangkunegaran princedom's last administrative representative in the area. As a youth he had joined the tiny number of Javanese elites who gained an elite Dutch language education in Solo. This prepared him to work toward national independence during the Japanese occupation and ensuing revolution against Dutch occupying forces after World War II. After serving in the nation's first government he retired back to Gudhangan in 1966 to live modestly from inherited land which supported his household – himself, a wife, and adopted daughter – and the families of two sharecroppers.

Pak Mulya's lowland experiences made him something of a local sophisticate, but I believe that for most villagers his aura of inherited traditional status was more noteworthy. All save the youngest villagers addressed and referred to him, for instance, as *pak béhi*, a now old-fashioned phrase combining the short form of the still common kin term *bapak*, "father" (see chapter 6), and the traditional official title *ngabéhi*.

(See J. Errington 1988:136–39.) Together with this distinctive form of address, Pak Mulya received from villagers one of the varieties of polite Javanese speech called *básá*, which I discuss in the next chapter. Though far from polished by Solonese *priyayi* standards, such *básá* usage was by local standards entirely respectful of Pak Mulya's age and station. Pak Mulya returned the ordinary, "low" style of Javanese called *ngoko* to those with whom he was at all familiar and to whom he counted as superior.

The other Gudhangan resident with a similar aura of traditional distinction was Pak Tirta, who shared with Pak Mulya a yard and a princely great-grandfather. Pak Tirta, slightly older than Pak Mulya, had never left the village for long. He had forgone advanced schooling to work as a supervisor at the local tea plantation and manage his own family's landholdings. He was very much a leading local figure: the pioneer of local planting of clove trees, head of the local Red Cross, and deviser of a system of pipes to route water from uphill directly and conveniently into neighborhood kitchens; as an active figure in local affairs his support was often sought out by local government officials. But his authority was most conspicuously and broadly spiritual, in ways I sketch below.

Together, Pak Mulya and Pak Tirta counted less as "local nobility" than as personal representatives of Solo the exemplary center, summoned up by Pak Iman in text 2.1. Their presence as inheritors and mediators of a *priyayi* ethos was perhaps most clearly in evidence on occasions when they exhibited their distinctive fluency in the most refined, high styles of *básá* Javanese. Such language, spoken rarely in face-to-face village interaction, was more appropriate in formal, semi-public gatherings like those I discuss in chapter 5. In the mouths of figures like Pak Mulya and Pak Tirta, high *básá* Javanese was then evocative of the elevated ethos which continues to be salient in village life. Such polished "high" Javanese speech sometimes figures in occasions of state business, but in Gudhangan serves more regularly and crucially in neighborhood gatherings focused on collective spiritual study and practice.

Gudhangan is home to one chapter of a far-flung organization called Pangestu, among the largest and best known of several such Javanese groups devoted to the study of life through the nature of the human interior state (J, I: *batin*). Among these mystical, so-called *kebatinan* groups, long associated with traditional *priyayi* culture, Pangestu is distinctive for its close relation to the same princely house of Mangkunegara from which Pak Tirta and Pak Mulya are descended. So it was entirely natural that Pak Tirta should be the head of the local chapter of Pangestu, and represent it to the organization's central office in the compound of the princely house in Solo.

According to the organization's official history, the godhead – Sang Guru Sajati (J: lit., "the great, true teacher") – made its teachings known in 1932 through the voice of one Raden Soenarto, a low-ranking member of the princedom's court. His voice then served to animate God's words in appropriately formal and literary, but nonetheless low Javanese *ngoko*, appropriate for talk by superior to inferior.³ In Gudhangan, weekly Pangestu meetings circulated between members' homes and, because they were attended by members of all save two households, served also as occasions when other local business could be done by the government's neighborhood official. And although the role of moderator shifted every six months or so, the central speaker and explicator of Pangestu's text and doctrine was always Pak Tirta.

Pak Tirta at these times spoke polished, high *básá* Javanese. It served not as a conversational speech genre, but the formal authoritative idiom of morally fraught discourse. In theme and style, then, his speech resonated with the elevated ethos of the exemplary center of Mangkunegara's palace: its distinctively polished forms tacitly underwrote his authority as the local intermediary between a local community and a version of Solo more narrowly and spiritually figured as an exemplary center.

High *básá* Javanese served also in broadly analogous venues in Mulih. But these superficially similar gatherings need to be contextualized further, and as a different kind of collective response to the state's osmotic presence.

Local identities, national religion

Mulih and Gudhangan share a subprovincial administrative apparatus, but lie in different village administrative districts (*kelurahan*). The head of Gudhangan's district – known as *pak lurah* or *pak pálá* – counted himself an agent of national development, as attested by his assiduous efforts to prepare for the village competition sketched above, and to acquire a middle school for his district. For present purposes his actions and conduct with local people can be said to fit the general pattern of the "modernist" or development *lurah* (*lurah pembangunan*) described by Ward Keeler (1987:89–96) in another part of south-central Java.

Mulih's *lurah* cut a rather different figure. Born and raised locally, he was known for supernatural sensibilities and power which he assiduously cultivated through ascetic practices and intimate contact with the district's autochthonous spiritual powers. The esoteric side of his work often led him rather far from office and home, but his absence was not construed as negligence. Rather it showed his concern for local welfare as understood in local terms. So did his choice of everyday dress: an old-fashioned Javanese jacket and tied headwrapping (not the elaborate *priyayi* variety) which bespoke his roots in and allegiance to local ways of life. Support and respect were due to *pak lurah* in Mulih for his work to gain governmental recognition for the villagers' claim to the official status of Hindus.

The vast majority of Indonesians and Javanese, including those in Gudhangan, count officially as Muslims, however readily they may accede to the label "statistical Muslims" (*Muslim statistik*). Attendants at weekly Pangestu meetings, for instance, count for administrative purposes as Muslims even if they do not attend mosque, pray, or observe the fasting month. But lowland reformist movements are making Islam an increasingly tangible presence in the area. The call to prayer emanating from the new, government-sponsored Gudhangan mosque is now amplified, and reaches ears further upslope in hamlets like Mulih. Reformist Muslims have likewise worked to do away with "superstitious" ritual practices centered on local spirit shrines, and so have made Islam's new, state-sponsored presence of a piece with other newly proximate lowland influences.

For this reason, claims to official recognition of Hindu status in the Mulih area can be seen as an indirect, collective assertion of local difference, and as focal for efforts to create solidarity and autonomy in the face of the broad external forces for change. Villagers in Mulih and its environs must accede to state requirements that Indonesian citizens espouse one of five state-sanctioned religions. But they have done so by supporting an agreement, brokered with the provincial government by *pak lurah*, to be recognized as living in a Hindu area.

By 1986 this official religious identity was well established and focal for bringing villagers together within communities and across generations. Virtually all residents of Mulih crowded into one household or another for biweekly Hindu religious services, which were conducted almost entirely in the same refined, *básá* Javanese used by Pak Tirta at meetings of Pangestu. So those meetings were dominated by the hamlet's only two residents who (as far I could tell) spoke high *básá* Javanese fluently. The slightly senior of these was a man of about thirty who farmed, like his neighbors, and was a barber at the local Saturday market. He had lived with relatives in Karang Pandan long enough to complete middle school, a level of education far above that of most adult people in Mulih who (like many in Gudhangan) had no formal schooling at all. *Pak lurah* had officially confirmed his status as Mulih's religious teacher.

Hinduism in Mulih's administrative district entails nominal membership in Parisadha Hindu Dharma, the national Hindu organization which is supervised by the national Department of Religion. Official government sanction and support has brought with it standard religious texts and official standards for doctrinal transmission. Hinduism, as a regular subject of school instruction, is taught by a Hindu teacher in the local elementary school with textbooks approved by the Department of Education. In this way, archaic Old Javanese is made an exoteric subject of instruction, rather than the esoteric province of a priestly elite.

Locally constructed contrasts between Hinduism and Islam resonate broadly with the kinds of geosocial differences and ambivalences cataloged above. Islam is overtly exogenous, but Hinduism, in local perceptions, is its autochthonous predecessor. The reference point (*kiblat*) for Muslims is the distant city of Mecca, which they are enjoined to visit at least once during their lives; villagers in Mulih and its environs have for their own sacred center the local, ancient Hindu–Javanese monument Candhi Cetha, which stands still further up the slopes of Mt. Lawu. And if Muslims recognize classical Arabic as the language of their sacred scripture, Old Javanese (*kawi*) counts as the analogously sacred, esoteric language of local Hindu scripture and practice.

In 1988, the emerging religious community of Mulih began to build its own temple (*pura*)[4] with support from the national organization Parisadha Hindu Dharma. When I saw it in its beginning stages – a stone floor, low walls, and a statue of the Hindu god Wisnu riding the mythical bird Garuda – I remarked to my Mulih host that it looked much like temples I had seen in Bali. He proudly told me of the priestly official from the Department of Religion who had been sent from Bali to spend a week helping to plan and consecrate the site. In this way he also ensured homogeneity between this newly official bit of Hindu territory and Indonesia's "core" Hindu area. (Balinese readily acknowledge and highland Javanese frequently note that Balinese traditions and scriptures originated in pre-Islamic Java.)

Old Javanese scripture increasingly figures in local religious practice, thanks to the crucial mediation of Indonesian institutions and language. This is because the preeminent experts in that language are Balinese, whose teachings can enter the community via the national school system and its supraethnic national language, Indonesian. By sponsoring Hinduism locally, the state is able to foster a kind of institutionally asymmetric pairing of national and "local" languages – new and old, national and ethnic – which brings religious and linguistic identification under its institutional aegis.

The state has interposed itself in this formative process in more obvious ways. In 1991 the temple was officially opened by provincial, district, and subdistrict government officials. As reported in the national monthly publication of Parisadha Hindu Dharma, the head of the provincial organization for Central Java then "received" the temple from the head of the subprovincial governmental district (the *bupati*, himself apparently a Muslim), who said that "the Hindu community [in the area] may not be nervous about speaking and participating actively in the wider field of development [*pembangunan*] in all facets of life"[5] ("Bupati" 1993:21). As official Hinduism has been assimilated to the institutional logic and legitimizing ideology of the state, its temple has become indirectly symbolic of the state's capacity to mobilize and regularize even this otherwise peripheral bit of Indonesian national space.[6]

Institutional groundings for language

In this chapter I have sketched Javanese and Indonesian relative to shifting upland landscapes and senses of community. I have given only slight attention to those languages' structures in order to foreground their ambiguous, sometimes conflicted places in shifting modes and perceptions of lowland authority. I have pointed out some obvious ways that Indonesian's ascendance has not led to the demise of Javanese, particularly its elevated, refined, *básá* varieties, which have been adapted to shifting contexts as part of Javanese elite traditions more generally.

I have likewise sought here to avoid a linguistic version of what Gupta and Ferguson call the articulation model of cultural change. They use this notion to argue against descriptions of peripheral communities which "posit a primeval state of autonomy . . . which is then violated by global capitalism" (1992:8). Such an understanding lacks fit with the shape of change in villages like Gudhangan or Mulih, where Indonesian is far from being cleanly superposed on a sociolinguistic *tabula rasa*. In the next two chapters I develop this linguistically underdifferentiated sketch to frame Javanese as a symbol of the prenational exemplary center, and Indonesian as an instrument of the power and ideology of the nation-state. The result is a picture of conflicted, socially fraught language change which is bound up with distinct senses of community, authority, and territoriality.

3
SPEECH STYLES, HIERARCHY, AND COMMUNITY

Negárá máwá tátá, désá máwá cárá.
The exemplary center is ordered, villages have their ways.

This chapter sketches the Javanese speech styles with an eye to the differing significances they take on in different communities and interactional contexts.[1] In it I neglect much of their structural complexity to foreground instead the shifting values of polite *básá* Javanese, and their links to the political culture of the exemplary center. My aim is a sketch of Javanese on a sociolinguistic landscape more heterogeneous and less stable than either dominant elite conceptions or some received scholarly accounts would suggest.

The chapter's epigraph is an aphoristic observation on distinct, territorially grounded senses of social organization in different locales in Central Java. Its first phrase links the exemplary center – the *negárá*, which has *nagari* (mentioned in chapter 2) for a stylistic variant – with explicitly ordered status hierarchies: overtly defined "orderings" of status relations characterized the elite *priyayi* communities in Surakarta, and simultaneously distinguished them from others in surrounding, subordinate communities.

The glossing phrase for *máwá tátá*, "is ordered," can be read in two ways, which can help to thematize two faces of this sociolinguistic "order." One is broadly interactional: use of speech styles was normatively ordered in accordance with presupposed status relations, and especially status differences. These helped make elite *priyayi* talk an interactional mirror and mediator of traditional, king-centered hierarchies. The other sense of "order" is broadly dialectal: it pertains to the relative values of speech which is more refined and "ordered" in accordance with context-free, aesthetic norms and ideals. *Priyayi* speakers were distinctively able to im-person-ate such ideals of refined, ordered conduct, manifesting in their persons exemplary qualities recognized as such across contexts and communities. I have described linguistic aspects of these orderings in some detail in J. Errington 1985 and 1988.

The phrase *désá máwá cárá*, in contrast, can be taken to allude to talk as part of the "ways" or "customs" (*cárá*) which are shared and transmitted among members of village communities (*désá*). *Cárá* can be glossed most broadly as "way of doing things," and the phrase *cárá Jáwá* can refer more specifically to Javanese custom, ways of dressing, and ways of speaking. John Pemberton treats this adage as a part of a larger, nineteenth-century Javanese elite effort to reify and regiment an otherwise unruly, heterogeneous "plenitude of practices" which was grounded in otherwise "unordered," perhaps unorderable spheres of village social life (1994:137). Here, though, I place more weight on a broader, fluid sense of *cárá*, as a means for considering conversational life as a "plenitude of practices" which itself is heterogeneous, transient, and contingent enough to elude easy reification as (linguistic) "order" or "custom."

Such a gloss helps develop a more agonistic reading of this aphorism as commentary on sociolinguistic difference and inequality between superordinate exemplary centers and subordinate rural communities. This "plenitude of practices" is in the first place not subject to uniform evaluation; not all aspects of verbal conduct are equally specified for prescriptive ordering. I suggest here that some aspects of speech which are secondary or non-salient make for a kind of "looseness of fit" or skewedness between elites' and villagers' understandings of the appropriate uses and intrinsic values of talk.

I consider here just the broadest such differences between speech style use in the traditional Surakartan *priyayi* community and in villages like Gudhangan and Mulih sketched in chapter 2. I juxtapose these two ways of using speech styles – as doubly ordered markers of overt hierarchy on one hand, and as customary conduct more diffusely bound up with intracommunity relations on the other – to show how they resonate with patterns of difference which Brown and Gilman (1960) described between "group styles" of personal pronoun use to mediate "power" and "solidarity." A similar contrast helps here to consider language ideology and use as reflexes of prenational Surakarta's territorial logic, and as mediators of dynamic, quasi-agonistic relations between its center and at least some of its peripheries. I suggest that sociolinguistic inequality was traditionally "ordered" within the territoriality of the exemplary center, but in ways which countenanced variable understandings of language difference on either side of this geosocial divide.

Style structure

This sketch must begin with preliminary, minimal attention to the broadest structural dimensions of style difference in Javanese. Since the

Table 3.1. *Examples of Javanese address styles*

"Is this yours?"

High *básá*	1	Meniká	menápá	inggih	kagungan	panjenengan?
Low *básá*	2	Niki	nápá	nggèh	gadhahan	sampéyan?
Ngoko	3	Iki	ápá	yá	dhuwèk-	-mu?
		THIS	QUESTION MARKER	YES	POSSESSION	YOURS

early nineteenth century, and in part for political reasons taken up in chapter 4, language scholarship in Java focused on what Dutch authors then called the most "cultured" (*ontwikkelde*) versions of Javanese, by which they meant the "language types" (*taalsoorten*) used among the Surakartan courtly elite. Scholarly attention to these elaborate forms of usage thus contributed to Surakarta's ideological primacy, touched on in chapter 2, and enabled assumptions that usage in this tiny fraction of Javanese society could be taken as paradigmatic for Javanese as a whole. Most accounts of the Javanese written since have likewise taken as reference points the most highly developed, *priyayi* repertoires of speech styles, and so too *priyayi* understandings of interaction and hierarchy (see J. Errington 1985, 1988).

The speech styles are commonly presented as a kind of paragrammatical system of referentially and grammatically comparable elements, which combine and contrast in regular patterns. With more or less elaborate versions of the array exemplified in table 3.1, authors have described stylistic variants on "the same" Javanese sentence along a structural *cum* aesthetic continuum, independently of contexts of use or identities of users.

At the continuum's "low" end are the "unrefined" (J, I: *kasar*) style elements and modes of speech, like sentence 3, which are called *ngoko* in the literature. In the "middle" – which is the gloss of choice for *madyá*, a term common in the literature – are sentences like 2. This term very clearly serves the classificatory strategy of locating all these styles on a double cline of structure and refinedness. Sentence 2 is "above" (more refined than) *ngoko*, but "below" (less refined than) the "highest," most polished (J, I: *alus*) styles like sentence 1 in table 3.1. This is usually called *krámá* in the literature.[2]

This comparative and contrastive mode keys to the semantic similarities between the elements in each column (or paradigmatic set) in table 3.1, which are conveyed by English glosses below. At the same time, each element partially distinguishes the style of the sentences, read horizontally, of which it is part.

Details of such systemic approaches are less important here than their basic, shared difference with the commonest ways Javanese speakers describe the speech styles. Speakers' practical points of view key more to interactional relations between speaker and addressee than to structural difference, and so not to scalar arrays so much as a basic, interactionally grounded bifurcate relation: between the "style" called *ngoko* (like sentence 3) on one hand, and all others called *básá* (like 1 and 2) on the other.

From this perspective, *ngoko* is not the lowest segment on a stylistic and aesthetic continuum. It is in fact the "basic" language, antecedent to and structurally foundational for all its relatively polite *básá* complements. *Ngoko* can be thought of as developmentally primary in that it is learned as a "first" language, prior to *básá* styles.[3] It is the medium of internal thought and feeling, the most im-mediate or "natural" means for ex-teriorizing or ex-pressing subjective, occasional states. All *básá* styles, on the other hand, are acquisitionally secondary and pragmatically augmentary: they serve generically to mark and presuppose a speaker's stance of polite awareness, *qua* speaker, to some interactional other as addressee.

James Siegel foregrounds this founding pragmatic distinction by likening *básá* to a distinct second language, "in the sense that it is not the speaker's 'own' language. Identification between the 'self' or speaker and his [*básá*] speech is avoided" (Siegel 1986:17). *Básá* speech thus marks an other-oriented mode of self-presentation. To speak to an addressee to whom politeness is owed is to match one's "own" words to his or her sensibility. *Básá*, as generically other-oriented conduct, thus contrasts with *ngoko* which, "by being *ngoko*, announces that it takes no cognizance of the hearer" (ibid.:24).

An abstract but useful way to describe this founding contrast between styles is as a relation of pragmatic markedness. *Básá* can be said to be grounded in and generically marked, over and against *ngoko*, for what Karl Bühler calls the appellative function of speech (1990:35), that is, for address of an interactional other. To contrast *ngoko* with *básá* as a non-polite, perhaps impolite mode of address, is to focus on the absence of such regard conveyed because it is "not-*básá*." This is its "minus" reading within the markedness relation.

But interactional concerns for overtly addressed others are bracketed in the sphere of "internal" states and thought. In this sphere, *ngoko* never contrasts saliently with any variety of *básá* since it is itself the "basic" medium of thought. "[T]o speak to oneself in *krámá* [*básá*] is absurd . . . since it raises the question of who is being honored" (Siegel 1986:22). When interactional self/other relations are bracketed, *ngoko* is neither polite nor impolite; then it takes on its superordinate or "zero" reading in the markedness relation. Figure 3.1 schematizes *ngoko*'s double role as

Speech styles, hierarchy, and community

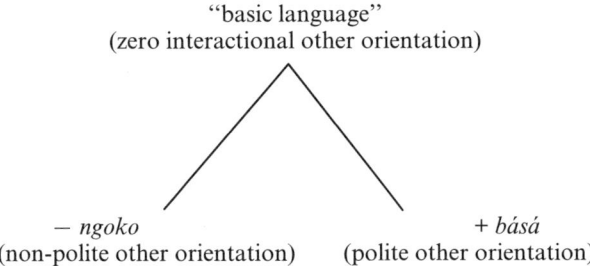

Figure 3.1 *Generic markedness relations between speech styles*

medium of interactionally and noninteractionally grounded language use; it diagrams the most basic, pragmatic difference to which these commonest Javanese terms apply. I return to this distinction in chapters 8, 9, and 10 in sketches of interactional dynamics, in which *ngoko* can serve a double mediating capacity.

For his Surakarta-centered reflections on selfhood, speech, and authority, Siegel finds it useful to deal with *ngoko* and *básá* (which he calls *krámá*) as categorically separate, internally unitary "languages." In this way he adopts a much simpler picture of style variation than is common elsewhere in the literature. My concerns here, though, are best served by making use of two structural subdistinctions between styles of *básá*. One was presented as the minimal distinction between styles I henceforth call "low *básá*" (sentence 2 in table 3.1) and "high *básá*" (sentence 1 in table 3.1). The other distinction is between subvarieties of low *básá*, illustrated in figure 3.2, which is relevant for discussion of bilingual usage in chapter 7.

The commonest elements of *básá* styles are lexical items, like the adjective *awis*, which stand in a binary, either/or contrast with a "basic" *ngoko* synonym (like *larang*). Both can be said to share a gloss ("expensive"). As Uhlenbeck (1978:284) points out, these commonest, two-member lexical sets predominate in the relatively frequently used "core" vocabulary of the language.

But there are also a few three-way stylistic alternations, like those between proximal demonstratives in column 1 in table 3.1 ("this"), and question markers in column 2. These more elaborate, three-member sets are concentrated in the language's grammatical and deictic apparatus, and serve to distinguish the *básá* styles I call "high" and "low." "High" elements of such sets, like *meniká* and *menápá*, mark relatively refined styles of address like sentence 1; the less polished, "low" *básá* styles are generally called *madyá* in the literature (though rarely by "ordinary" speakers) and are marked by terms like *niki* and *nápá*.

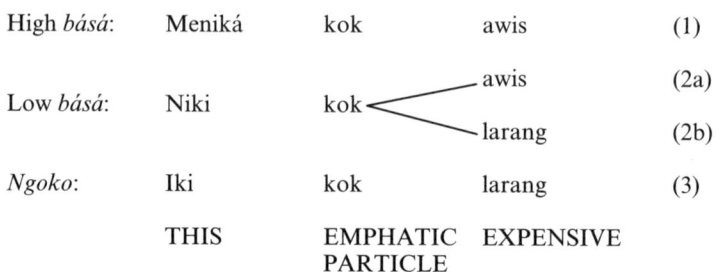

Why, this is expensive!

Figure 3.2 *Structural relations between styles of* básá

Low *básá* substyles in turn can be of two sorts, like 2a and 2b in figure 3.2, depending on their referential elements. Low *básá* elements, like *niki* and *nápá*, can combine with either *ngoko* or *básá* members of two-member sets, like *larang* and *awis*. As a result, styles of speech can be relatively "higher" (like 2a) or "lower" (like 2b). This secondary opposition, within low *básá*, depends on the double combinability of words like *larang* and *awis* with their respective *ngoko* and *básá* cognates on one hand (*iki* or *meniká*) as well as low *básá* elements (like *niki*) on the other.

Further details of speech style structure, which are taken up in the extensive literature on *priyayi* usage, can be ignored here,[4] where it is more relevant to consider the tacit narrowing of perspective in much of the literature, such that non-*priyayi*, non-exemplary usage is accorded the residual status of less elaborate variant. Received scholarship helps tacitly to residualize non-elite usage, and to subject it to what Gal and Irvine call erasure, which "renders some persons or activities or sociolinguistic phenomena invisible" (1995:974). The rest of this chapter considers and redresses the effects of this ideologically grounded erasure.

Exemplary users, exemplary uses

The speech styles' most immediate significances can be conveniently sketched with respect to dominant *priyayi* usage, and with recourse to Brown and Gilman's well-known account of second-person pronoun usage in Western European languages. Their famous model (1960) can be mapped conveniently and transparently onto the common substance of descriptions of exemplary elite use in Solo up to the turn of the twentieth century. Speech styles' interactional significances were then realized in

$$
\begin{array}{ccc}
\textit{ngoko} & \rightleftharpoons & \textit{ngoko} \\
\text{low } \textit{básá} & \rightleftharpoons & \text{low } \textit{básá} \\
\text{high } \textit{básá} & \rightleftharpoons & \text{high } \textit{básá}
\end{array}
$$

Figure 3.3   *Traditional exemplary repertoire/use*

patterns of reciprocal exchange. These were cocreated as parts of ongoing social relations schematized in figure 3.3.

Exchange patterns, represented by "horizontal" half-arrows, could be more or less symmetric. "Vertical," more or less asymmetric exchange – of some *básá* style for *ngoko*, or low *básá* for high *básá* – presupposed status differences between speech partners, such that "higher" styles were spoken "up" the hierarchy by inferiors in return for some relatively "lower," less refined style spoken "down." Maximally asymmetric patterns of exchange – e.g., of sentences like 1 and 3 in table 3.1 – presupposed maximal status differences.

Literature dating from 1920 or so conveys a sense of highly stratified elite networks, in which all varieties of *básá* served to mark and mediate finely distinguished status differences. Interactionally relevant status differences were the rule rather than the exception in traditional elite circles. This was because socially ordered descent and official status combined with kin relations and age in ways which had clear, ubiquitous correlates in asymmetric patterns of *ngoko/básá* exchange. Textual evidence suggests that low *básá* was then addressed to intimate superiors – for instance, to husband by wife, or elder sibling by younger – in return for *ngoko*. (See J. Errington 1985:46–51, 1988:22–84.)

Relatively symmetric exchange, on the other hand, could modulate the relative intimacy or formality of interaction between equals or near equals: "higher," more refined styles would elevate and make interactional engagement more ceremonious. Symmetric exchange of *ngoko*, the basic language, was the mark of intimacy. In all these uses, speech styles mediated hierarchy and interactional intimacy through what Michael Silverstein calls their "principal ideological function" of "deference-to-Addressee" (1995:283). At the same time, fluency in these social *cum* linguistic techniques was learned as part of a broader range of social demeanors, and so "cultivated" within a kind of "natural sensibility" (Bourdieu 1984:255). *Básá*, spoken fluently, was a little like a mask worn successfully enough to dissimulate its secondary nature, and to advertise none of its generically augmentary, "not-*ngoko*" nature. For this reason, properly refined speech was not just appropriate for an addressee and structurally well formed; it was also flexible (J: *luwes*) enough to convey a sense of transparency between observable conduct and internal nature. It evinced that sense of "relaxation within tension," in Pierre Bourdieu's phrase (1982, 1984), which bespeaks the embodiment of a state, rather than the conscious application of learned technique.

Bourdieu alludes to such socialization processes as inscribing recognition and mastery of language "in a practical state, in dispositions which are impalpably inculcated, through a long and slow process of acquisition" (1991:51). What he calls a domestic mode of acquisition served to restrict transmission of refined *básá* competence quite self-evidently and "naturally" to elite circles. This restricted distribution gave high *básá* significance not just in terms of situated appropriateness, but as the restricted, superordinate part of a stratified system of competences and statuses. "Differences in the mode of acquisition" of refined language made it possible for use of high *básá* to be perceived as an index of "differences in nature" of speakers, exemplary and non-exemplary alike (Bourdieu 1984:68).

This secondary significance of usage (especially high *básá*) was powerful because it was tacit. It manifested competence (or incompetence) in verbal technique as a secondary index of a speaker's social background (see Silverstein 1995:284). *Básá* usage which counted as inadequately refined ("high") for a given addressee in a given context could be construed not just as inappropriate in context, but also as indicative of an aesthetic *cum* moral deficiency on the part of a speaker. This "essentialist" misrecognition, as Bourdieu (1984:24) puts it, allowed mastery of verbal technique to be diagnostic of intrinsic nature. So too self-evident, iconic linkage between language use and user contributed to *priyayi* hegemony, conferring the appearance of "necessity to a connection" between speech and speaker "that [is] only contingent" (Gal and Irvine 1995:973). Construed as a mark of upbringing, and cultivated internal nature, high *básá* helped to naturalize social differences and the authority of elite speakers (J. Errington 1984).

These paired significances of high *básá* could emerge most clearly in uncommon but telling occasions of interaction across the sociolinguistic divide between elites who controlled high *básá*, and non-elites who did not. Non-elites then beheld in a speech partner someone who controlled just the kind of speech which they themselves should address to that speech partner, but could not. One instance of this dilemma, and a solution to it, was related to me by an elderly *priyayi* woman of Surakarta, who told me of trips she took with her father to a distant plantation in the 1920s. She went along, by her own account, so that villagers would feel less embarrassed (*pakéwuh*) when called on to respond to her father's questions. Because her father knew that the villagers' best but none-too-high *básá* was inadequately polished for address to him, a high official, he brought his adolescent daughter as a kind of surrogate addressee, to whom they could address their low *básá* responses while he attended as bystanding audience. (This is also a first example of the kinds of ambiguous, shiftable participant relations which I discuss at length in chapters 8 and 9.)

During this era, political change was already affecting the status of *priyayi* in Surakarta, and shaping the perceived social values of high and low *básá*. One effect of these changes, which I have discussed in J. Errington 1985, was a revaluing and devaluing of "low *básá*" as it came to be identified not just as less refined but as "substandard," outgroup usage. *Priyayi* increasingly had recourse to low *básá* only in their dealings with non-intimate inferiors, especially non-elites. As recently as the early 1980s, older *priyayi* in Solo still evinced biases against low *básá* as language typical of those who "know no better," i.e., who lack control of high *básá*.

Surakarta's development into an urban center has seen the ongoing erosion of traditional *priyayi* political and cultural primacy, and a concomitant loosening of traditional links between elitehood and competence in high *básá*. As traditional status distinctions have been overshadowed by a regnant egalitarian ethic, *priyayi* find themselves obliged to deal with non-intimates who do not accept linguistic marks of their traditional inferiority by accepting *ngoko* in asymmetric exchange for some style of *básá*. *Priyayi*, on the other hand, find that the logic of style exchange makes unacceptable their use of high *básá* to persons incapable of reciprocating that usage. To arrive at some non-intimate but symmetric pattern of *básá* exchange, traditional elites now have recourse to the same low *básá* genres which are commonly used among other non-elite urbanites, and in the village communities discussed below.

For the remnants of traditional elite *priyayi* circles in contemporary Surakarta, *básá* usage curiously mirrors that between tongue-tied peasants and the father of my elderly acquaintance in the 1920s. High *básá* continues to be distinctive of a speaker's status and indicative of regard for an addressee; but traditional elites in Solo the urban center are now obliged to adopt a self-perceived out-group guise when they speak low *básá* "out" of their in-group, and "down" (rather than "up") the social hierarchy. I schematize this transitional situation in figure 3.4, parenthesizing "low *básá*" to indicate that ambiguities accrue to its use by conservative elites: it counts as relatively stylistically polite in comparison with *ngoko*, yet relatively unrefined and covertly dialectal in comparison with high *básá*.

As traditional elite circles have become attenuated, their younger members have come to interact more, and more equably, with other Indonesian urbanites. Even parents who have been vigilant in educating their children in high *básá* recognize that its interactional usefulness is

```
high básá  ⇌  high básá  ↑
----------------------------
(low básá  ⇌  low básá)
----------------------------
ngoko      ⇌  ngoko       ↓
```

Figure 3.4 *Contemporary conservative elite Javanese use*

increasingly restricted. As low *básá* has become more ubiquitous in their dealings outside family circles, it has become less salient as a linguistic mark of social background.

In chapter 5 I return to this marginalization of high *básá* in the sphere of face-to-face interaction, which indirectly informs its new uses in quasi-public venues, and its new values as an emblem of new versions of Javanese ethnic tradition. More directly relevant here, though, is another somewhat ironic upshot of such change: as high *básá* is increasingly detached from everyday interaction, patterns of speech style use in the urban center seem increasingly to resemble longstanding patterns of use in village communities.

Speech styles at the periphery

From the hierarchized, hierarchically superordinate exemplary center, lack of competence in high *básá* could be perceived as a kind of deficiency which was endemic among those down the social hierarchy, and away from the exemplary center.[5] But this view is not fully shared or matched by understandings of *básá* usage in communities like Gudhangan and Mulih. Certainly Solonese elites are correct in describing villagers as largely unable to speak refined, high *básá*, as I learned first-hand when I first ventured to use it conversationally in Gudhangan and Mulih. I was then not just a foreign curiosity but a kind of linguistic nonesuch, having inadvertently created a situation similar to that my older consultant described to me as occurring between her father and peasants. I elicited reactions from older villagers which may have been much like those she recounted: nervous laughter and embarrassed mumbling.

So I was obliged to improve very quickly my skills in low *básá*, the preferred medium of polite talk in everyday, face-to-face dealings. In these villages, low *básá* is exchanged symmetrically between unfamiliar and sometimes even somewhat familiar equals, or is exchanged asymmetrically for *ngoko* between unequals. This latter pattern occurred in the usage transcribed as text 2.1, for instance, when Pak Iman gave Endhang *ngoko* in return for low *básá*. Status differences are not interactionally irrelevant in village life, but less finely differentiated and marked; they key more to samenesses and differences in relative age and kin status than to ranks in official or descent hierarchies.

Notable in this regard was the common interactional pattern between "ordinary" villagers and their local traditional elites, Pak Mulya and Pak Tirta. These notables gave their covillagers *ngoko* or low *básá*, and generally received in return some version of low *básá*. No one evinced much concern, so far as I could tell, that low *básá* might be inadequately refined to these representatives of the exemplary center. This appears a significant point of contrast with attitudes of older, conservative, city *priyayi* who count as Pak Mulya's and Pak Tirta's age-mates. Speakers in Gudhangan evinced little feeling of embarrassment over their limited *básá* repertoires, and little sense that low *básá* was an inferior substitute for high *básá*, even to covillagers of high traditional status. Low *básá* is rather the broadly appropriate mode of polite conduct, acceptable by and to covillagers of notable status.

In this respect, usage in Gudhangan appeared to be informed by tacitly different, more fluid understandings of *básá*'s values; its use was part of a "group style," in Brown and Gilman's (1960) phrase, different from that of exemplary elites. From the exemplary center, such usage might seem a pale, derivative imitation of high *básá*. But within the village community itself, low *básá* is a locally, self-evidently appropriate mode of verbal politeness, learned and transmitted within households and used in the community at large.

This does not mean that high *básá* is unknown in village life, as chapter 2's sketch indicates. I described there (and return in chapter 5 to) high *básá*'s place in village life as an exemplary object of aesthetic appreciation. But its use then was broadly ceremonial, and in contexts where most villagers participated as parts of audiences for relatively circumscribed, quasi-ritualized, and non-dialogic high *básá* talk. At gatherings of Pangestu and Hindu Dharma, high *básá* speech enhances not just a speaker's exemplary demeanor, but the shared sense of gravity of these occasions. Then *priyayi* notables who are also covillagers engage in quasi-public, monologic speech, assuming roles as local representatives of the distant exemplary center.

As a speech genre which is thus not just distinctively refined but distinctively public, high *básá*'s appropriate uses and institutional values seem to stand in the sort of broadly bifurcate relation to other styles, low *básá* and *ngoko*, which can be schematized as in figure 3.5.

The solid horizontal line in figure 3.5 can be taken as representing the double distinctiveness of high *básá* usage in village milieux. On one hand, high *básá* is distinctively appropriate for authoritative, non-conversational contexts, and for addressing collective, non-responding audiences; it thus falls outside the kinds of dynamic patterns of interactional

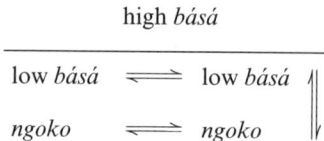

Figure 3.5 *Contemporary urban/village usage*

exchange involving *ngoko* and low *básá* sketched earlier. On the other hand, high *básá* is distinctive of its users' statuses in rural communities. In Gudhangan, for instance, Pak Tirta and (occasionally) Pak Mulya serve as local spokespersons at formal gatherings, im-person-ating an exemplary aesthetic of conduct. It is no coincidence that they act in such quasi-ceremonial capacities at quasi-corporate gatherings which are licensed by non-local institutions, and often involve the presence of outsiders.

Such privileged linguistic usage mediates between a local community, whose members are otherwise bound together in more mundane day-to-day experience, and the larger, supravillage polity centered on a privileged locus of that language: the courtly circles of the exemplary center. In figure 3.5, then, the significance of the dimension of verticality – "above" and "below" the line – differs from that in previous figures and in table 3.1. It suggests a bifurcation like that between Charles Ferguson's (1959) diglossically related "high" (H) and "low" (L) language varieties; here "high" *básá* stands over and against other, "lower" *básá* varieties and *ngoko* alike. Notwithstanding the partialness of its fit with such usage (J. Errington 1991) a broad notion of diglossia helps to foreground tacitly different divisions of linguistic labor in peripheral villages like Gudhangan and Mulih on one hand, and in exemplary elite circles of Solo on the other. Village communities, as sites of "local diglossia," can be thought of as conforming to the territorial logic of the exemplary center while maintaining a distinct, covertly autonomous understanding of the relation of language to personal worth. These patterns of usage can be seen, then, as arising not through overt resistance to elite dominance – that is, through some overt or explicit counterordering of language use – but in tacitly enacted, locally transmitted ways of talk.

Linguistic distinction at the center and periphery

I have sketched here two hierarchically related, overlapping, but distinct logics of Javanese speech style use. One is informed by the dominant logic of the social "order" within a Javanese "aristocracy of language and culture." In this elite sphere, language use was embedded in a broader, stratified system of tastes and competences which served, tacitly and powerfully, to naturalize *priyayi* cultural dominance. By linking an ethos of interaction and a logic of sociolinguistic inequality, the speech styles (especially high *básá*) were doubly grounded in the apex and center of the territory over which *priyayi* had authority.

From their superordinate perspective, distinctively subordinate ways of speaking in peripheral communities were easily residualized or "erased"; a distinct, tacit logic of high *básá*'s values and appropriateness could be ignored. But in villages, high *básá*'s exemplariness could set it off from everyday life and so from low *básá* and *ngoko* talk. Admirability does not necessarily translate there into perceived emulability, and makes for an alternate understanding of linguistic hierarchy which fits better more commonalistic understandings of status, and is better grounded in the tacitly reproduced, relatively autonomous village norms of low *básá* as a polite verbal demeanor.

If such distinct understandings of language and community in fact coexisted at the centers and peripheries of prenational south-central Java, that condition contrasts significantly with the sorts of social and linguistic homogeneity associated with the rise of the nation-state. Theorists otherwise as different as Benedict Anderson and Ernest Gellner (whom I discuss in chapter 4) have underscored the relation of nationalism and linguistic sharedness among a citizenry, and developed different reasons for emphasizing the linguistic homogeneity within national territories which are defined by state borders (see Anderson 1991:163–85) rather than exemplary centers. I consider some of these connections in the next chapter's sketch of codeveloping Indonesian language and polity.

This quasi-agonistic, center/periphery relation can be contrasted with Bourdieu's institutionally grounded description of sociolinguistic inequality in state-centered societies. In his view, the division of linguistic labor in peripheral villages I sketched above appears to be partially reproductive of an elite-defined hierarchy of competence and taste. High *básá*'s "scarceness" as symbolic capital then informs the distinctive ceremoniousness of local elite voices. In this way, it appears to be "part of the paraphernalia which always announces the sacred character, separate and separating, of high culture" (Bourdieu 1984:34).

Bourdieu views such "legitimate practices, i.e., the practices of those who are dominant," as the *standard* which "[a]ll linguistic practices are measured against" (1991:53). This assertion is of a piece with the broader argument in his well-known book *Distinction* (1984) that state-sanctioned schools enable misrecognition of difference between two kinds of social sensibilities: some are internalized or "cultivated" in the domestic sphere of the home on one hand, while others are acquired as pedagogically objectified knowledge in educational institutions. In this way he argues that state-supervised educational systems function to disguise class-linked differences between two modes for acquisition of culture, and to reproduce misrecognizable symbolic dimensions of class difference.

This economistic argument presupposes the state's uniform presence as a regulator of uniform symbolic and economic "capital," and in this respect has been cogently critiqued by Kathryn Woolard. She plausibly disputes the enabling assumption that sociolinguistic hierarchies are always incorporated into uniform, "fully integrated" symbolic and economic "markets" (Woolard 1985:739–43). Bourdieu's state-centered argument, she suggests, already partakes of the dominant point of view it seeks to explicate; by overgeneralizing the power of institutional hierarchies, it residualizes solidarities which can be tacitly maintained in and through the linguistic usage of dominated, "vernacular communities" (ibid.: 743–45).

South-central Java's "premodern" polities present an instance of such a disjunction, one which is grounded in distinct constellations of institutions and a non-national (or prenational) territorial logic of the exemplary center. (Compare in this regard Smith-Hefner 1989.) One linguistic reflex of this center–periphery disjunction is villagers' routine, unembarrassed recourse to styles of low *básá* for address of elders and local notables, who themselves control high *básá*. The distinct, local sense of appropriate usage at these subordinate but semi-autonomous peripheries is worth quickly illustrating with recourse to a few empirical particulars: variation and change in personal pronoun use.

I have sketched elsewhere longstanding patterns of shifting personal pronoun use among the *priyayi* elite of Surakarta (J. Errington 1988:111–51). Relevant here is their rural complement: recurring, targeted appropriations of distinctively elite pronominal usage by speakers further "down" the social hierarchy. (Broadly analogous changes in kin terms are discussed in chapter 6.) From at least the early nineteenth century up to the very recent past, a cumulative effect of such appropriation has been the repeated assimilation of formerly deferential elite personal pronouns into the repertoires used in commoner communities, and their concomitant replacement by new forms in courtly circles. This pattern is crudely summarized for second-person pronouns in table 3.2.

For contemporary Surakartan elites, the use of *sampéyan* by their nineteenth-century forebears for equals and superiors would be striking, because nowadays it is stereotypically part of low *básá* usage by and to speakers of markedly lower (traditional) status who do not control high *básá*. Non-elites appropriated this distinctively polite form: by around the turn of the century it had progressively displaced *ndiká* in rural polite

Table 3.2. *Changing uses of polite second-person pronouns*

	c. 1920	c. 1960	c. 1980
Elite:	sampéyan	panjenengan	panjenengan
Villager:	ndiká	sampéyan	sampéyan/panjenengan

usage. By the 1920s, a new term, *panjenengan*, had come into elite usage as *sampéyan*'s replacement. *Panjenengan* in turn has undergone much the same appropriation (and, from the elite's point of view, devaluation).

Such patterns recall Bourdieu's description of "title inflation" in England which, he says, shows how members of a dominant group are similarly unable to "conserve their position, their rarity, their rank except by running to keep their distance from those immediately behind them, thus jeopardizing the difference which distinguishes the group immediately in front" (Bourdieu 1984:161). He calls it a linguistic reflex of

an integrative struggle and, by virtue of the initial handicaps, a reproductive struggle, since those who enter this chase, in which they are beaten before they start, as the constancy of the gaps testifies, implicitly recognize the legitimacy of the goals pursued by those whom they pursue, by the mere fact of taking part.

(1984:165)

But Bourdieu's economistic interpretation of these specifics appears overbroad against the backdrop of broader, relatively stable differences in usage of speech styles sketched above. Figured against relatively stable differences in *básá* usage, this "integrative struggle" over personal pronouns seems both highly targeted and interactionally keyed. The "goals pursued" are locally situated, because they are bound up with concerns to show deference to addressees within and to members of one's own community, and not necessarily just to members of the exemplary elite. It shows how interactionally crucial elements have been selectively targeted for emulation and, cumulatively, for appropriation.

This highly specific form of lagging emulation, not part of a diffuse effort to emulate an exemplary ideal, is a kind of appropriative raid on resources which are relatively salient and useful for showing respect by local criteria, in local communities of space and time. This narrow but crucial aspect of etiquette use centers on relatively pragmatically salient elements (J. Errington 1988) for which the interactional stakes are high, but also locally constituted.

Suitably foregrounded, this narrow sphere of pronominal politeness throws into relief broader, territorially linked differences between shared senses of the values of Javanese speech styles. I have sketched those differences here as being grounded in the sense of hierarchical order (*tátá*) on one hand, and locally constituted and transmitted ways (*cárá*) of showing politeness on the other. In chapter 5 I return to high *básá*'s public, authoritative use with an eye to this quasi-agonistic relation. But in such use, high *básá* is often counterposed with Indonesian, which has come into ascendance along with the developmentalist ideology and territorial logic of the New Order.

4
NATIONAL DEVELOPMENT, NATIONAL LANGUAGE

> The monopoly of legitimate education is now more important, more central than is the monopoly of legitimate violence.
>
> (Gellner 1983:34)

In south-central Java, Indonesian is a national but un-native language. It lacks self-evident politically or culturally salient attachments to a primordial, native-speaking community.[1] That very un-nativeness has been key to the success of Indonesian language development, a state-fostered drive to "reduce arbitrary social and linguistic heterogeneity through the fast growth of functional heterogeneity within a single language" (Neustepny 1974:37). That same success licenses visions of incipient language shift like Someya's, quoted in the introduction.

But such programmatic, state-centered evaluations do not speak to the ways that the larger project of development might shape perceptions and uses of Indonesian by its un-native speakers; nor do they consider Indonesian's role as a positive and not just an un-native factor in the growth of an Indonesian national identity. To speak to these questions, and redress these gaps, I sketch here Indonesian's sociohistorical grounds, and consider its potential as a symbolic resource for modernist, nationalist ideology. Because Indonesian's values have derived from its groundings first in a colonial and now in a national state apparatus, I consider first its historical place in each as a "nexus of practice and institutional structure" (Abrams 1988:58).

To consider nationalism and developmentalism as facts which might shape understandings of that language in use, I then recruit the self-styled "philosopher of industrialization," Ernest Gellner (1964:72). His abstract, theory-driven account of language, modernity, and nationalism helps here to explicate the New Order's self-legitimizing developmentalism, and to locate Indonesian in that project. This is because his technodeterminist vision of what I call language "standardism" resonates in broader, telling ways with New Order development ideology and practice alike.

Colonial Malay, national Indonesian

Indonesian has historical roots in dialects of Malay spoken natively on both coasts of the Straits of Malacca (Sumatran and Malayan) and the neighboring Riau Islands. "Malay" (I: *bahasa Melayu*) can thus refer to the language of a distinct ethnicity, as used by older Mulih villagers (mentioned in chapter 2) who referred to Indonesian (in Javanese) as *básá Mlayu*. Non-native dialects of Malay also served as *lingua franca* throughout the archipelago well before the Portuguese made their way to the spice islands – the Malukus of what is now Eastern Indonesia – in the sixteenth century. By some accounts pidginized Malay varieties, sometimes called "market language" (I: *bahasa pasar*), were used as far north as the coasts of the (present) Philippines and southern Japan, as far west as the coasts of Madagascar, and throughout what is now the Indonesian archipelago.

There is no date on which Indonesian can be said to have been born from Malay, but it does have an identifiable baptismal event: the celebrated "meeting of youth" (*Rapat pemuda*) on October 28, 1928, in Batavia, then capital of the Dutch East Indies. (A convenient source for general background is Moeliono 1993.) There and then an ethnically diverse, Dutch-educated native intelligentsia jointly adopted a nationalistic program and simultaneously renamed Malay (*bahasa Melayu*) as Indonesian (I: *bahasa Indonesia*), language of their nation-to-be. Their famous "Oath of the Youth" (I: *Sumpah Pemuda*), still repeated on its anniversary every year across the country, conferred public, formal recognition on the project of a unified people (*satu bangsa*) speaking one language (*satu bahasa*), in a single homeland (*satu nusa*). It does not now ring hollow, as Indonesian has come to be far more widely known than was the variety of Malay standardized and propagated under Dutch aegis, which they appropriated to the nationalist cause.

This legitimizing 1928 periodization elides "standard" Malay/Indonesian's colonial genealogy. Different forms of Malay had been widely used for centuries by Dutch traders, missionaries, and military, and later by colonial administrators. Because access to Dutch was severely restricted for "natives," longstanding controversy persisted among interested parties as to which variety of Malay would best serve their several purposes. The shape of this debate reflected the nature of the Dutch presence: as the spice trade decreased in profitability, they shifted their exploitative focus to inland agricultural and human resources on Java and Sumatra, thereby giving issues of administrative communication new immediacy. After the Dutch East Indies Company (Vereenigde Oostindische Compagnie, or VOC) ceded power to the colonial government of the Netherlands East Indies, language issues became increasingly important for efforts to increase knowledge of and extend control over local "native" affairs.

These language problems were complex in south-central Java's agrarian kingdoms, which controlled a fertile rice plain suitable for cultivating sugar, tobacco, coffee, and other profitable exports. In the late eighteenth and early nineteenth centuries, colonial officials found themselves confronted by a dilemma: because colonial policy kept Javanese largely ignorant of Dutch, Dutch were obliged to learn the technically challenging, interactionally pivotal Javanese speech styles, especially for dealings with courtly elites. These were among the most immediate reasons for early moves to codify and teach Javanese to Dutch officials. By the middle of the nineteenth century, colonial efforts to train Dutch officers in Javanese had been largely abandoned, and communication across this colonial divide, as in other parts of the Dutch East Indies, commonly involved marginal, non-native, and non-prestigious varieties of so-called "service Malay" (*dienstMaleisch*).

It is enough to note here a dichotomy which recurrently figured in debate on the colonial language question: choosing between "pure" or high Malay and "low, common, and intelligible (although degenerate) language" (Valentyn, quoted in Hoffman 1979:66). By the early nineteenth century, practical needs for a codified administrative vehicle converged with the possibility of recovering a "pure," high form of the language which was held out by the ascendant discipline of philology. Political and intellectual forces increasingly combined to promote the "self-consciously proprietorial attitude of didactic Dutch scholarship toward the language from the mid-nineteenth century on" (Hoffman 1979:78). There arose a unique group of colonial administrators – *taalambtenaren*, or (in Teeuw's translation 1973:112) "linguistic officers." By practicing what Teeuw calls a "unique combination . . . of . . . pure [linguistic] science and applied science oriented to social needs" (ibid.:9), they created what "an extraordinary symbiosis of scholarship with the metropolitan politics of a colonizing state" (Hoffman 1973:22).

These state linguists' pioneering forerunner was the historical linguist H. N. van der Tuuk, whose extensive field research was in turn directly inspired by his "heroes in the field" (Teeuw 1971:xviii), the Indo-European philologists Bopp and Grimm. Van der Tuuk was among the strongest sponsors of the philological project of reconstructing with precision the "pure" forms of original Malay, and his status as a scientist lent considerable force to his practical arguments that, in the absence of a properly established standard for pure Malay, Dutch officials were learning an illegitimate "babble" Malay devoid of value and no one's first language.

The rise of international trade, burgeoning port cities, growing print media, and a new administrative infrastructure, together with the rhetoric of a colonial *mission civilatrice*, all made feasible and institutionally necessary what Dutch linguists made intellectually desirable: a Dutch-promoted school Malay which was rationalized, uniform, and cohesive, "an identical idiom . . . understood and spoken everywhere" (Fokker 1891, quoted in Hoffman 1979:84–85). Out of this multifaceted process of colonial growth arose a variety of standardized Malay which was partially selected and partially constructed by and for the colonial state.

A standard Malay orthography was fixed at the turn of the century by van Ophuysen, whose work in the mainland "Malay heartland" led to the codification of a "general, cultured Malay" (*algemeen beschaafd Maleis*). In 1908 a colonial office called the Balai Pustaka was established to provide reading materials in "good" Malay (as well as major ethnic languages) for "a new class of potential readers, with different living and reading habits, with different expectations with regard to books, based on their school experiences" (Teeuw 1973:112).[2] This literary publishing arm of the state soon became a major force in "a long-term project to homogenize and unify Malay" (Maier 1993:55). Novels, poetry, and criticism produced by the Balai Pustaka were exclusively in Dutch-propagated, standard school Malay, and so excluded markedly Islamic or Chinese literature in favor of Western-accented visions of modernity and humanism. This agency's literary products were offered to a market created largely by the state's own educational system, a community of Malay speaker/readers who were likewise largely employed, directly or indirectly, by the colonial system. If school Malay was artificial or "stiff," this was a correlate of its "stability and uniformity" (Teeuw 1973:120). "[D]ominated by Balai Pustaka," *bahasa Melayu* "provided a solid and trustworthy foundation for the building of the present-day national language" (ibid.:124).

In his chronicle of the rise of school Malay, Maier usefully deploys Bakhtin's observations on the centripetal effects of standardizing social authority to discuss "awareness of standardized language in a network of schools" (1993:55). He points out that the ascendance of this print-mediated variety did not eradicate other geographically and socially variable varieties of Malay which were simultaneously developing in other communities:

This particular kind of Malay was strongly associated with Dutch Authority, and while embitterment about the socio-political and economic situation merely increased, the natives often referred to it with the term *Bahasa Belanda* (Dutch) rather than *bahasa Melayu*; not all of them by any means felt compelled to use it.
(1993:57)

Observers have long noted the coexistence of "low" Malay dialects, which in recent years have led some to allude to this split as one between "high/low" forms in a diglossic relation (e.g., Moeliono 1994:377). A more detailed sketch of this relation was written in the early 1960s by a leading Indonesian literary figure and (then) Communist propagandist, Pramoedya Ananta Toer. In his historical account of Indonesian's "evolution" he describes the social grounds for the split between two kinds of what he calls "pre-Indonesian" (*basa pra-Indonesia*) – "working" language (*basa kerdja*) and "school Malay" (*Melayu sekolah*):

> Working language is the language of work, and so the practical language which can be used at any time. Unlike the standard language, whose development was strongly supported if not cultified by the Dutch, working Malay developed on its own, growing steadily, practical and available whenever needed . . . Working Malay spread more widely and dynamically, and so has become an important topic for sociolinguistics [*sic*]. From a sociolinguistic [*sic*] angle, one can observe several structural features which distinguish it from writings in the standard language, for instance, their respective intonation, vocabulary, syntax, and their respective ideolects.[3]
>
> . . .
>
> School Malay or standard Malay is often called official language. This is the product of language which has been cultivated, thriving in school circles. As a political matter, it needs to be recalled that this language was the means of communication between the colonial government and the people, for conveying all orders, regulations, and rules to be obeyed. Because of that, school language was useful only for those who were educated to become civil servants or their groups. The language developed in civil servant circles, among the officials, above all teachers, fertilizing the seeds of the bureaucrat.[4]
>
> (Pramoedya Ananta Toer 1963)

Remarkable not just for the Indonesian neologism *sosio-linguistik*, which Pramoedya seems to have coined in 1963, this account identifies the institutional grounds for this double development of Malay. "Low," "market," "working" Malay served in polyglot urban communities which were only indirectly or incidentally penetrated by particular institutions and agents of the colonial regime.

The commonest of these common dialects evolved along with Batavia, which over three centuries was transformed from trading fort into the burgeoning commercial and administrative center for the Dutch East Indies. At the center of this original plural economy – where ethnic, economic, and linguistic lines of division stood in virtual congruence – "working language" was the quintessential urban mode of "intercommunication which spread the whole length of Indonesia's coasts, in the harbors, markets, shipyards, offices, until, eventually, it developed into the language for working" (Pramoedya Ananta Toer 1963).[5]

This split reproduced itself in the sphere of print through low Malay print culture, which developed largely independently of canonic, school Malay grammar or genres:

the [high] Malay press was usually headed by "experts" in Malay, that is to say, teachers or former teachers. This definitive separation between Malay and pre-Indonesian was augmented by the siding of those with power with Malay throughout the Dutch colonial era, and this led to complications and disputes within society simply because of the modes of use of these two kinds of language.[6]

(Pramoedya Ananta Toer 1963)

These social and linguistic complexities underlay the "Oath of the Youth," which was pronounced in the same "school Malay" which it anointed as Indonesian.

In the 1960s Pramoedya envisioned a proper Marxist synthesis between these dialectically related social spheres and languages. But the same political upheaval which eventually consigned him to internal exile led to a very different linguistic and national development in which the ambiguities of Indonesian's roots in colonial history still surface, albeit in muted ways. Compare in this regard two statements drawn from different editions of the official governmental rules for standard Indonesian orthography:

Since rules for spelling Indonesian with Latin characters were established in 1901 on the basis of work by Ch. A. van Ophuysen . . .[7]

(Departemen pendidikan dan kebudayaan 1972:i)

Since rules for spelling Malay with Latin characters were established in 1901 on the basis of work by Ch. A. van Ophuysen . . .[8]

(Departemen pendidikan dan kebudayaan 1979:i)

The 1972 edition's reference to the standard spelling system of Indonesian (*bahasa Indonesia*) retrojects the language's origins into the Dutch scholarly and colonial project, well before the legitimizing 1928 baptismal event. The implications of this colonial–national link seem to have given pause to the officials in the Indonesian Department of Education and Culture, and led to the 1979 edition's revised reference instead to *bahasa Melayu*, "Malay language."

Such terminological shifts are symptomatic of problematic continuity between the "Malay" language project of the Dutch, and the "Indonesian" project of the New Order. Similar ambiguities emerge in popular nationalist accounts of Malay/Indonesian's social history, which conflate the modern 1928 baptismal event with a proto-national, ante-historical Malay/Indonesian ur-community.[9] Analogous ambiguities figure even in the writings of Indonesia's most famous and outspoken modernist, S. T. Alisjahbana. He wrote early in the nationalist period, for instance, that "Chinese had at the beginning of the Christian era come to Indonesia [*sic*] and encountered a kind of Indonesian [*sic*] lingua franca in these islands, which they called Kwenlun" (Alisjahbana 1956:6).[10] Such passing allusions to an "Indonesian lingua franca" resonate broadly with visions of a proto-national community, intimating without claiming an Indonesian proto-nationality.[11]

In Java, at least, such rhetorical slippage now helps to elide Indonesian's historical relations with colonialism, and with present-day dialects of Malay spoken natively in present-day Malaysia by their conationals, in Sumatra (numbering about five million), and in coastal communities on other Indonesian islands. The New Order's success has exerted centripetal, homogenizing forces for propagation of a version of *bahasa Indonesia* which answers well to Pramoedya's description of "school language."

Modern, native Indonesia(n)

The declaration of independence in 1945 brought Indonesian into ascendance as a national language under Sukarno's charismatic presidency. But factionalism, corruption, and economic stagnation ultimately made untenable his position between the powerful Communist Party and the fiercely anti-Communist military. His government collapsed with the bloody September 30th movement of 1965, which came to be known by the politically salient acronym GESTAPU (from Gerakan September Tiga Puluh) under the New Order, for which it was a founding event. Factions of the Indonesia military responded to the kidnapping and killing of six generals and a lieutenant, ostensibly by Communists, by seizing control of the government and, over ensuing months, overseeing the massacres of hundreds of thousands of ostensibly Communist Indonesians by their fellow citizens. From this bloody chaos emerged the military dominated New Order state (Orde Baru, as opposed to Sukarno's Old Order, the Orde Lama). The New Order, headed by Suharto, has overseen and guided all aspects of state policy – political, economic, social, and linguistic – in a concerted drive to mold Indonesia to its imagined vision of modern development.

Nationalist and developmentalist ideologies have been brought into strong convergence by the New Order as it implements massive modernization projects in all parts of the nation. One of the twin ideological underpinnings of the state's largely unilateral, authoritarian, top-down actions is secondarily relevant here: the nativist, quasi-ethnic encapsulation of an Indonesian transcendental essence called Panca Sila (lit. "the five ways"). Panca Sila was Sukarno's formulation of pan-Indonesian beliefs and social values but has come to be, in the New Order's own English phrasing, a national ideology.[12] It consists of five general social principles – Belief in One Almighty God, Nationalism, Humanitarianism, Popular Sovereignty, and Social Justice. During the "Old Order" Alisjahbana characterized Panca Sila as

a means of uniting various political ideals and objectives . . . the compromise represented by the Pantjasila was of first-rate importance. But as a logical construct or as a reflection of the internal realities of Indonesian government, it was obviously untenable . . . In spite of official acceptance of the Pantjasila, all the parties ignored it when it came down to the level of practical politics, and, as in other democratic states, fought only for their own goals and ideals.

(Alisjahbana 1961:148–49)

But the New Order has transformed it into a litmus test for actions which it deems inimical to the state, that is, as *anti-Panca Silais*. Panca Sila's ubiquity, rhetorical power, and contextual malleability in public discourse help to qualify New Order definitions of what is Indonesian, and so what is non- or anti-Indonesian.

Panca Sila is now complemented by an ideology of modernism and development, *pembangunan*. This is the other major ideological force which the New Order mobilized to motivate and legitimize its vision of a modern future and policy decisions, many with massively disruptive effects on local communities like those sketched in chapter 2. The vision of a radically new era with which *pembangunan* rhetoric is joined is evident in another of Alisjahbana's later remarks:

The Indonesia yearned for by the new generation is no continuation of [the kingdom of] Mataram, no continuation of the kingdom of Banten, no continuation of the kingdom of Minangkabau or Banjarmasin. In their thoughts, Indonesian culture is likewise in no way a continuation of Javanese culture, of Malay culture, of Sundanese culture or any other.

(Alisjahbana 1977:42)[13]

In such epochalist formulations – clearly of a piece with visions of language shift – development ideology serves to figure ethnic diversity less as a problem to be solved than a condition to be abandoned, or allowed to recede on the historical horizon as Indonesians advance into a modern national future. In this respect it coarticulates clearly with predictions of ethnic language death, like that issued by Someya for Javanese, discussed in the introduction.

Pembangunan has been a keyword in almost three decades of New Order modernist discourse. President Suharto acceded to the title "Father of Development" (*Bapak Pembangunan*, as opposed to Sukarno, who was the self-styled "voice of the people"). Development rhetoric can be "development communication" (*komunikasi pembangunan*) and the press, in fulfilling its national duty – under more or less overt but always effective government surveillance – operated as a proper "development press" (*pers pembangunan*). General Benny Moerdani, a central figure in the New Order military and political elite, periodized Indonesian history into the revolutionary period (*periode perang kemerdekaan*) and development period (*periode pembangunan*), effectively eliding the Sukarno era's historical salience. However questionable its status elsewhere in the post-Cold War era, "development" was an enduring, crucial rubric for legitimizing New Order social, political, and economic policy, and for its moves to subdue resistance to its decisions.

Indonesian, the "language of development" (*bahasa pembangunan*), was likewise intimately bound up with the New Order's fortunes, as is clear from one of Suharto's very first unilateral decisions: a 1965 Presidential Instruction which mandated the government-supervised building and staffing of elementary schools throughout the country, particularly in rural areas. These have been a primary institutional means for New Order dissemination of Indonesian to the citizenry as primarily "a school-mediated, academy-supervised idiom" (Gellner 1983:57). As part of *pembangunan*, state language policy has long been framed in terms consonant with those which serve in other spheres of modernization. Issues of language development (*pembangunan bahasa*) and the "politics of the national language" (*politik bahasa nasional*) are regularly framed as aspects of political integration and social control:

> The concept of national community cannot be fully realized if there is not one national language ... A nation-state [*negara*] that has one common language known by its entire populace will be more progressive in development, and its political ideology will be safer and stabler.
>
> (Burhan 1989:77)[14]

In such self-evidently policy-oriented, state-sponsored contexts, Indonesian is tacitly located among the "targets" or "objects" of institutional treatment, to be "developed" through conscious, rational, policy-oriented actions by the state and its agents. Because it is symbiotically bound up with the nation-state's infrastructure, Indonesian can be an object of state manipulation and superposed, "top-down," on otherwise diverse ethnic communities.

The general tenor of New Order development rhetoric can be considered here by foregrounding one way it differs from its Old Order antecedents. Ariel Heryanto has critically reviewed tropes of "development" over thirty years of intellectual discourse, and perceptively traced a broad thematic shift from organic to mechanical conceptions of change (1985, 1988). Focal in this transition has been a move from organic metaphors of *perkembangan* to an architectonic or mechanical rhetoric of *pembangunan*.

Kembang "flower" and *perkembangan* (roughly, "flowering") were keywords in much pre-New Order discourse on a "NATURAL PROCESS of change, which is motivated primarily by some INTERNAL necessity, enforced primarily by its own INTERNAL energy, its pace and extent being PROPORTIONAL to its own nature" (Heryanto 1985:49–50). This earlier version of "development" is redolent of Romanticist visions of language and nation, and had its earliest and most eloquent expression in Alisjahbana's Romanticist writings, like the following:

A culture begins to bud, when there grows up within a society a conviction of the truth of a certain system of values . . . the ability of a culture to develop is not unlimited, for every culture contains within itself the dialectic of all growth. As the papaya seed, which sprouts in the fertile soil and joyfully thrusts up through it to greet the beneficent rays of the sun, must experience, the further it rises up out of the earth, an increasing remoteness from the soil, from which its roots suck up the sap, that makes it grow, so every culture that gives expression to a definite system of values, must eventually experience the limits to the possibilities of its further development.

(Alisjahbana 1961:3)

In the 1950s (roughly the period during which this passage was written) the "organic" discourse of *perkembangan* coexisted and interarticulated with the more mechanistic, instrumental discourse of *pembangunan*.

Heryanto reads *pembangunan*'s ascendance over *perkembangan* from a variety of New Order writings, which convey a dominant vision of agentive, instrumentalist, and rational social change:

[i]n essence, *pembangunan* does not refer to things in nature or natural processes. On the contrary, it refers to an exploitation of nature, as of human beings. In essence, it denotes CRAFTMANSHIP as well as ENGINEERING, with the chief emphasis on yielding MAXIMAL PRODUCT, in the most EFFICIENT pace and manner possible, by bringing EXTERNAL forces to bear upon the object, *bangunan*.

(Heryanto 1985:50–51)

Implementing *pembangunan* is a matter of constructing a new whole from manufactured parts, "like a person building a house" in Suharto's own words (1971).[15] Under the New Order, then, Indonesian can fairly be called a project of "language engineering," a phrase which fully captures the state's position as the backer, architect, and executor of the linguistic aspects of nation-building.[16]

Theories of nationalism, ideologies of development

Modernist proponents of Indonesian like Someya and Alisjahbana assume what they do not demonstrate about linkage between Indonesian's institutional and ideological grounds on one hand, and putative qualities of Indonesian usage – directness, clarity, effectiveness – on the other. Those connections may be rhetorically self-evident within the New Order's discourse of *pembangunan*, but are less obvious if one searches interactionally situated talk for practical correlates of that ideology. To consider Indonesian usage as a socio-symbolic field which might be tacitly shaped by the *doxa* of *pembangunan*, prior explication is needed for links which might be plausibly drawn between developmentalist ideology on one hand, and conversational practice on the other.

Ernest Gellner helps articulate this relation by bringing issues of institutional change, language, and subjectivity together in his theorization of nationalism. He argues that standard, national languages are infrastructural for modern state institutions, and prerequisite for rational, context-independent modes of thought. Gellner diagnoses nationalism as an upshot of modern economic and political formations, and sees in it the kind of collective representation which allows modern states to worship themselves in particularly naked form. In his view, modern political and economic constellations subsist on and support the cultural and linguistic homogeneity which states foster, and which nationalisms symbolize.

From Gellner's distanced, debunking perspective, Panca Sila and the ideology of *pembangunan* appear to serve together an Indonesian version of the "deception and self-deception of nationalism," obscuring the "mechanisms" of what "*really* happens" (1983:57) in nation-building. Whether or not members of the New Order technocratic elite responsible for *pembangunan* would accept Gellner's characterization of nationalism as a necessary (self-)deception, they have clearly recognized the crucial symbiosis between language development's effectiveness and the perceived authenticity of the national polity.

Gellner critiques and extends Durkheim's thesis on the division of labor by arguing that advanced industrial societies differ from what he calls advanced agrarian societies in their dependence on distinctively *generic* training.[17] So they require specifically secular literacy in a homogeneous language. Such linguistic competence can be developed only through a process of "exo-socialization [and] exo-education outside the local intimate unit . . . [This] makes the link of state and culture necessary" (Gellner 1983:38). So national languages subserve a state-supervised division of labor, in Gellner's view, and are symbiotically related to modern political and economic infrastructures.[18]

Gellner's account could serve as a kind of theoretical charter for New Order efforts to foster simultaneously an industrial infrastructure, and universal Indonesian competence and literacy through its state school system. In this respect Indonesia's success with Indonesian seems a paradigmatic example of what Gellner terms "the general imposition of a high [here, Indonesian] culture on society, where previously low cultures had taken up the lives of the majority . . . of the population." Thirty years of New Order government have yielded what Gellner calls "a . . . school-mediated, academy-supervised idiom, codified for the requirements of reasonably precise bureaucratic and technological communication" (1983:57).

Of interest here is Gellner's extension of this functionalist argument to the sphere of subjectivity, thought, and rationality. Invoking Max Weber, he argues that standard languages are not just infrastructural for communication within territorial boundaries and across institutional contexts; they are also necessary for objective, context-free, "modern" modes of discourse and thought. He asserts that modern national languages embody two conspicuous elements in Weber's notion of rationality. "One is coherence or consistency, the like treatment of like cases . . . the very soul and honor of the bureaucrat . . . The other is efficiency, the cool, rational gauging of means and ends, the spirit of the ideal entrepreneur" (Gellner 1983:20). But a national language counts more broadly as

> a universal conceptual currency, so to speak, for the general characterization of things . . . all facts are located within a single continuous logical space, [such] that statements reporting them can be conjoined and generally related to each other, and so that in principle one single language describes the world and is internally unitary . . . in our society it is assumed that all referential uses of language ultimately refer to one coherent world, and can be reduced to a unitary idiom; and that it is legitimate to relate them to each other.
>
> (ibid.:21)

Modern national languages are by this account exoteric, contextually uninflected means for autonomous thought and discourse, the verbal grounds for distinctively modern stances and the perspective of what Nagel (1986) has called a "view from nowhere."

Gellner's understanding of modernity can be thought of as keying to the referential capacities of language, and as corresponding to what Michael Silverstein calls standard languages' ideologically privileged "functional utility . . . as a means of representation or instrument of denotation" (1996:285). By abstracting language's capacity to describe states of affairs from interests of users and contexts of use, Gellner develops a positivist perspective on the idea of a standard language as a "referential system sensitive to nature and blind to society" (Gellner 1994:51).

Gellner's self-acknowledged partiality to neat models makes his argument a categorical, clear-cut, and useful supplement to overtly ideological New Order framings of nationalism and modernity. By suggestively linking standard national languages with modern modes of language use, he explicates what is otherwise tacitly assumed about Indonesian and Indonesian's "modernity." His is thus a useful frame for particulars of Javanese Indonesian usage which are taken up in following chapters: not for explaining Indonesian's values, but for interpreting its use in emergent forms of bilingual interaction.

So too it is worth relativizing his abstract, logico-deductive argument to his own authorial position and social context. This can be done by briefly noting his recourse to Basil Bernstein's influential sociological research (e.g,, Bernstein 1971) on the educability of working-class children in Britain. There is tacit but important linkage here to Gellner's allusion to differences between "our" modern, national languages, and those of prenational polities. The latter sort of language serves in a premodern, "self-enclosed community" in which people "communicate in terms whose meaning can only be identified *in context*," as a kind of "'shorthand' or 'restricted code'" (Gellner 1983:12). This allusion to "restricted code" – a quasi-empirical moment in a broadly logico-deductive argument – draws tacitly but clearly from Bernstein's efforts to explain why working-class children do poorly in British schools.

Relevant here is a protean, problematic leitmotif which runs through Bernstein's work: his distinction between the context-embedded, covert, unobjectified "restricted codes" which he asserts are used in working-class families, and the less contextually tied "elaborated codes" used among members of the middle class. Bernstein's several versions of this distinction are less important here than their common implication for Gellner's invocation of it. Were it the case that members of premodern, prenational communities indeed use "restricted" codes, then Gellner's account of difference between the national/modern and prenational/premodern polities would show a telling, troubling homology with class-linked distinctions in at least one (presumably) modern nation-state. And if even paradigmatically modern national societies harbor communities of "restricted code" users, then Gellner must be construed as describing or prescribing a potential, rather than an actual, state of social organization.

If it is not read in this teleological way, Gellner's account accords the United Kingdom, for instance, the status of an incompletely modern nation, which has yet to reach the end of the long hard road of progress to nationalism (and so, as Sartre's ironic definition of progress has it, which leads to "us"). Class differences appear to prevent adequate "exosocialization" through schools, and permit or oblige individuals to reside in "closed" communities. If Gellner's account in this regard appears utopian, it nonetheless has practical political uses, clearly illustrated by the New Order's own rhetoric of *pembangunan*. The New Order presented itself as the necessary force behind a collective move to a developed, modern Indonesian future which is incipient but also indefinitely deferrable.

Considered with an eye to Gellner's theorization of national modernity, then, predictions of language shift like Someya's, quoted in the introduction, can be seen as the academic complement to New Order development ideology. They are grounded in the condition which Gellner seems to explain but actually prescribes, and which, as a national future, legitimized New Order actions in the present.

As an explicator of the otherwise taken-for-granted nature of "modern" language-and-thought, Gellner foregrounds epistemological correlates of the *doxa* of development and modernity; he thus provides a privileged view of Indonesian, the peculiarly un-native language of nation and state, as an ideologically freighted symbol which is increasingly entering into everyday interaction. This referentialist theory/ideology sharply contrasts with the structure and practical logic of Javanese speech level usage sketched in chapter 3. I foregrounded there the broadest grounding of the *ngoko/bása* distinction not in topics of speech or "characterizations of things," but in existentially grounded interactional self/other relations: the transient, situated, subjective, and occasional conditions of talk. Exactly these conditions of language use are bracketed in Gellner's theoretical account of distinctively modern thought in standard, national languages.

If *ngoko* and *bása* are (recalling Bühler's terminology) differentially privileged as expressive (of speaker) and conative (for addressee) in verbal practice, Indonesian stands over and against both, at least in Gellner's theoretical account, as distinctively and impersonally privileged for its referential significances. I return to this three-way distinction in later chapters to develop an interpretive strategy for considering aspects of bilingual, Javanese Indonesian usage.

5
PUBLIC LANGUAGE AND AUTHORITY

State ideologies of nationalism and developmentalism permeate Javanese communities, and serve to propagate the New Order's authoritative understandings of Indonesian citizenship. But its institutional forces for change are not aimed at straightforwardly devaluing Javanese-ness, or displacing antecedent understandings of ethnic community. The state appears instead to be working toward suitably domesticated versions of subnational Javanese ethnicity, one among others, under the unifying rubric of "custom" (I, J: *adat*). By selecting and promoting aspects of "tradition" deemed suitably emblematic of ethnic distinctiveness, the state can license those diacritics of collective difference, and locate them in particular segments of national territory which it controls. Just as national borders demarcate internally homogeneous, mutually exclusive citizenries, so can provincial and subprovincial borders be made primary reference points of distinction for internally homogeneous, subnational ethnic groups (see Anderson 1991:163–85).

This chapter first considers high *básá*'s shifting role as it is being developed into one such emblem of new versions of Javanese ethnicity in Central Java. I try to show here how, if high *básá* "has lost no ground in a period of nationalism and independence" (Siegel 1986:20), this has been possible only because of shifts in its institutional groundings and its emblematic significances for state-fostered understandings of Javaneseness. I sketch two faces of high *básá*'s emerging place, as it is reshaped by a new class of Javanese Indonesian elites. On the political side, this has involved official moves to "preserve" elite Javanese tradition in which high *básá* has been focal. But refined high *básá* can also be considered as a scarce ceremonial resource which is increasingly the purview of a class of professional speakers, and of value in ceremonial venues now sponsored by members of a new urban elite. Exemplary high *básá* speech can imbue these reinvented traditional contexts with an aura of exemplary dignity, yet at the same time it counts as a commodifiable skill.

I turn briefly in this chapter's latter part to high *básá* as a rhetorical resource for the figuring of authority through talk to peripheral village publics. There I sketch high *básá*'s salience for implementing and performatively enacting power in formal, monologic situations. This is also a way to broach issues of bilingual usage as it inflects the authority of public talk, and mediates shifting understandings of polity. Public talk, Javanese and Indonesian alike, can be considered in performance as potentially presupposing two distinct modes of public speakership on one hand, and two distinct senses of co-presence among those gathered as a collective addressee, or audience, on the other.

I develop this second interpretive sketch around three tiny texts of public usage. These are transcriptions of particulars of the sort readily residualized under "macro" profiles of "language development," and which serve to demonstrate the curiously hybrid, heteroglot character of much such public talk. They help show how rhetorically motivated switchings between high *básá* and Indonesian figure shifting modes of speakership, audiencehood, and relations of power between them.

Standards for exemplary language

Aside from social ideologues like Alisjahbana, quoted in chapter 4, few observers take seriously the notion that Javanese is threatened with imminent death through massive language shift to Indonesian. But this has not prevented the New Order from devoting considerable public attention to one purported, unfortunate effect of national development: decline in knowledge and use of high *básá*. New Order officials have framed this as a pernicious consequence of modernization, one which threatens the linguistic and cultural heritage of all Javanese. Their official response can be briefly considered here through the inaugural Javanese Language Congress (Kongres Bahasa Jawa) which was convened in 1991 in Semarang, capital of Central Java, at President Suharto's behest.[1]

Six hundred Indonesian technocrats, politicians, and intellectuals (mostly Javanese) met to discuss (mostly in Indonesian) the current state of the nation's dominant ethnic language (their native language) in the dynamic of national development. Suharto (himself Javanese) opened this widely publicized conference by urging the various language experts in attendance to discuss ways that Javanese philosophy, especially as contained in the Javanese orthography, could be used to develop and disseminate Javanese character. Claiming rather disingenuously to speak not as president of the republic but as a Javanese, he expressed his hope for the Indonesian people to possess the "noble spirit" necessary for "proper relations" among people, and between people and the environment, as well as between people and God.

It is enough here to adduce some of the broader concerns which recurringly figured in many of the papers delivered and discussed among attendants. All at the Congress, as one attendant put it to me, "lamented the disappearance of [exemplary, high] *básá*."[2] This major concern was linked, in turn, to their shared worries about widespread ignorance of Javanese orthography (the *hánácáráká*). Linguistic etiquette and literacy were thus recurringly identified as integral to the Javanese tradition (I: *tradisi Jawa*) but increasingly unknown by younger Javanese.

By portraying these oral and written traditions as being under threat, conference participants recurringly presupposed an ethnic past in which high *básá* and the *hánácáráká* were widely if not universally controlled by people of Javanese descent. But this is a picture of the Javanese past which seems at odds with the prenational situation, at least in the "heartland" of south-central Java. There, as indicated in chapter 3, high *básá* together with literary Javanese were traditionally the distinctive province of the traditional courtly elite. Knowledge of exemplary *básá*, as also discussed in chapter 3, was restricted enough to imbue users with an aura of exemplary status, and to index their participation in exemplary circles. Active and passive control of literacy was similarly restricted.

So any ongoing "loss" of this elite Javanese tradition would be better understood as a more limited change occurring among just those who would be its direct inheritors: descendants of traditional *priyayi* elite, who now mostly live in Indonesia's urban centers. The Javanese language conference's basic premises and stated goals therefore appear skewed with the prenational situation sketched in chapter 3. It seems less a search for ways to preserve a common, threatened heritage, and more an effort to propagate a public, official, standard version of a formerly ineffable, esoteric "noble sublime" (*adhiluhung*) (see Florida 1987; Pemberton 1994). High *básá* in this way is being framed as part of a Javanese past which is in danger of being "lost" as the inheritance of all Javanese Indonesians. In venues like this Congress, high *básá* and traditional literacy are effectively detached from the exemplary center – the apex of the traditional social hierarchy – and made state-sanctioned emblems of Javanese ethnicity in the nation at large.

The Congress likewise served to legitimize the New Order's stewardship over this tradition. Conference participants addressed Suharto's fond hope for the institutionally protected future of Javanese language (I: *bahasa*) and culture (I: *budaya*) by recommending that both be placed under the custodial aegis of the New Order's Department of Education and Culture, which was officially authorized to oversee the teaching of the language in state schools located in Javanese territory. As Javanese language (especially high *básá*) enters schools in Central and East Java, it takes on the status of "local content" (*muatan lokal*) in the state-established curriculum. Detached from courtly circles, it has been effectively defined relative not to exemplary centers but to ethnically homogeneous provincial territory; subordinated to the institutional logic of the nation-state, exemplary high *básá* becomes an object in and for standard, public culture.

This process can be read with an eye to Gellner's standardist logic of nationalism and language sketched in chapter 4. In prenational Java, high *básá* had a distinctly exemplary territorial locus, set off from and "not properly united" with its more mundane peripheries. It stood as part of a "hierarchically related sub-world" of "special privileged facts" and "insulated facts or realms," "sacralized and exempt from ordinary treatment" (Gellner 1983:21). With the demise of that prenational (and, in Gellner's scheme, pre-rational) language and polity, high *básá* can now be "reduced" to the national "unitary idiom" (in Gellner's words) which is Indonesian. Under the New Order's aegis, and via the Javanese Language Congress, the "sub-world" of high *básá* has been assimilated to the national language's exoteric standard, and to the "deception and self-deception" (in Gellner's phrase) which is the state's self-legitimizing tradition. High *básá* is then a newly public-ized object: local content for translocal national forms, and an aid in New Order efforts to define as "non-native" what it deems to be uncongenial side effects of development and modernization.

In this respect, spoken high *básá* is being subjected to much the same process as the literary Javanese (*kawi*) of Hindu scripture which is becoming the vehicle of exoteric education in villages like Mulih (see chapter 2). The project inaugurated at the Javanese Language Congress may or may not fall short of its goal of saving "ethnic tradition" for Javanese Indonesians. But it will not be a total failure if it serves to impress on them an enduring awareness of the simple fact of such an ineffable ethnic tradition, now sponsored by the state. Such an association would serve to legitimize the state as custodial successor to elite *priyayi* exemplars of that tradition. Minimal, emblematic associations between high *básá*, literary tradition, and Javanese ethnicity likewise help to mediate ambiguities of un-native Indonesian language and identities for the New Order, and in the New Order's terms.

Ritual commodification of high *básá*

Among the life cycle rituals to which Javanese allude with the phrase *ndhuwé gawé*, which literally means "have work," weddings stand out for their importance, elaborateness, and resource requirements. Ward Keeler (1987:141–65) has described well the major investments of money and energy which weddings require, and the concomitant needs of their sponsors to mobilize networks of kin and dependants to produce them. Wedding ceremonies bring kin concerns into convergence with broader status considerations, and advertise through their elaborateness their sponsors' access to capital and labor. But weddings also provide evidence of their sponsors' spiritual capacity or potency (Keeler 1987, following S. Errington 1983) to attract numerous and high-status guests. These attendants sit as subdued, more or less attentive witnesses to a carefully choreographed sequence of ritual events. They collectively ratify not just a solemn event of marriage, but their host's social potency and status.

Since the rise of the New Order, this distinctly familial sphere of ritual practice has "preoccupied cultural imaginations in New Order Java" (Pemberton 1994:198), and become focal for new, ceremonial versions of *priyayi* dress, conduct, and speech in ceremonial productions. Of central interest here are the changing saliences of exemplary, high *básá* speech genres within those ceremonies as verbal means for imbuing them with a distinctive sense of dignity and refinement.

In these semi-public venues, highly elaborate and refined variants of high *básá* – sometimes called in Javanese *básá rinenggá*, "adorned language" – are increasingly the province of a new class of professional masters of ceremony called *protokol* (a Dutch borrowing) or *pranátá-cárá* (an archaicized neologism). John Pemberton has described very well (1994:197–235) these paid spokespersons' skill in providing indefinitely long, inconspicuous, yet elegant running commentary on ritual proceedings for a gathered audience. Such talk is open to aesthetic evaluation by aficionados for its internal stylistic consistency, as well as the number and plausibility of its distinguishing archaicisms. Among the most sought after and best paid of these new ritual specialists, by no coincidence, are men linked through kinship or office with traditional Solonese courtly circles. But their services have become increasingly professionalized and detached from palaces, and so too have their relations with weddings' sponsors become increasingly contractual. Ideally refined and exemplary high *básá* is less and less a mark of its speakers' intrinsic character as it becomes the stock-in-trade of a new class of ritual specialists.

Flowery, formal varieties of high *básá* have also been commodified and quasi-standardized in print media. Manuals on the numerous intricacies of "authentic" Solonese wedding rituals are commonplace in book stores all over Central Java (at least), and commonly include examples of the kinds of flowery, high *básá* which is normatively used at crucial ritual junctures.[3] The popularity of such manuals suggests an enduring awareness (at least among urban Javanese) of extrinsic points of reference for properly staged "Javanese" weddings. So too exemplary high *básá*, as an integral feature of such events, is ever more self-consciously associated with this circumscribed, standardized ritual of ethnicity.[4] Although exemplary high *básá* usage continues to be imbued with a sense of high status, in south-central Java and elsewhere that sense of status has shifted along with the institutional grounds of the urban elite class which sponsors its use.

Speakers, sponsors, and audiences

In urban centers, at least in my experience, the state's public business is carried out in Indonesian; high *básá* is appropriate for semi-public rituals of domestic life, like the weddings touched on above. But in at least some village communities high *básá* is a central resource for public representations of the state's authority. This curiously official use of an ethnic language needs to be considered here as complementary to the kinds of Indonesian usage which, on the face of things, are normative for talk by Indonesian officials, in overtly Indonesian venues, about Indonesian topics.

Such bilingual usage can be considered in light of its antecedents and (possible) analogs in non-Indonesian events such as the community gatherings sketched in chapter 2.[5] I suggested there that exemplary *básá*, in use at gatherings held under the aegis of Pangestu (in Gudhangan) or Hindu Dharma (in Mulih), could performatively invoke the traditional sanctioning power of Surakarta, the distant exemplary center. As privileged knowledge held by distinctively competent speakers, it simultaneously conferred dignity on topics of import, and on the persons gathered as a collective, local addressee. As a "natural" index of intrinsic refinedness, I suggested in chapter 3, it could distinguish its speakers' suitability in such roles not as social skill but a "status attribute" which enabled a distinguished person to "display himself [*sic*], [and] present himself as embodiment of some sort of 'higher' power" (Habermas 1989:7).

Anderson (1972) has drawn on Javanese historiographic tradition to characterize this "higher power" as being evident, so to speak, only in its absence. Paradigmatic in this regard is the image of an unmoved, unmoving king, whose oversight and will is manifested only mediately, beyond the more obvious ambit of his detached seclusion. By this political cultural logic, Anderson suggests, the locus and nature of power can be known only as it is indirectly manifested through its delegates, not directly from its source.

In a broadly similar manner, Keeler describes rituals like weddings as presupposing a relation of what he calls "dissembled control" (1987:163) between quiescent, inactive ritual sponsors, and those who work actively on their behalf. So too Pemberton characterizes sponsors of ritual events as "invisible figure[s] behind the scenes" whose "implicit spiritual reach" (1994:222) is evident in the smooth coordination of others' efforts.

A sponsoring power's "dissimulation of exertion" (Keeler 1987:141) extends to the sphere of talk. In these various ceremonial spheres, ritual spokespersons are understood to re-present and ventriloquate their sponsors' interests; so they are licensed as what Goffman (1974, 1981) calls animators for these silent, sanctioning principals. Exemplary *básá*, publicly used, can thereby disclose a source of authority which it subserves, and can presuppose an exemplary speaker's relation to it. Such an authorizing source of power need not otherwise be identified, nor be understood as having a human locus: the authority of words uttered at the Pangestu meetings described in chapter 2, for instance, is underwritten by the authority of words which were authored by the Godhead (Sang Hyang Sejati), ventriloquated by a human mouth, and then reproduced as the text of *Sasangka Jati*.

If public exemplary Javanese usage manifests and mediates such authority-laden relations between sponsors and utterers of refined speech, then it simultaneously presupposes a particular kind of relation between that refined speaker and the unspeaking, co-present collectivity which is an audience addressed. In village venues like those sketched in chapter 2, these small, peripheral publics are composed of individuals who are bound to each other in perduring relations of kinship, acquaintanceship, and neighbor-hood. Before, after, and during such events they count to each other as what Schutz calls consociates; they share a community of space and time, and "grow older together" (1967a:165) before and after coparticipating in the role of audience.

Relations between consociates contrast, in turn, with the radically anonymized relation between cocitizens of the nation-state, which is at least tacitly presupposed when state representatives address groups of persons in standard Indonesian. Public Indonesian speech, as the conduit for information encoded in standardized forms across homogeneous national space, does not invoke consociateship so much as the "horizontal comradeship" of Anderson's nationally imagined community (1991:7). As an imagined community it is essentially anonymous, and partakes of the kinds of social relations which Schutz placed under the rubric of contemporaries. Notwithstanding their shared social biographies, villagers count in "public" Indonesian events as citizens, and as such are recruited to audiences which are tiny, gathered fractions of the nation's diverse populace, on a tiny bit of national territory.

The perceived authority and "publicness" of exemplary *básá* needs to be contrasted in parallel manner with that of public Indonesian speakership, which is underwritten less by speakers' distinctive competences or character than by rights and duties grounded in state hierarchies. These transparent institutional grounds for authority are otherwise self-evidently present in everyday life, like the hierarchy of ranks which is superposed across national territory. Because public Indonesian language and authority are overtly linked to state institutions, they are ostensibly uninflected for personal characteristics of speaker or the identity of a collective addressee.

This contrast between high *básá*'s and standard Indonesian's institutional grounds and modes of "publicness" is crude but sufficient to consider their joint use as presupposing or rhetorically figuring different kinds of authoritative relations. It provides a general strategy for contrastively reading a few tiny texts of generically and topically "mixed" talk, and interpreting each as inflected for different, situated dimensions of public speakership and audiencehood. Two of these texts are records of markedly bilingual performances, more and less felicitous; they can be juxtaposed here with an eye to the broader question of convergence between "ethnic" and "national" guises for the authority which is assumed with and through public speakership.

But both these texts show how formal, public speech can seemingly lack the kind of "code consistency" which Judith Irvine has pointed to as characteristic of formal speech. Such consistency, she suggests, restricts a speaker's ability to "detach himself from the social persona implied by one type of usage and suggest [through use of another code] that persona is not to be taken quite 'for real'" (1979:777). In this way Irvine brings Goffman's dramatistic perspective to bear on the "seriousness" of institutionally demarcated contexts for verbal self-presentation. In fact, such seriousness can be felicitously and multiply inflected. Such bilingual usage similarly diverges from Bakhtin's description of the generically homogeneous, monoglot, "authoritative word," which is located "in a distanced zone, organically connected with a past that is felt to be hierarchically higher" (Bakhtin 1981:342).

A wedding speech

The New Order's saturation of rural communities, touched on in chapter 2, can be read in part from the entry of Indonesian language into local, ostensibly domestic ritual occasions. Text 5.1 shows how Indonesian language, topics, and agendas can come to be interpolated in the otherwise public, exemplary *básá* talk which is normatively appropriate in wedding ceremonies. In this way words ostensibly uttered in the name of a ritual sponsor take on the sanctioning authority and interests of the state, in form and content alike.

Text 5.1
Wedding address

Má, ingkang kaping tigá inggih meniká
pinter macak. Pinter macak
ing ngriki inggih meniká pinter
ngetrapaken busáná, utawi ngadi sarirá.
Sanajan bahanipun sanès bahan
ingkang mewah, sanès bahan
ingkang awis sanget, menawi pinter
macak meniká, trepipun ageman ndadosaken
utawi ndamel luluting kakungipun.
Pinter macak meniká mboten namung
nedahaken anggènipun busáná kémawon,
nanging pinter ngatur isèn-isèning
dalem: méjá, kursi, gambar-gambar lan
sanès-sanèsipun dipuntátá rapi.
Má ingkang kaping sekawan pinter *masak*.
Pinter *masak*, sanajan tá bahanipun
mirah, mboten bahan-bahan ingkang
awis. Menawi pinter *masak* lan
cekap *gizi*nipun saged
ndamel maremipun kuláwargá sedáyá.
Má ingkang kaping gangsal, pinter manak.
Pinter manak ing ngriki mboten
ateges kerep anggènipun nglairaken
putrá, meniká babar pisan
mboten mekaten ingkang kulá kajengaken.
Pinter manak meniká, saged
ngatur *jarak*ing *kelahiran*, saged
ngatur *jarak*ing *kelahiran*. Yen saged ngatur
*jarak*ing *kelahiran*, mboten
teges saben tahun wonten, saben tahun
wonten, inggih tigang tahun utawi langkung
saweg wonten. Meniká naminipun pinter
manak.
Milá *saran* kulá dhumateng sang penganten
mangké yèn sampun dipunparingi
momongan sepisan, lajeng tumut *Ka Bé*.
"*Keluarga kecil yang berbahagia.*"
Pinter manak ugi
njagi *pendidikan* lan *kesehatan*ipun
wiwit saklebeting guwágarbá ngantos
dumugi déwasanipun . . . Sang pengantin
sarimbit ingkang kawulá mulyakaken,
meniká wau pepindhanipun mboten sanes
inggih meniká saking *Pé Ka Ka*. Kados
sampun cekap, atur kulá ingkang
katujokaken dhateng penganten sarimbit.
Taksih wonten wekdal, sang penganten
kekalih, sumrambahipun para rawuh
kakung wiwah putri, kulá nyuwun wekdal
badhé nyekar . . .

[1] *Má* number three is
"clever at dressing." Clever at dressing
here means clever at
wearing clothes, or attiring the body.
[5] Although the material is not material
which is luxurious, is not material
which is very expensive, if one is good at
dressing, the fittingness of apparel will
cause or make deep love in your husband.
[10] Good at dressing does not just
pertain to clothes alone,
but good at arranging the contents of the
house: table, chair, pictures, and
so on all organized neatly.
[15] *Má* number four is good at *cooking*.
Good at *cooking*, even if the ingredients
are inexpensive, not ingredients which are
expensive. If one is good at cooking and
it has sufficient *protein*, it can
[20] make the entire family satisfied.
Má number five, good at having children.
Good at having children here does not
mean often giving birth to
children, that is not at all,
[25] not that which I intend.
Good at having children is being able to
control the *spacing* of *births*, being able to
control the *spacing* of *births*. If one is able
to control the spacing of births, it doesn't
[30] mean each year there's one, each year
there's one, rather three years or more
before there's one. That is called good at
having children.
So my *advice* to the happy couple,
[35] later if you've been granted
your first child then use *Ka Bé*.
"*The small family is the happy one.*"
Good at having children is also
watching over *education* and *health*,
[40] starting from inside the womb through
adulthood . . . Happy couple
whom I honor,
this just now nothing other than
according to *Pe Ka Ka*. This seems
[45] sufficient, my words which are
directed to the newlyweds.
There is still time, newlyweds
both, and honored guests,
gentlemen and ladies, I beg time
[50] to sing . . .

The speech represented by text 5.1 occurred at a 1986 wedding celebration in the environs of Purwareja, west of Jogjakarta, which was neither particularly spectacular nor overmodest by local rural standards. Few of the two hundred guests seated on rented folding chairs seemed to pay much attention to this speech as it came over the loudspeaker system.

Pak Siswa, a man of about fifty-five, was a qualified spokesperson as kin to the groom's father, and a retired school inspector of local repute. But his speech is undistinguished by professional city standards. While devoid of inadvertent low *básá* forms, it is likewise sparsely populated by the kinds of archaic terms and elegant phrasings which distinguish the most exemplary, professional high *básá* usage associated with urban elites. Early in the segment transcribed here (lines 1–4) Pak Siswa addresses the new bride on the topic of making her appearance pleasing, using the very common term *macak*, which he then glosses with the more refined high *básá* (but also Indonesianized) phrase "to apply/use clothing/adornment" (*ngetrapaken busáná*), and then the still more literary *ngadi sarirá* (line 4). So too he tends to use the common *básá* first-person pronoun *kulá* (at lines 25, 34, 45, 49) rather than the more archaic, elegant *kawulá* (which occurs only once, at line 42).

Notwithstanding his only moderately, inconsistently elevated verbiage, Pak Siswa's speech is by local standards fittingly and distinctively refined; it confers dignity on him, his audience, and the occasion as a whole. But his speech takes on a didactic tone which would also be inappropriate in a more refined, urban setting. This occurs toward its conclusion, where he broaches a markedly Indonesian theme in Indonesian language. Text 5.1 begins at the point when he begins to impart advice to the newlyweds by playing off a bit of received Javanese wisdom regarding prototypically male vices: the "five *má*" (*má limá*), which are proscribed as threats to domestic life. These are all activities referred to with words beginning with the sound /m/ and, save one, the syllable *má*.[6] Pak Siswa creates a kind of mirror set of five prescriptions for virtuous female conduct. So for instance the third of his prescriptions is skill in *macak* ("self-adornment"). To make the fourth *má* (line 15) fit both form and theme, Pak Siswa has recourse to the Indonesian word *masak* "cooking" rather than Javanese *ngulah-ulah*.

But he left the most important *má* for last, and gives it most of his attention: *manak* (line 21), "having children" and the need to do so infrequently. There is nothing subtle in his allusion at line 36 to *Ka Bé*, acronym for the state's birth control program (*Keluarga Berencana*), or in his quotation of that program's Indonesian language slogan: *Keluarga kecil yang berbahagia*, "The small family is the happy one." This is the concluding point of his speech, not just as delegate of the ritual sponsor in whose name he is speaking, but also an Indonesian (-speaking) agent for the New Order's domestic education program (line 44): *Pé Ka Ka*, acronym for *Pendidikan Kesejahterahan Keluarga* "education for family happiness."

This generically hybrid usage was judged by the person who recorded it as of mild interest at best, neither striking nor awkward. In fact the deployment of Indonesian within Javanese here seems to have augmented the rhetorical force of Pak Siswa's didactic speech, transforming a bit of Javanese moral wisdom into a lesson on good citizenship. In form and content, then, such talk can be read as a passing index of the state's ongoing penetration of semi-public rhetoric, ceremonial events, and domestic life alike, as touched on briefly in chapter 2.

Verbal events like these seem to show the state's ability to insinuate its claims on villager-citizens into local collective life, and to superpose the duties of citizenship onto family-linked roles. Against a broader social backdrop, then, the seeming felicitousness of Pak Siswa's bilingual talk can be seen as a public, performative correlate of New Order ongoing assimilation of high *básá* to its own institutional purview.

Bureaucratic Javanese?

Text 5.1 suggests an ongoing, smooth engagement between high *básá* and standard Indonesian, and so too the capacity of un-native authority and language to enter ethnic occasions and communities. But this consonance appears more contingent than necessary in light of language like that in text 5.2. This bit of usage shows that dissonances can arise from juxtapositions of these two languages: between the genres of speech spoken, and between their speaker's relation to an audience of fellow villagers who are also citizens.

This awkward bit of formal speech was recorded during an event in which official state interests had to be introduced, topically and generically, into a tiny, intimate gathering. This is a meeting of male heads of households at the smallest, most local level of administrative oversight, the neighborhood of forty or so households called the *rukun tetangga*, or *RT* (pronounced *èr té*). (Indonesian segments are italicized; Javanese are not.)

The speaker recorded here is the administrative head of this unit, the state's lowest-level, unpaid representative who acts as a kind of *primus inter pares* known and addressed as Pak RT (roughly, "Mr. RT"). He and his neighbors met biweekly as comembers of the government-sponsored group referred to by the Indonesian acronym Kelompencapir. This is an acronym for *Kelompok pendengar, pembaca, dan pirsawan*, which can be glossed briefly as "Gathering of listeners,

Text 5.2
Kelompencapir/Gathering of listeners, readers, and viewers

Déné syarat-syaratipun mangké dados *ketua* sáhá *pengurus* èr té menika: setunggal, nggih meniká ingkang *bertakwa terhadap Tuhan yang maha ésa*, nggih meniká setunggal. Bab *tugas kepengurusan*, setunggal inggih meniká *bertaqwa terhadap Tuhan yang maha ésa*. Kaping kalih nggih meniká, *setia* sáhá *taat kepada Pancasila* sáhá *undang-undang dasar empat puluh lima*. Kaping tigá nggih meniká *setia* sáhá *taat kepada negara dan pemerintah*. Sekawan nggih meniká *berkelakuan baik, jujur, adil, cerdas dan berwibawa*. Lajeng E: *tidak pernah terlibat langsung atau tidak langsung* wontenipun *pengaruh gerakan Gé tiga puluh S/PKI*, sáhá *underpol*ipun, *underpol* meniká *bawahannya dari pada Pé Ka I*. Ef: *tidak dicabut hak pili*hipun *berdasarkan keputusan pengadilan*. Dados *hak pili*hipun *tidak dicabut*. Gé nggih meniká *sehat jasmani* lan *rochani*nipun. Ha: *dapat membaca dan menulis* aksárá latin. I: *telah bertempat tinggal tetap sekurang-kurangnya nam bulan dengan tidak terputus-putus*. Menika *syarat-syarat*ipun. Dados *bertempat* wonten mriki *sedikitnya enam bulan tidak terputus-putus*. Lajeng *yang dapat ditunjuk menjadi pengurus rukun tangga seluruh*ipun *warga sebagai yang dimaksud maksud ayat satu dan dua adalah penduduk setempat warga negara terdapat terdaftar pada kartu keluarga*. Pokokipun meniká ingkeng saged dados inggih meniká *penduduk asli*, nggih meniká *penduduk* ingkang sampun kagungan *Ka Ka, Kartu Keluarga* kados kálá mbèn meniká. Meniká párá sedhèrèk *syarat-syarat*ipun. Mbok menawi mbenjing mangké utawi mbenjing badhé ng*leksana*kaken *pemilihan* meniká kedah *memenuhi syarat* menika, awit meniká dipun, a, dipun*sah*kan saking *menteri dalam negeri*.

[1] As for the requirements to become *head* and *supervisor* of the neighborhood: one, that is *devotion to God Almighty*, that is
[5] one. As for *duties of administration*, one is *devotion to God the Almighty*. Number two, that is, *faithful* and *observant of Pancasila* and *the constitution of forty-*
[10] *five*. Third, that is *faithful* and *loyal to nation and government*. Four, that is *good conduct, fair, just, clever, and authoritative*. Then E: *never involved directly or*
[15] *indirectly* in the *influence of the movement of G thirty S/PKI*[1] or their *underpol*, "*underpol*" are subordinates of the *PKI*. F: *the right to vote has not been revoked on the basis of a*
[20] *court verdict*. So the *voting rights haven't been revoked*. G: This is *healthy in body* and the *mind*. H: *can read and write* Latin letters. I: *have lived in place permanently at least six*
[25] *months without interruption*. Those are the requirements. So *residing here* [means] *at least six months continuously*. So *those who can be designated neighborhood heads, all* of them [are]
[30] *members as meant by the intent of stipulations one and two are local residents, citizens found listed on the family register*. The main thing is, those who can are
[35] *native residents*, that is *residents* who have a *Ka Ka, family register*, like before. Those, siblings, are the *requirements*. Perhaps another day later or in the future
[40] will be *carried* out *an election*, [candidates] *must meet* these *requirements*, because these have been, uh, have been *official*ized by the *minister of the interior*.

readers, and viewers," i.e., consumers of (state-sponsored, state-supervised) mass media. Kelompencapir meetings circulated between members' households, much as did those of Pangestu in Gudhangan, and Hindu Dharma in Mulih. Unlike those meetings, however, Kelompencapir meetings in this hamlet (at least) were attended by just male heads of households. They also served as convenient venues for transmitting information from subdistrict and village head's offices to neighborhoods, as does Pak RT in text 5.2.

The tenor of this meeting is slightly less formal than that of the larger village meeting (*rapat desa*) which I discuss later. This is evident from Pak RT's use in his opening statement (not presented here) of a formal term of collective address which glosses as "siblings" (*párá sedhèrèk*) rather than "fathers" (*párá bapak-bapak*). Pak RT normally uses high if not maximally refined *básá* in addressing Kelompencapir meetings, as shown by his typically formal greeting, expression of thanks to the host, apology for errors, and reading of the meeting's agenda.

But at this point in the meeting in question it was incumbent on him to introduce as a first item of business a directive, in Indonesian, from the central minister of the interior (*menteri dalam negeri*). This communiqué dealt with new regulations for candidates for the new RT position to be created when the neighborhood is subdivided to accommodate its expanding population. Pak RT reads these regulations as they are written, in Indonesian, and so animates words quite transparently authored and authorized by agents of the state.

Pak RT presumes at least passive knowledge of Indonesian on the part of his audience, as is evident from the way he reads but does not directly translate these regulations (save for the word *underpol* at lines 17–18, which he is at pains to clarify). But he nonetheless works throughout to frame this considerable amount of Indonesian verbiage (italicized in the text) with a sustained Javanese discourse, into which key Indonesian phrases and words are interpolated. Because he is unable to assimilate them wholly into "his own" Javanese form of address, there emerges from his talk an awkward feeling of doubleness in speakership, speech, and audiencehood.

This dissonance could be diagnosed, along lines suggested by Bakhtin (1981), as arising between two distinct, noncompatible authoritative modes of discourse. Written Indonesian regulations embody the authority of a bureaucracy, what Gellner calls "coherence and consistency (like treatment of like cases, the soul and honor of the bureaucrat, orderliness)" (1983:21). The other is the distinctive refinedness of exemplary high *básá*. That generic dissonance suggests a broader lack of fit between hierarchical state/citizen relations on one hand, and mutualistic expectations of locally gathered consociates on the other. Pak RT tries to elide this gap as he shifts back and forth between official, written Indonesian and Javanese. At lines 18–20, for instance, he reads directly regulation F – *tidak dicabut hak pilihnya berdasarkan keputusan pengadilan* – without a Javanese gloss, but then repeats the two key phrases (*hak pilih*, "voting rights," and *tidak dicabut*, "not withdrawn") within an utterance otherwise marked as exemplary Javanese (by *Dados* "so, thus" and *-ipun* "genitive marker" at lines 20 and 22).

This stylistic dissonance was reflected likewise by Pak RT's halting, hesitant manner, which lacked the flowing smoothness characteristic of properly refined Javanese speech. It suggests a sense of difficulty and tension in his self-location, with and through speech, between his authority's source on one hand, and his audience on the other. Bilingual address of these smallest of audiences can thus create a palpable sense of disjunction between words of the state addressed to citizens, and the received idiom of consociateship addressed to a group of neighbors who "grow older together." When a speaker like Pak RT is officially obliged to animate a generically non-Javanese message, he feels but can only partially mitigate the lack of fit between message and venue. He cannot totally elide underlying incompatibilities between his double role as official and neighbor, or straddle the generic *cum* social disjunction between Indonesian and Javanese speakership.

Exemplary Javanese in an Indonesian event: the *rapat desa*

Talk like Pak Siswa's in text 5.1 can be read as an instance of modern Indonesian's entry into the public life of rural Javanese but also more strongly, perhaps, as a harbinger of its eventual displacement of high *básá* as the language of politics and community alike: a kind of language subshift in the public sphere. However congenial with broader, developmentalist visions of language shift, these predictions seem premature or forced in light of public speech like that at the event recorded and transcribed as text 5.3.

This use of public speech is superficially anomalous, like that in text 5.1, but in a different way. It shows high *básá* in public use, by state officials, at state-sponsored gatherings, to discuss state business. Such usage may seem curiously deviant or retrograde for those with broadly developmentalist expectations about language shift, and throws a different light onto questions about generic figurings of authority in public speech.

In 1986, in a district north of the city of Surakarta, the village head (*lurah*) convened a public meeting of household heads – normatively male, as shown by the vocative in line 1 (*bapak-bapak*, lit. "fathers") – about the fiscal status of the village. (In fact many others, male and female, were present at this event.) *Rapat desa* ("village meeting") is an Indonesian rubric entirely appropriate for this gathering, given the status of its convener and his topic of discussion: the district's fiscal status (*keuangan desa*, lines 3, 14, 19). Yet this phrase, along with *tahun anggaran* ("budgetary year," line 4) are the only Indonesian phrases in

Text 5.3
Rapat desa/village meeting

Panjenenganipun párá bapak-bapak. Bilih ing sakmangké kulá badhé ngaturaken wontenipun *keuangan desa* ing *tahun anggaran* séwu sangang atus wolungdásá gangsal, séwu wolung atus, séwu sangang atus wolung dásá nem, ingkang kawiwitan wulan April tahun wolungdásá gangsal dumugi ing wulan Maret tahun wolungdásá nem. Sadèrèngipun kulá ngaturaken wontenipun *lapuran* kula salebetipun setunggal tahun, ing samangké mbok bilih anggènipun ngaturaken sáhá ng*lapur*aken wontenipun *keuangan desa* salebetipun setunggal tahun dhumateng párá bapak-bapak sedáyá, mbok menawi wonten kekiranganipun. Kulá nyuwun pangapunten awit bilih sadèrèngipun kula *lapur*aken, wonten ingkang kedah mlebet *soal keuangan desa*, nanging dèrèng saged mlebet. Dados janipun sampun setor dhumateng désa, nanging kabektá dèrèng cethá, pramilá ing samangké nyuwun pangapunten dhumateng párá bapak-bapak . . .

[1] Honored gentlemen. Now I will present the *village fiscal* situation in the *budgetary year* one thousand nine hundred
[5] eighty-five, one thousand eight hundred, one thousand nine hundred eighty-six, which began the month of April, year eighty-five through the month of March, the year of eighty-six.
[10] Before I present my *report* for the entire year, at present perhaps [my] presentation and *reporting* of the *village fiscal* situation in the year
[15] to all you gentlemen, perhaps there will be shortcomings. I beg forgiveness, because before I *report*, there is a *problem* [with] *village finances*,
[20] but can't yet be entered. So actually they're deposited to the village, but [as they] are not yet clear, therefore at present [I] beg forgiveness to the gathered gentlemen . . .

otherwise exemplary *básá* speech, which even excludes the Indonesian numbers for amounts and calendar dates (lines 4–9) otherwise common in casual Javanese interaction.

It seems apposite to call such usage official yet exemplary, given locutions like that at line 10, at the end of this bureaucrat's prefatory remarks about district finances. He is at pains first to note that a lag in bookkeeping is beyond his control, and prevents him from fully and accurately presenting monthly figures. By dwelling on what seems in the larger scheme of things a minor accounting problem, he shows himself a punctilious keeper of books, and a worthy functionary in the administrative framework where such matters have significance.

But he flanks this explanation (at lines 16–17 and 24) with a locution which I render as "(I) beg forgiveness," *(Kulá) nyuwun pangapunten*, and which is a paradigmatically polite *básá* formula to convey one's concern for others, awareness of one's own possible inadequacies, and all due humility. Deployed in such public usage, the utterance of this phrase can throw into relief what one hopes will be (or has been) a flawless performance, to which that apology may draw attention and may also punctuate. And if he advertises an official's concern for procedure, he also dissimulates any personal interest he might have in the matter at hand. By formulaically marking concern not just for bureaucratic competence but also proper fit between exemplary conduct and public context, the speaker can heighten the dignity of the event together with his own self-presentation.

In this way, *pak lurah*'s use of high *básá* seems not to mitigate or disguise the non-Javanese-ness of his Indonesian authority so much as to assimilate or ethnicize that authority in a crucially public venue. By doing the state's business in elevated ethnic manner, he re-presents the state's institutional framework through an exemplary Javanese tradition, at the same time figuring his audience as members of a local community. Exemplary Javanese speech lets him disclose a covert source of authority and legitimacy which he does not claim.

Such exemplary Javanese talk can be construed as figuring the state as a silent, absent, sanctioning source of potency, which indirectly licenses the transposition of exemplary high *básá* speech genres into a modern "public" venue. As a strategic self-presentation, this adoption of traditional guise by the state's "public" representative seems to blur differences between the authority which is institutionally presupposed by the content of his words, and performatively enacted through its forms.

Languages' authority

High *básá*'s relative scarceness in Javanese interactional life has shaped its values on the new, national scene as a symbol of ethnic identity, and a mediator of new forms of authority. As an icon of Javanese culture and identity, I have suggested, it has been subject to increasing standardization and commodification in the larger process of "national development." On one hand, the New Order has made its prenational exemplariness salient for national development, through official events like the Javanese Language Congress. Through that Congress (and its 1996 successor) high *básá* has been subjected to institutional treatment as part of a new version of Javanese (linguistic) tradition, effectively subordinated to the logic and rhetoric of New Order developmentalism. On the other hand, an urban Javanese Indonesian elite class has introduced highly refined high *básá* into its new economy of ceremonial production, and so to a new kind of Javanese ritual context which distinguishes its new class of professional speakers, and their elite employers, from those in lower and more rural sectors of society.

High *básá* appears in a different light in public village contexts, where it can serve as complement and subordinate to Indonesian in authoritative, state-backed talk. Public uses of the two languages play out in more ways than can be considered here, but the bits of verbiage presented above help suggest how they presuppose distinct but interanimating modes of public speakership. Indonesian and Javanese have contextual saliences which vary between what Jelin might call the most "solemn, institutional" gatherings (such as that recorded in text 5.2), and others (like text 5.3) which verge on "the individualized, familiar, habitual, micro-climactic of daily life" (Jelin 1987:11).

Developmentalists might see little reason to differentiate between such contexts and uses. Events like those partially presented in texts 5.1 and 5.2 might count as different facets of the state's ongoing, osmotic entry into village and domestic life; their generically hybrid character could be seen as a residuum of premodern understandings of authority and community which are soon to disappear. Then such curiously bilingual usage appears interstitial and transitional to the national era, in which monologic Indonesian will mediate state power for the nation's citizens.

From this point of view it is difficult to make sense of an Indonesian official's use of high *básá* like that recorded in text 5.3, which can only seem rhetorically anomalous. I believe such events can be focal mediators for local versions of national development, and as such are more than epiphenomenal of large-scale institutional forces. They can also be read as points of convergence between different understandings of publicly enactable authority and collective identity, as transient episodes in what Anderson called the "*project* for the assumption of 'modernity' within the modalities of an autonomous and autochthonous social-political tradition" (1966:89).

I have framed texts of these events in non-local terms and elided many particulars: biographies of relations between speakers, sponsors, and audiences; aspects of the settings in which they were recorded; the longer speeches from which I excised them; and so on. I have tried in this way to foreground the broader saliences such public talk might have as a mediator of distinct senses of authority and community, and the ways high *básá*, over and against Indonesian, makes for usefully ambiguous, shiftable re-presentations of authority, community, and territoriality.

6
INTERACTIONAL AND REFERENTIAL IDENTITIES

A useful way to broach the give-and-take of everyday conversational life is through the commonest Javanese Indonesian ways of speaking of the persons who are parties to speech. These involve kin terms and personal pronouns, which Javanese commonly use to refer to speaker and addressee, participants in the interaction in which uses of both kinds of terms figure. These aspects of talk are thus bound indexically and referentially to interactional process and self/other relations. For that reason they can throw a narrow but revealing light on Indonesian's entry into formerly monolingual Javanese interaction and communities.

Javanese and Indonesian kin terms, like those in many other Southeast Asian languages, are commonly used to speak of persons spoken to and bring an idiom of siblingship and seniority into a broad range of interactional relations. Rather than try to catalog the full expressive range of these interactional resources, I present emergent, syncretic aspects of kin term use with an eye to two broader kinds of social change. Some kin terms which once counted as Javanese have effectively been Indonesianized through their tacit links with new, territorially grounded understandings of ethnic and national identity. A few other kin terms, distinctively foreign in provenance and urban in association, have entered urban usage as diacritics of new, class-linked statuses in Java and elsewhere. Both patterns of variation and change can be considered with an eye to the shifting modes of territoriality sketched in chapter 2.

This chapter's other major concern is personal pronouns used to refer to the persons ("I" and "you") who are presupposed as participants (speaker and addressee) in their use. The double referential and social situatedness of their use was broached in chapter 3 to describe speech style use with Brown and Gilman's (1960) model of the "pronouns of power and solidarity." This was possible because the Javanese speech styles' social significances are realized in patterns of exchange which correspond to those presupposed by personal pronouns' referential and social significances alike: reciprocal, alternating enactments of speakership and addresseeship which "you" and "I" perform for each other.

I focus here on narrow points of pronominal use: differences which speakers appear to be tacitly *creating*, and not just accepting, in their use of Javanese and Indonesian pronoun repertoires. I foreground what seems a stylistic impoverishment of Indonesian personal pronoun repertoires as enhancing the "flatness" of Indonesian interaction in contrast to Javanese. This pattern of non-use, largely unnoted by speakers or observers, deserves attention as an unobtrusive but real point of resonance between the standardist ideology of language discussed in chapter 4 and concrete immediacies of conversational practice.

Syncretic uses of Javanese (?) kin terms

Examples of usage presented earlier in this book have already illustrated the central role of kin term use in acts of interactional reference to addressees. Of interest here are broad patterns of change in such kin term use which have emerged with the nation-state's ascendance, and the exemplary center's decline. The upshot is usage which counts as socially syncretic: interactional moments in which the saliences of talk's provenances, ethnic and national, are bracketed.

This change has involved the disarticulation of repertoires of formerly Javanese kin terms from titles of office and descent, which were in turn of a piece with the prenational hierarchies grounded by the exemplary center. They have been revalorized in and through Indonesian institutions so as to be appropriate in broader ranges of contexts, and relative to more diffuse understandings of social status. Within communities, and across lines of social difference, these syncretic kin terms have given rise to more socially and linguistically homogeneous forms of interaction.

This process is most evident for *ibu* and *bapak*, erstwhile Javanese terms listed in the first two rows of table 6.1. These terms once had very different social significances in Javanese interaction, but have come by different routes to be comparable forms of syncretic Javanese–Indonesian usage. This convergence can be sketched with recourse to table 6.1's broad historical and social distinctions between "prenational" and "contemporary" on one hand, and between "elite" and "non-elite" on the other.

Ibu and *bapak* now count throughout the nation as respectful Indonesian terms for respected adult men and women. In Java, at least, *bapak* is a neutral term for unfamiliar adult males, not necessarily deferential or intimate. As such it has "Mister" as an equivalent of choice even among Javanese who know no other English.[1] But *bapak*'s development into polite usage in Javanese and Indonesian alike has been shaped by the demise of other terms which (like *ibu*) once were highly deferential in import. To emerge as *bapak*'s counterpart, on the other hand, *ibu* has widened considerably in appropriate use, well beyond reference to and

Table 6.1. *Changing patterns of kin term use*

Gloss	c. 1920 Non-elite	Exemplary elite	Non-elite	c. 1980 Urban elite (to kin)
mother	(si)mbok, mak–(bi)yung	(i)bu	(i)bu–mbok	mami
father	(ba)pak	(ba)pak (+ title)	(ba)pak	papi
parent's older brother	(si)wá	pak dhé	pak dhé	om
parent's younger brother	(pa)man	pak lik	pak lik	om
parent's older sister	(si)wá	bu dhé	bu dhé–mbok dhé	tante
parent's younger sister	lik, bibi	bu lik	bu lik	tante
elder sister	yu	mbak(yu)	mbak(yu)–yu	mbak(yu)
elder brother	(ka)kang	(ka)kang (+ title)	(kang)mas–kang	(kang)mas

Note: Parentheses enclose the syllables of "full" forms which are commonly elided in casual or intimate speech. Dashes mark alternations between relatively innovative–conservative terms.

address of female adults of the highest traditional status as in prenational Java.

Bapak's narrowest, most concrete sense, glossable as "male progenitor," is unambiguously carried when it is inflected with a possessive suffix. In idiomatic, now stereotypically rural Javanese usage, this involves the genitive marker -*né*,[2] as in example 1, where it appears together with its similarly suffixed, comparably rural Javanese counterpart *mbok* "mother" (discussed later).[3]

    1. Nyusul mbokné karo bapakné, rak nang káná ndhisik.
        [He] followed his mother and father, [they] went there first.

At the same time, *bapak* alternates with vocative *pak*, which can have a less formal, perhaps less respectful feel. (This pattern of vocative use, which secures uptake with a prospective speech partner, is matched in parenthetical use of both terms to identify an already established addressee.) Older elite Javanese, for instance, expressed a preference for use of *pak* to address lower-status male adults such as pedicab drivers (as in sentence 3) over referential *bapak* (as in 2). Where sentence 2 can (in appropriate contexts) refer to non-speech partners, sentence 3 (all other things being equal) identifies addressee as referent.

    2. *Bapak* rak wis takgèkki tá?
        Bapak [you] I've already paid, right?
    3. Rak wis takgèkki tá *pak*?
        Haven't I already paid [you], pak?

In a specifically Javanese repertoire of kin terms, *bapak* can contrast with other terms which more finely modulate social relations. A younger adult who becomes relatively familiar with an older adult, for instance, might switch from address with *bapak* to the markedly Javanese *pak dhé* "parent's older brother" (see table 6.1) as an address form. In the words of one of my informants whom I observed make this shift with a mutual acquaintance, this treats a speech partner like "real family," and confers a more clearly ethnic cast on the relation.

In prenational Javanese usage more broadly, and in unaffixed form, *bapak*'s broadest interactional senses were shaped by coavailable titles of royal descent and office with which it could be combined or contrasted. In the prenational era, then, respectfulness conveyed by (*ba*)*pak* and other kin terms discussed below was commonly augmented with titles (usually in short form) in compound forms like *pak béhi*, mentioned in chapter 2. To address someone with *bapak* instead of a title, or without appending a title element to that term, could mark that addressee as an adult male who otherwise had no status worthy of note.

Ibu, quite unlike *bapak*, was highly and unambiguously honorific usage in prenational Java, normatively reserved for first wives (not concubines)[4] of the highest-ranking *priyayi* men. It contrasted then with the much more commonly used (*si*)*mbok*, which was then roughly comparable (as example 1 above suggests) in social import with *bapak*, and which could similarly be used in combination with title elements. But following the demise of the royal court, and its system of titles, these two terms have had quite different fates. *Ibu* has effectively displaced *mbok* as polite but not necessarily deferential usage in otherwise Javanese and Indonesian speech alike. *Mbok* consequently has come to feel markedly rural and lower-class, appropriate for speech to and of uneducated village dwellers.[5]

In this way *ibu* has become *bapak*'s counterpart as an Indonesian designation for female parent, and a neutral term of address for educated adult women. This broad, city-centered shift in use of both terms has entered rural south-central Java as part of the state's ongoing penetration of village communities. More intense contact with this innovative pattern of use has made it increasingly familiar to and prevalent among younger villagers in Gudhangan and Mulih, not all of whom are bilingual. The leading edge of such change centers on the small group of teachers and office workers in the area who are themselves bilingual and are normatively addressed and referred to as *bapak* or *ibu*. But where many uneducated, monolingual village men might similarly be addressed (in Javanese) as *pak*, their female counterparts are still commonly called *mbok*.

Younger villagers' awareness of these social differences is illustrated in text 6.1, drawn from discussion which I recorded during a rehearsal for a play which some Gudhangan teenagers were producing with help from an experienced lowland actor and director, Surya (S). He had interrupted a scene to discuss one actor's (C) use of *bu* (in low *básá* Javanese) in response to a summons from his mother (A). Several other attendants (X, Y, Z) participated in the ensuing discussion, which alternated between low Javanese (in roman typescript) and Indonesian (in boldface). The text begins at a point when actors are rehearsing a scene which begins with Téjá (vocative form Já) beings called by his mother.

It may have been the artificial performance/rehearsal context which induced C, as Téjá, to use *bu* (short form of *ibu*) in low *básá* to his "mother," at line 2, in much the manner C himself would have responded to a summons from a teacher at school. Surya intervenes to ask in Indonesian (at line 10) about its appropriateness compared with *mbok* or *mak* (another markedly rural, dialectal variant). As these young adults deliberate, they allude directly to socioeconomic differences associated with the terms. The joking suggestion of *mami* at line 9 alludes to new forms of distinctively urban elite usage which I consider below.

Text 6.1

A: Já! Téjá! Cobá réné lé.	[1]	A: Já,[6] Téjá! Come here, son.
C: Enten nápá *bu*?		C: What is it, *bu*?
[Surya interrupts]		
S: Ha *mbok* ápá *bu*?		S: Now, [should he use] *mbok* or *bu*?
Mbok ápá *bu*?		*Mbok* or *bu*?
X: *Mbok* waé.	[5]	X: *Mbok*.
Y: *Mak, mak* yá isá, *mak*.		Y: *Mak, mak* will do, *mak*.
Z: *Mbok* aé.		Z: *Mbok*.
S: Aksiné *mbok*.		S: *Mbok* is good.
X: "*Mami*" aé. [laughter]		X: *Mami*.
S: Mana yang lebih wajar	[10]	S: What's more natural
pada keluarga mlarat,		in a poor family,
pada keluarga mlarat seorang		in a poor family, [does] a
anak terhadap ibunya		child to his/her mother
memanggilnya "*mbok*" apa		call "*mbok*" or
"*mak*" apa "*bu*"?		"*mak*" or "*bu*"?
X: "*Mbok*."	[15]	X: "*Mbok*."
D: Yang banyak itu "*mbok mak*"		D: What's common is "*mbok*" [or]
itu.		"*mak*."
[C repeats the line]		
C: Enten nápá tá *mbok*?		C: What is it, *mbok*?
[B interrupts]		
B: Nèk "*mboké*"?		B: What about "*mboké*"?
D: "*Mboké*," ájá – "*mboké*."		D: "*Mboké*," don't – "*mboké*."
[the scene resumes]		
A: Já! Téjá!		A: Já, Téjá!
C: Nggih *mbok*?		C: Yes *mbok*?

Ibu is known by these young villagers, then, in Javanese and Indonesian alike, as keying to status on the contemporary social landscape. Its ongoing transformation from deferential Javanese to standard Javanese Indonesian can be similarly read from an anecdote related to me by one young villager about her male cousin who, after returning from a year spent in Jakarta, addressed his monolingual aunt, her own sixty-year-old mother, as *ibu* in Javanese. His mother's dubious reaction was "Why, that's palace usage!" (*Lho, rak cárá ningrat kuwi*). She was discomfited by use which was intended to be polite and, in her nephew's mouth, undifferentiated for class, nationality, or ethnicity. But in her ears, that same usage had prenational, ethnically inflected status connotations of traditional elitehood.

More important here than the nuances of such usage are the institutional forces which have brought *bapak* and *ibu* into convergence as comparable, standard, syncretic forms of usage. The role of conspicuously modern institutional contexts and a quasi-egalitarian ideology in this transformation is conveniently evident in an observation by Ki

Hadjar Dewantoro, a progressive member of high courtly circles of Jogjakarta, prominent proto-nationalist, founder of the famous Taman Siswa educational system, and Indonesia's first minister of education and culture:

> We used the terms "Bapak" and "Ibu" because we considered that the terms of address currently in use, "Tuan" [Sir], "Njonjah" [Madam], and "Nonah" [Miss], and the corresponding Dutch terms, "Meneer," "Mevrouw," and "Juffrouw," and also the terms in use in Java, such as "Mas Behi," "Den Behi," and "Ndoro," which implied superiority and inferiority of status, should be abolished from Taman Siswa. We introduced the use of the terms "Bapak" and "Ibu" not only for when pupils spoke to teachers but also for when younger teachers spoke to older ones. We never once spelled this out as a "regulation," but this kind of appellation soon came to be used in educational institutions across Indonesia.
> (quoted in Shiraishi 1992:161–62)

The upshot of this institutionally grounded change has been both terms' effective detachment from their distinctively Javanese origins, and their conversion into standard Indonesian.

In other parts of Indonesia *bapak* and *ibu* may count as conspicuously un-ethnic usage, and be associated with official contexts or institutions which underwrite them as parts of Indonesian. Certainly New Order institutions underwrote the paternalist style of rule often called *bapakism*, as well as the emerging phenomenon which has been called *ibuism* in recent critical discourse on gender relations in modern Indonesian political culture (Djajadiningrat-Nieuwenhuis 1987; Suryakusuma 1996; Anderson 1996). (Both of these terms are derived, fittingly enough, with a suffix borrowed from Dutch or English.) But by the same token both terms have returned to south-central Java as usage which is native yet national, and in everyday use represent interactionally crucial syncretisms.

Two other kin terms, *mbak* ("elder sister") and *mas* ("elder brother"), are similarly spreading from city to village communities in Java, and similarly obtrude (for older rural Javanese, at least) not so much as distinctively Indonesian as distinctively modern usage. Table 6.1's bottom two rows crudely summarize this change as it has involved shifting uses of other terms as well.

Mbak and *mas* once counted as distinctively statusful Javanese, but are now penetrating rural communities and repertoires as syncretic Javanese Indonesian forms. *Mbak(yu)* derived historically from the phrase *mbak ayu* (lit. "pretty mother"), formerly in common Surakartan usage (at least) for polite reference to and address of childless, post-adolescent girls and women. *Mbakyu* in turn has two short forms, usable vocatively/ parenthetically and in combination with other elements. One is *mbak*, which counts primarily as its stylistically informal version; the other is *yu*, which is distinctly rural, uneducated, and low-status in feel. (See J. Errington 1988:138–39.) A convenient example of the *mbakyu/yu* alternation in rural usage is 4 below, drawn from conversation among villagers in which G has asked A for information about the identity of Tanem, about whom A has been speaking. A has natural recourse to both forms in her response.

4. G: Tanem ki sing ndi tá yá?   Which Tanem, huh?
   A: Mbakyuné   The *mbakyu* [elder sister] of
      yu Daliyem kaé.   *yu* Daliyem.

Genitivized with *-né*, the "full" form *mbakyu* refers here to a kin relation. The short form *yu*, combined with the referent's name, Daliyem, is a form of address which contrasts with innovative, tacitly urban *mbak*. This is a clue, then, to the social background of A as an older, monolingual speaker.

Present-day uses of *mbak* and *yu* broadly parallel those of *ibu* and *mbok*: *mbak* is not so much honorific as polite in Javanese and Indonesian usage alike, whereas *yu* suggests a referent and perhaps speaker who are rural and stereotypically monolingual in Javanese. *Yu* is now increasingly associated with older, uneducated villagers with whose passing, perhaps, it will be entirely superseded by *mbak*.

Broadly similar patterns are shaping the appropriate use of *mas* ("elder brother"). In Central Java, at least, *mas* is preferred for reference and address to younger adult males, regardless of language otherwise used. But sixty years ago *mas* was a low-level title of nobility, combinable with titles of office (as in *mas béhi*, alluded to in the quotation from Hadjar Dewantoro above). *Mas* contrasted interactionally in prenational use with the comparatively non-statusful *bapak*, noted above, and could convey the speaker's awareness of and esteem for addressee's status. I have described elsewhere (J. Errington 1988:141–44) the ways that *mas* was appropriated outside elite circles, and spread in use to a broader range of communities and contexts. By the time of independence, it was well on its way to displacing *(ka)kang* as a kin term in many communities. Now *mas* has penetrated everyday usage, including that of monolingual villagers, so thoroughly that *kakang* counts as stereotypically rural, old-fashioned, specifically Javanese usage. All seventy-nine occasions of use of *kakang* in my recordings serve to refer to or address villagers with whom speakers were relatively intimate, who were of relatively low status and older than forty. As one younger village consultant remarked, "If I call someone *kang*, he must be kind of old, and someone I know fairly well."

Older rural villagers in Gudhangan and Mulih find themselves at a point of juncture between eras and kin term use: they sometimes find themselves using (*ka*)*kang* to local contemporaries but *mas* to younger, presumably less estimable males. My host in the village of Mulih, for instance, addressed older neighbors as *kang* but younger men and boys (including me) as *mas*, the form his own children likewise used among themselves (often in the forms *masé* and *masmu*). In such use *mas* is not evocative of traditional elites, but new ways of life.

Rural Javanese communities are thus being penetrated by innovative patterns of usage which may be statusful but are not exemplary, and which are associated with an urban more than an exemplary center. So too they are broadly syncretic in feel. This process is variable and unequally advanced within and across communities, as is apparent in a bit of usage I recorded in Mulih and reproduce here as example 5. In this speaker's usage, at least, *mas* seems to be "leading" *mbak* when she refers to a husband and wife, at least ostensibly of comparable social status, with the relatively innovative *mas* and more conservative *yu*:

5. Lha kulá ngertiku ndhèk mbèn Well me, I know before
   mas Kus niku bojoné *yu*   *mas* Kus, the spouse of *yu*
   Tun kaé, aku sing ruh ngono   Tun, I saw him,
   kuwi nyang klurahan.   going to the lurah's office.

Broadly similar changes are shaping use of the increasingly old-fashioned kin terms listed in the first column of table 6.1 – (*pa*)*man*, *lik*, (*si*)*wá*, *biyung* – which are increasingly rural, old-fashioned, and specifically Javanese in feel. As they are progressively displaced by newer forms, listed in table 6.1's middle rows, they are giving way to usage which may be of "native" provenance but is not now exclusively Javanese.

In non-Javanese communities, use of *mas*, *mbak*, and similar forms may distinguish a speaker as being of Javanese ethnicity (although there is reason to suspect that they are spreading beyond Javanese ethnic territory, and to use among speakers of other ethnicities).[7] But within the more local frames of reference which are relevant here, these terms count as equally appropriate in otherwise Javanese and Indonesian talk, and have no salience as markers of national or native identities. Any distinctiveness of their use hinges, rather, on a contrast keying to urban–rural usage difference, which appears to be of diminishing salience as newer, city-based terms enter younger villagers' usage.

These patterns of lagging emulation only partly resemble shifts in pronominal use sketched at the end of chapter 3. Kin terms now entering villages are syncretic and distinctively modern, rather than exemplary in source or deferential in import. Their use is grounded less in respect for the addressee's status than in felt comembership in newer kinds of communities. As such, these shifting patterns of kin term use are not really part of an "integrative struggle," or mechanisms for reproducing received social distinctions. They are instead mediating larger patterns of sociolinguistic change as tiny, transient, yet intimate reflexes of the forces which are shaping the sociolinguistic landscape.

Urban elites, kin terms, and another "reproductive struggle"

These shifts, taken as a whole, appear to be progressively leveling linguistic marks of the territorially linked status distinctions sketched in chapters 2 and 3. As parts of simpler, territorially homogeneous repertoires of terms for persons, they are presumably fostering more egalitarian modes of interaction envisioned early in the nationalist era by progressives like Dewantoro. So too one could diagnose these as developments which serve to promote what Gellner calls the "blindness to society" he claims is characteristic of modern national languages.

But to diagnose Javanese–Indonesian kin term use in this way is overbroad, if one ignores very different patterns of innovation ongoing in Surakarta the urban center. New patterns of usage there reflect another social dynamic, and the rise of a Javanese Indonesian urban elite class. Terms listed in table 6.1's final column can be framed in this respect as distinctive of modern, urban, middle-class usage.

These terms are all distinguished by their shared Dutch provenance and, at least in Surakarta, their distinctively Western manner of use, primarily or exclusively to and for one's own kin. *Papi* and *mami*, for instance, like their Dutch cognates, serve to refer to and address one's "own" biological father and mother (rather like "dad" and "mom"). Both have become common usage among younger educated speakers of my acquaintance in Solo, and are widely enough used to be recognized (thanks to mass media) even among rural villagers as distinctively modern and urban. Shared recognition of their meanings and social saliences was presupposed, for instance, by the joking suggestion which a village youth made in text 6.1, that the son in the play use *mami* to his mother. *Tante* and *om* are likewise stereotypically Jakartanese, in use for family and non-family alike, but as far as I can tell are used in Surakarta (at least) more restrictedly to and for "genuine" kin, or comparably intimate members of one's family circle. Educated Solonese elites among whom I observed this use all characterized it with reference to Jakarta, and judge it equally appropriate in Javanese and Indonesian speech.

Viewed as both (or neither) ethnic or national, this usage appears as broadly syncretic as that discussed earlier. But insofar as it is class-linked, use of terms like *mami* and *papi* works against the homogenizing grain of those other patterns of change. It recalls more strongly shifts in pronominal usage discussed in chapter 3, insofar as it distinguishes a distinctively new, urban social status. But this narrow site for what Bourdieu calls an "integrative struggle," which "dominated classes allow to be imposed on them" (1984:165), is not re-producing old distinctions so much as it is producing new ones. Grounded in a distinct (Western) logic of kin term usage and a new, socioeconomically grounded sense of class, this second pattern is syncretizing ethnicity and nationality within new, national forms of social hierarchy.

So these two broad changes in kin term usage seem quite different: the first reduces linguistic marks of social difference between city and villager, while the second emerges as a correlate and marker of urban class difference. Together, though, they represent different reflexes of the broad, underlying shift in territoriality which I sketched in chapter 2, and which is engendering new hierarchies in the Javanese part of the national landscape. As rural areas are increasingly penetrated by city-based institutions and language, kin term use is becoming less differentiated for ethnicity and nationality. At the same time, the rise of a Javanese Indonesian middle class is accompanied by new usage taken over from their urban, Jakartan (so, Indonesian) counterparts.

Complementary patterns of pronominal usage

In response to my various queries about differences between their two languages, Javanese commonly alluded to Indonesian's lack of stylistic elaboration as making it simple (I: *sederhana*), bland (I: *tawar*), or plain (I: *polos*) in comparison with Javanese. But, at least as normatively described, Indonesian does incorporate a few interactionally crucial stylistic distinctions in its personal pronoun repertoires. Textbooks, dictionaries, and grammars of Indonesian, for instance, commonly note the "informal" and "formal," "familiar" and "polite" personal pronoun variants set out in table 6.2.[8]

The social meanings of use of first- and second-person pronouns, which are of focal interest here, can both be conveniently characterized with the Brown and Gilman model of singular (T) and plural (V) pronoun usage, discussed in chapter 3. In this way "familiar" *aku* and "formal" *saya* can be said to contrast as do the Javanese *ngoko* and *básá* styles, including their respective first-person pronouns: *aku* on one hand, and *kulá* and *dalem* on the other. So too, on the face of things, the relatively familiar Indonesian second-person pronoun *kamu* (like *engkau*, a dialectal variant) contrasts with *anda* as does the *ngoko* term *kowé* (cognate with *engkau*) with relatively polite *básá* forms *panjenengan* and *sampéyan*.[9]

But actual Indonesian usage suggests that these structural parallels are merely prescriptive, because speakers consistently avoid using *aku* and

Table 6.2. *Indonesian personal pronoun paradigms*

	First person	Second person	Third person
Familiar/informal			
possessive/nominal	-ku	-mu	-nya
passive	ku-	kamu, kau-	di-
elsewhere	aku	kamu, (eng)kau	dia
Polite/formal			
(all environments)	saya	anda	beliau

kamu. The results are non-obvious but notable patterns of non-use which offer clues to broader contrasts between Javanese and Indonesian interactional dynamics. Javanese speakers' comments on Indonesian's "plainness" in fact fit with their own avoidance of that language's interactionally keyed stylistic nuances. These "flattened" interactional dynamics, not just accepted but created, fit the modernist ideology of language sketched in chapter 4. As such they deserve brief documenting here.

Most convenient evidence that *aku* counts exclusively as an element of their native language are instances of switching between the two languages in which speakers likewise switch between first-person pronouns. In the examples transcribed below, Javanese usage is in roman typeface; Indonesian is in italics. Boldface is used for tokens of Javanese first-person pronouns.

6. *Tempat saya* **tak**tukokké blanjan . . . bol voly, bal tendhang, cakram, peluru kaé **tak**tukokké kabèh. Mbok **aku** dipikir nèk sekolahan káná, yá, ming, *kecuali, saya rugi waktu,* kesel. Yá ming **aku** sok gelem ngétokké dhuwit sing sifaté, upamané nggo ápá, *kegiatan anak.*

   [1] *At my place,* **I** bought them, got . . . volleyball, kickball, a discus, shotput,
   [5] I bought all those for them. So **I** should be thought of in that school there, right, but, *aside from, I lose time,* tired. Yeah only **I'm**
   [10] sometimes willing to put out money which is for, for instance, for, uh, *the kids' activities.*

7. Mbok kon nggáwá **aku** waé, *saya itu sudah tiga puluh tahun.*

   Why not tell him to carry **me**, *I'm already thirty years old.*

8. Ning nèk juki panemu modhèlé kolah ngéné **aku** wis moh, **aku** gemang. **Aku** ra mundhur *soal pembangunan, saya tidak*

   [1] But if asked an opinion about money for the pool I won't, I don't want to. I won't back off the problem of
   [5] building it, *I won't*

	mundhur, tapi untuk membicarakan model kolah **aku** *is, saiki wis meneng. Kono angger ketemu ngrembug dhit kolah ngrembug piyé-piyé* **aku** *is meneng.*	[10]
9.	**Aku** *mau iyá omong wingi kan*, Pak Ustaji *bareng karo* **aku**. *Saya kira ya omong waé wong sisan iyá kalau diamati.*	[1] [5]
10.	Ora *langsung nglamar ke Perancis*, **tak**kirá *lancar diterima malahan. Saya ini ndak ngapusi, tenan kok.*	
11.	Sebab *saya menilai tidak* kok *tegesé ngremèhké* nggih, *tapi umumnya orang yang masuk suster yang seratus persen tumbuh dari hati nuraninya, karena dia hanya betul-betul akan mengabdikan dirinya ke dalam proyek kemanusiaan, sesuai dengan panggilan agamanya, itu ya kira-kira lima persen*, hem, ora **ku**ngenyèk no ora, ning *dalam pengalaman saya* lho, **aku** *wis tahu nganti nyang Salatiga kono, kono lak okèh daérah ngono kuwi.*	[1] [5] [10] [15]

back off, but as for discussing money for the pool, I've *already, now [I']m quiet. If they meet to discuss money for the pool, discuss however,* I *stay quiet.*	
Just yesterday I *was talking, right*, Pak Ustaji *was along with* me. *I thought, yeah, it's just talk, the first time, and yeah if you examine it.*	
[If he] doesn't apply directly to France, [he] I *think would be accepted quickly, in fact. I'm not kidding, for real.*	
Because [as] *I see it, it's not to belittle them, right, but generally women who become nuns one hundred percent from their innermost hearts, because she only, truly will devote herself to humanitarian projects according to her religious calling, that's maybe five percent*, uh, I'm *not mocking, no, but, in my experience, right,* I've *been to Salatiga there, there's lots in that area.*	

Among some 2,000 tokens of use of *aku* in my corpus of transcribed material, only six could be construed as integral parts of otherwise Indonesian usage; four of these occur in speech of non-native Javanese, and the other two appear to be parts of code switchings which are discussed in chapter 10. On the other hand, that same corpus contains some 370 occasions of self-reference with Indonesian *saya* by and to persons who otherwise exchange *ngoko* styles (with *aku*) of Javanese.

Broadly similar differences in second-person pronoun usage can be demonstrated for use of Indonesian *anda* and *kamu*, although their situated interactional senses differ from those of their Javanese counterparts (the *ngoko* pronoun *kowé* on one hand, and *básá* pronouns *sampéyan* and *panjenengan* on the other). *Kamu*'s felt familiarity makes it appropriate for address of intimates to whom one otherwise uses *kowé* when speaking Javanese. This is illustrated by examples 12 and 13. Passage 12 below, in *ngoko* (roman) and Indonesian (italicized), is spoken to a "you" (in Indonesian, *kamu*) who has joined an ongoing encounter with a mutual acquaintance. (The utterance cited begins with a pun on Indonesian *sarjana*, a title for a college degree holder, and Javanese *sarjáná*, a cognate glossable here as "scholar.") Example 13, extracted from a later point in the same interactional sequence, is entirely in *ngoko* with *kowé* to the same addressee, and concludes a story that speech partner has just told. Such use of *kamu* seems to presuppose the same sort of interactional intimacy which accrues to use of *kowé*.

12. Allah *sarjana* ápá sarjáná,
    sarjana ki ketárá lho. *Kamu itu*
    melihat orang berilmu dengan
    anu, kuduné isá
    mbédakké lho.

    Oh Lord, a *BA* or a scholar, a
    BA, it's apparent, y'know. *You*
    see someone knowledgeable with,
    uh, [you] should be able to
    distinguish [them], y'know.

13. Upámá isá, isá milèh ngono
    yá anggerá milèh kowé no,
    kowé rung tau roh tá,
    bojoné.

    If [one] could, could choose like
    that, better you choose,
    you've never seen her, right,
    his spouse.

But in another respect *kamu* differs from *kowé*. Example 14 shows how *kamu* can serve not just in reference to an "actual" speech partner, but to an indefinite anonymous or hypothetical addressee, as can "you" in English (as in "You never know"). This is evident from fully Indonesian example 14, where it serves this function along with first-person pronoun *saya*.

14. Kadang-kadang lalu
    menyalahken kepada pemudi itu.
    Jadi cinta itu bukan hanya
    cinta saja *kamu* dengan *saya*
    saja.

    Sometimes then [they]
    fault that girl.
    So love is not only
    love just of *you* with *me*
    alone.

I have neither observed nor recorded analogous uses of *aku* and *kowé* in Javanese.

Indonesian *anda* stands quite apart from all these other terms in provenance and appropriate usage. It was purposely coined and propagated early in the national era to the specific end of displacing elaborate pronominal markers of traditional status differences, and so helping to modernize Indonesian interaction through the Indonesian language. In fact *anda*'s present viability is probably due in large part to the efforts of its most visible champion, the same Takdir Alisjahbana quoted in chapter 4 as the foremost Indonesian ideologue of developmentalism. In his view, *anda* held the promise of a modern form of reference, "blind to society," which would subserve the rise of an egalitarian interactional ethic.

But its current place in Indonesian usage, at least among Javanese, hardly fits that vision: it has not displaced its antecedents so much as become their peripheral complement. *Anda*'s feel for Javanese, at least, was well captured by one speaker's description of it as "advertising language" (*bahasa iklan*), which alludes to the sense of interactional detachment and anonymizing disengagement it presupposes. For this reason it is far less commonly appropriate in face-to-face interaction than is *kamu* or use of a kin term.

So by the same token *anda* is differentially appropriate, as in example 15, for use in the same sort of unmarked, indefinite sense expressed with *kamu* in 14.

15. S: Ada kemungkinan malah anda tersangkut.   S: There's a possibility in fact you're implicated.
    M: Ada kemungkingan malah anda ikut mendukung atau ikut melindung terdakwa.   M: There's a possibility in fact you helped support or helped protect the accused.

In another context, a speaker similarly models an act of hypothetical Indonesian address (see chapter 8) to her superior in the Indonesian Department of Education. Its final, *ngoko* element is italicized.

16. Pak, gini ya pak ya, "Anda mau membantu saya, saya ingin ke luar Jawa" *ngono*.   Pak, like this, pak yeah, "Will you help me, I, I want to leave Java" *like that*.

So *anda* clearly does not contrast with "informal" *kamu* as do the "polite" Javanese second-person pronouns (*sampéyan* or *panjenengan*) with ordinary ngoko *kowé*.

This superficial review suffices to ground a central observation: that Indonesian personal pronoun repertoires, as used among Javanese, are not just simple, but simplified in relation to their native usage. Speakers do not exploit pre-given stylistic contrasts among Indonesian pronouns, and so create a kind of antisyncretism between the pronouns which are important interactional mediators in their national and native languages. In this respect, a more accurate summary of current usage than that in table 6.2 is given in table 6.3, where parentheses mark relatively peripheral elements of each repertoire.

Such phenomena of non-use, and the kind of stylistic *cum* interactional flatness they promote, are by their nature inconspicuous. But like watchdogs which do not bark, they provide clues to broader interactional dimensions of bilingualism, and their relations to the modernist language ideology of Indonesian sketched in chapter 4. They suggest a broader pronominal trope for the interactional identities assumed and performed in Indonesian, over and against styles of Javanese, *ngoko* and *básá*.

Table 6.3. *Javanese vs. Indonesian personal pronoun usage*

	Javanese	Indonesian
First person	aku/kulá/(dalem)	(aku)/saya
Second person	kowé/sampéyan/panjenengan	kamu/(anda)

Another pronominal trope

To pursue broader significances of this relatively narrow aspect of interaction, it is worth recalling the parallel I drew in chapter 3 between the referential meanings of personal pronouns, and the social meanings of the Javanese speech styles. "Polite" *básá* speech styles, I suggested there, are generically weighted for what Bühler calls the conative or expressive function of speech, and so presuppose a speaking stance relatively weighted for an addressee, a "you." Over and against these pragmatically marked styles stands the "basic" *ngoko* style, which counts as the un-polite language of the speaking self, a medium of thoughts and feelings irregardless of whether they are uttered for some co-present addressee. (I invoke this distinction again to describe aspects of Javanese conversational practice in chapters 8 and 9.)

Given these broad links between the referential meanings of personal pronouns, and the social meanings of speech styles, a place is available for the patterns of Indonesian pronoun non-use sketched here. If they contribute to interactional flatness – less situated, more anonymizing modes of speech – then they make for usage which is doubly skewed with Javanese, at once un-ethnic and im-personal.

This broader complementarity – between *ngoko* and *básá* on one hand, and Indonesian on the other – can also be pronominally troped by calling Indonesian the detached, "third-person" way of speaking. As a way of speaking it is tacitly weighted, by provenance and institutional grounding, for what Bühler called the referential functions of speech.

To think of Indonesian as the language of neither thee, nor me, but of "it,"[10] is suggestive for questions about its place in Javanese versions of the Indonesian "project of modernity." It suggests that Indonesian is available for relatively specific modes of conversational engagement, which allow speech partners to bracket Javanese interactional identities; it appears that this interactional difference brings the national language into line with its ideological grounds and makes its use, in Woolard and Schieffelin's phrase, "more like itself" (1994:70). In chapter 10 I invoke this broad pronominal metaphor in a sketch of other, broader aspects of bilingual Javanese–Indonesian interaction.

7
LANGUAGE CONTACT AND LANGUAGE SALAD

Javanese commonly describe their "mixed" bilingual Javanese–Indonesian usage as *bahasa gadho-gadho*, a phrase fairly translated as "language salad" or, following Buchori (1994), "hybrid language." It combines Indonesian *bahasa* "language" (cf. Javanese *básá*) with Javanese *gadho-gadho* (now, effectively, an Indonesian borrowing) which refers to a dish of lightly cooked or raw vegetables, mixed together on a plate and covered with peanut sauce. As a humorous, dismissive, or pejorative alternative to "mixed language" (I: *bahasa campuran*), *bahasa gadho-gadho* recalls labels which have been coined for bilingual usage in other communities,[1] as well as "word salad," a linguists' designation for randomly mixed, ill-formed, and unpatterned combinations of grammatical and lexical material.

The hallmark of *bahasa gadho-gadho* is inclusion of lexical material from one language (usually Indonesian) in use of the other, either in grammatically assimilated forms which I discuss in this chapter's latter part, or more extensive code switchings which I sketch in chapter 10. But "mixed" lexical usage is not the only distinguishing mark of such "mixed" Javanese–Indonesian speech. A range of common accentual and grammatical reflexes of Javanese native speakership in Indonesian usage can fairly be called "contact phenomena," insofar as they are distinctive of Javanese dialects of Indonesian. But their social significances need to be considered with an eye to Indonesian's un-native character, which makes them interactionally negligible as diacritics of speakers' ethnicities.

The term "language contact" is commonly associated with Uriel Weinreich (1953), who used it for the systemic effects which antecedent knowledge of one language can have on acquisition and use of another. In this way he made language contact a phenomenon of individual bilingualism, and developed a rubric for the study of how one's native (ethnic) language shapes acquisition of a second language, especially with respect to "interference" in the latter's sound system (giving rise to an "accent") and grammar ("dialect").

The "Javanese–Indonesian case" eludes Weinreich's seminal formulation because he tacitly (and, in most cases, fairly) presupposed such deviation to be describable with recourse to native-speaking usage, an extrinsic ground for his monolingual "norms." But in the absence of such "native-speaking" Indonesian models or targets, many aspects of Javanese–Indonesian usage elude his characterization of interference, because they do not count as deviant with respect to some native exemplar. In use by Javanese to Javanese, Indonesian counts more as what DeVries calls the "vague ideal norm" (1988:125) of a national language, which is always tacitly in need of practical, native-speaking supplement.

More recently, the historical and comparative linguists Sarah Thomason and Terence Kaufman (1988) have developed a different sense of language contact: as grounded in dimensions of intergroup relations, which shape patterns of acquisition and (perhaps) transmission of (formerly) non-native languages. In this way issues of difference and change in language structure are extended beyond individuals' knowledge to sociohistorical circumstance. When language contact is framed as part of "the sociolinguistic history of speakers" (ibid.:35), interference and borrowing can be framed as outcomes of the "cultural pressure," "numerical and political dominance" (ibid.:67), and "prestige or economic forces" (ibid.:77) which shape broader social contact.

In their schema, "borrowing" is a notion extended beyond lexical usage (*bahasa gadho-gadho*'s hallmark) to "deeper," structural phenomena which Weinreich might have called interference, and which occur in more intense degrees of social contact. In their view, such borrowings count as adaptations of non-native elements, and can serve in the long term to maintain a native language, albeit in altered form. Borrowings contrast with phenomena of "substratum interference," that is, systematic alterations in the structure of one language, usually superordinate, in long-term, intergenerational processes which lead to its displacement of another, usually a subordinate, in language shift.

In the absence of a locally salient Indonesian native-speaking community, this ambitious comparative scheme lacks clear, direct fit with the scene of "contact" between Indonesian and Javanese. On one hand, the lack of Indonesian native speakers means likewise that there are no locally salient reference points for gauging degrees and kinds of interference in Indonesian usage among Javanese. On the other, this lack of a south-central Javanese native (-speaking) Indonesian community means an absence of the kinds of sustained contact between collectivities which shape interference, convergence, or borrowing.

Insofar as neither scheme shows good fit with Javanese–Indonesian language salad, both of these comparative schemes direct attention to another sphere of "contact," neither cognitive nor collective: the sphere of face-to-face interactional and conversational contact which both languages can mediate. Under such an interactional profile there obtrude two "contact phenomena" which otherwise seem quite disparate.

One involves use of discourse particles which might seem negligible from a code-oriented perspective, but are nonetheless integral to the same interactional dynamics which are crucially mediated by the personal pronoun and kin term use discussed in chapter 6. I sketch a few of these particulars here to show how their transient, situated significances create another syncretic sphere of Javanese Indonesian usage. Their peripherality for native-speaker understandings of what counts as "mixed" usage can be portrayed here as giving them a broad interactional significance which, like Edgar Allan Poe's purloined letter, is hidden in plain sight.

The other much more obvious phenomenon is "mixed" lexical usage, especially in sometimes heavy borrowing of Indonesian lexical items into otherwise Javanese talk. But as alternative or complementary referential resources, these un-native vocabularies can be seen as assimilated to the antecedent structures of Javanese speech styles, sketched in chapter 3. Considered (like Javanese lexicons) as structurally secondary diacritics of styles of address, these Indonesian lexical elements appear to be tacitly syncretized to distinctively Javanese interactional dynamics.

Discourse particles and lexical items, quite different aspects of "salad language," can be brought together here with an eye to broader questions about how their situated significances are informed by their provenances, native and national. Characterized together, they help show how emerging Javanese Indonesian bilingualism lacks fit not just with received approaches to language contact, but also with socially interested visions of language shift.

Syncretic discourse particles

Javanese, Indonesian, and many other Malayo-Polynesian languages[2] have extensive repertoires of discourse particles which index their users' subjective states, and so can be thought of as psychoostensives (J. Errington 1988:222). Because they mark the situated relevances of referential material to which they are attached, they are endowed with functions which can be called, with Bühler, broadly conative (i.e., other-oriented) and emotive (i.e., self-expressive). They are thus integrally bound up with interactional self/other relations, and the interactional dynamics in which they are situated. Being neither referential nor glossable, they are also relatively elusive for direct, abstract characterization (Silverstein 1976). In this respect they can be counted as what Gumperz calls contextualization cues, which are "[h]abitually used and perceived but rarely consciously noted and almost never talked about directly" (1982:131).

I cannot provide a full catalog of discourse particles in either Indonesian or Javanese,[3] or a fine-grained description of all their functional significances, in the manner of Schiffrin's (1987) study of English discourse markers. It is enough here to make operational, *ad hoc* recourse to Bühler's basic distinctions, introduced in chapter 2, between referential, expressive, and conative functions of speech (which, as Schiffrin notes [ibid.:337], have direct correspondences in her own framework). To demonstrate the pervasive, osmotic quality of these particles in Javanese–Indonesian usage, I present examples of these Javanese particles in otherwise Indonesian usage, and of Indonesian particles in otherwise Javanese verbiage.

Two of the commonest Javanese particles, *lho*[4] and *kok*, can be presented together as "bivalent," because they take on complementary indexical significances in complementary environments. At beginnings of utterances – and sometimes referential phrases in other environments, in the case of *kok* – both index something about the speaker's stance or feeling *vis-à-vis* the states of affairs ensuingly spoken of. At the ends of phrases or utterances, on the other hand, *lho* and *kok* index the speaker's concern that the addressee be aware of the significance or salience of what has been said. They then serve appellatively (Bühler 1990:35) or conatively (Jakobson 1960:355) to index the speaker's concern for the addressee's stance to a state of affairs spoken of.

Prefatory, expressive *kok* marks surprise at and sometimes doubtful concession of a state of affairs, what Schiffrin (1987:28) calls a change in informational state. Though its best functional analog in English is often intonational, it can be glossed very broadly as "How is it that . . .?" Learning for instance that a servant has returned from the kiosk with two batteries, rather than the three she was instructed to buy, the mistress of the house may remark *Kok loro!?* (*loro*, J: "two"). Translatable as something like "You only got two?" with sharp intonational rise, or "How/why is it [that you only got] two?!," it may signal the speaker's desire for an explanation. Were the servant to respond that the price of batteries had risen, and the money provided was insufficient, the mistress might say, as much to herself as to anyone else *kok larang* (*larang*, J: "expensive") – roughly, "How expensive!" – signaling surprised acceptance of a state of affairs of which she was not previously aware.

Example 1 and many following are taken from a single extended discussion, otherwise entirely in Indonesian, about the fall of the Marcos regime in the Philippines in 1986. W has just described a Marcos underling's action with the term *pemborosan* (I: "wastefulness"). C marks his disagreement by topicalizing and disputing that choice of term with prefatory *kok* and another Javanese particle, *tá*, touched on later.

1. W: Mengingat pemborosan.　　　W: Considering [the] wastefulness.
   C: *Kok* pemborosan *tá*,　　　　C: [Why do you say] Wastefulness?!,
   　　kesetiaan.　　　　　　　　　　　[rather] loyalty.

Lho, uttered with falling intonation at an utterance's beginning and followed by a brief pause, marks speaker's surprise or doubt at some state of affairs, rather like the English interjection "well" with falling intonation. Prefatory *lho*'s functional similarity to prefatory/expressive *kok* is indirectly evidenced by their frequent co-occurrence: *lho* initially marks surprise, and *kok* follows grammatico-referential material referential of the matter in question. So in otherwise Indonesian example 2, *lho* indexes surprise at a prior remark and *kok*, inserted between the topic phrase (*orang-orang itu*, "those people") and comment phrase (*mau menerima . . .*, "want to receive . . .") indicates the thematic relevance of the question which follows.

2. *Lho*, orang-orang itu *kok*　　　*What*, those people *why should*
   mau menerima yang sekian　　　[they] want to receive so
   banyak itu?　　　　　　　　　　much [money]?

In postposed position, *kok* punctuates and emphasizes a speaker's view on some state of affairs which is referred to in the immediately preceding material, and his or her concern that its truth or relevance be recognized by the addressee. In example 3, for instance, P is jokingly responding to a friend's remark that they and their friends, although college graduates, are like high school students in their tastes. He uses conative, postposed *kok* complementarily with prefatory, expressive *lho*.

3. *Lho*, kita itu lain lagi *kok*.　　　*Well*, we're different, *y'know*.
   Seperti Pak Dibyo itu.　　　　　Like Pak Dibyo.

As a marker of the end of an utterance or phrase, *kok* can also mark a potential transition point for the roles of speaker and addressee.[5]

At the close of a topic phrase or utterance, *lho* indexes the salience of what has been just been conveyed for an addressee, and indexes the speaker's concern that s/he take heed. It can then have an advisory, admonitory, or urging feel, as in example 4. (For other examples see text 10.1, lines 12 and 150.)

4. Tahu kehidupan malam　　　　Get to know the night life,
   gitu *lho*.　　　　　　　　　　　like that *y'know*.

Lho and *kok* are both ubiquitous and integral parts of Javanese and Indonesian talk alike, and important means for molding interactional dynamics in both.

Lha and *wong* are two other Javanese particles which appear only at utterances' beginnings, and serve there to index a speaker's sense of fit between her or his addressee's prior knowledge or expectations on one hand, and some state of affairs encountered or spoken of on the other. In this respect both recall Schiffrin's descriptions (1987:202) of English "so" as functioning to convey a result causally related to extrinsic events or states, inferentially related to information known to the speaker, or motivationally related to some course of action.

Lha can index an expectation confirmed, a conclusion drawn, or a cause for action described. It can have as least-bad translations into English like "didn't I tell you," "well of course," "so," or "just as I thought." Example 5 below is drawn from the same Indonesian discussion of Philippine politics which supplied examples 1 and 2 above: S, making a point hard on the heels of M's remark, uses opening *lha* to emphasize connectedness between the situation to which M alludes and Enrille's circumstances.

5. M: Enrille, dia mengatakan bahwa "saya itu merasa berdosa terhadap Cory dan masyarakat Filipina, sebab yang melaksanakan penipuan suara adalah saya atas perintah Markos." Itu dalam suaranya. Berita itu kok dirasa-rasa sekarang *rádá*[6] berbalik arah.

   S: *Lha* ya *tá* orang tuanya, bagaimanapun, katanya "kita warga di Filipina" itu *tá*. Orang tua Enrille apa bukan rakyat?

   M: Enrille, he stated that "I feel [I have] sinned against Cory and the people of the Philippines because the one who carried out rigging of the election was me, on orders from Marcos." That was in his voice. That news if [you] think about it now *rather* shifts direction.

   S: *Well* his parents, *right*? Whatever else, they said "We're Philippine citizens," *right*? Are Enrille's parents not of the people?

Lha is only used prefatorily and can serve, as in this example, to initiate speakership and effect a transition between roles of speaker and addressee.[7]

Wong (or *ong*) also indexes a sense of self-evident connectedness between context and the topic of the utterance it opens. It marks, perhaps more strongly than *lha*, a speaker's sense that the addressee should know and recognize that connectedness. It often functions together with utterance final, conative *kok*, as in example 6.

6. *Wong* saya punya pikiran *kok*.
   Of course I've got some thoughts, *y'know*.

All three particles can be combined for heightened conative effect, as in otherwise Indonesian example 7.

7. *Lha wong* dia itu melayani masyarakat *kok*.
   Well of course he's serving the people, *y'know*.

A close functional and expressive analog might be use of *duh* as English slang at the end of utterances (e.g., "I'm babysitting and can't go now *duh*").

One final particle, *tá*, needs to be mentioned here. It is probably the commonest in Javanese Indonesian usage, but also the most elusive for brief characterization. Broadly conative in function and phrase final in distribution, it marks the salience of words or phrases which it then punctuates, albeit less forcefully or specifically than do other particles. In the comment on Enrille in example 5 above, for instance, speaker S pairs *tá* first with *lha* to emphasize agreement with M, and then uses it in utterance final position to throw into thematic relief the relevant condition mentioned.[8]

These particles are Javanese in provenance, but no less common in otherwise Indonesian usage as markers of transient subjective states, or orientations to topics and addressees. But Javanese speakers (at least in south-central Java) also use somewhat smaller repertoires of Indonesian discourse particles in Javanese and Indonesian usage alike. I sketch patterns of use of two of these here: *lah* and *kan*.

Indonesian *lah* differs from Javanese *lha* in pronunciation, distribution, and expressive meaning. Where *lha* is pronounced with a breathy open vowel, Indonesian *lah* has a non-breathy vowel followed by voiceless aspiration. Where Javanese *lha* marks an expressive orientation in prefatory position, Indonesian *lah* functions as a kind of expressive postposition to words or phrases of particular topical salience, more like Javanese *tá*.

To show how *lah* now figures in otherwise monolingual Javanese usage, I present examples from a single, casual conversation in a village west of Jogjakarta, engaged in by several young, bilingual men. (Indonesian elements are in italics; all others are *ngoko* Javanese.)

8. Yá is kono*lah*, sakkarepmu*lah*.
    All right, over *there*, whatever you *want*.

9. Yá upamané bar anu,   Yeah, supposing after uh,
    kengantuken ngono*lah*   [you] get tired, *right*,
    terus klalèn   then become unaware and
    turu tekan ésuk.   sleep until morning.

10. *Sekarang* ngéné waé*lah*,   *Now* [it's just] like this,
    iki ngéné soalé kaya   it's like this, like
    Sungkono kaé terus ora áná   Sungkono's, if he has no
    pekarangané terus Sungkono   yard, then Sungkono
    kon nang ndi?   will be told to go where?

Indonesian *lah*'s entry into Javanese thus seems to be augmenting a repertoire of increasingly convergent, syncretic particles.

Kan is closely related to Indonesian *bukan*, which serves (roughly put) as a negator for nominal elements. Both can serve at the end of phrases, like English tag questions of the general form "is it/isn't it the case"? But *bukan*, besides being rarer in this use than *kan* (in my data and personal experience) cannot serve to foreground an element which it immediately precedes, as can *kan*.⁹ Among younger bilinguals, in otherwise Javanese talk, *kan* can appear in such positions with analogous expressive force. Below are just a few of almost two hundred examples from transcriptions in which *kan* appears in otherwise Javanese utterances (including utterance final position, as example 14 indicates).¹⁰

11. Lha kuwi *kan* áná dhit
    Pé Ka Ka tukokké jariké?

    Well, *isn't* there money from
    PKK to buy the clothes?

12. Dadi umpamané mácá telung
    surat ngono sing
    cendhèk-cendhèk ngono
    kan isá?

    So, for instance, read three
    letters, like that,
    short ones, [they]
    can, *right*?

13. Nèng klas siji limá.
    Siji-limá klasé *kan*
    regedé mboten umum.

    In class one-five.
    One-five, *isn't it*
    a really messy class?

14. Aku, thik
    ngomong, aku, aku
    gur pèk dami
    kan?

    I, what do you mean
    [I] said, I, I
    was just picking dry stalks
    [in the field], *right*?

Kan appears to figure in Javanese usage as functional analog and supplement to another particle of Javanese provenance: *rak*, which has similar expressive import in preposed positions. In example 15, for instance, *rak* serves, as might *kan*, to mark the salience of the following topic phrase (. . . *dhá olèh dhuwit*, "all get money).

15. *Rak* dhá olèh dhuwit, nggoné Man Kusen?
    Didn't [they] all get money, at Man Kusen's place?

Examples of usage containing *rak* and *kan* are useful for comparing their expressive significances. Examples 16 and 17 are otherwise *ngoko* Javanese, and show both particles alternating as markers of topical salience.

16. Iyá, yá wong limá las
    iku, cuma ketuané
    rak aku.
    Dadi bocah kuwi takok yá ápá
    énaké ngéné, *kan* mesti akhiré
    yá kuduné digolèki manèh?

    Yes, yeah, fifteen people,
    only the one in charge
    is me, *right*?
    So the kids ask how's
    the best way, *won't* it have
    to be looked for again?

17. Bocahé mbeling tá,
    dadi áná slènder,
    stom kaé pas liwat.

    The kid's naughty, right,
    so there's a steamroller,
    a roller going by.

Lha kuwi *kan* mulih sekolah, bocah-bocah ngetutké nèng mburiné, *lak*[11] iseng, tangané mlebu nggon kaé *lho*.	So then, *right*, going home from school, kids are following along behind, for the hell of it, *right*? His hand goes in there *y'know*.

But *rak*, unlike *kan*, can be semi-productively suffixed with -*an* at the close of a phrase or utterance, with broadly similar expressive force. Example 18 demonstrates this distributional complementarity between *kan* and *rakan* as markers of a conversationally salient point.

18. Sebab nèk dimusyawarahké kono *kan* rumangsá ndhuwé dhuwit anu *rakan*.	Because if put to discussion *won't* [they] feel they have money, uh, *right*?

Though fewer in number, these particles of Indonesian provenance are entering otherwise Javanese usage in ways which point to the emergence of a functionally unitary, syncretic repertoire. I have briefly cataloged these seemingly minor bits of "mixed" usage to foreground the absence of any felt "hybridity" which is created by the Javanese and Indonesian provenances of these discourse particles. Considered separately, each suggests a distinct pattern or sociolinguistic dynamic.

Taken in isolation, native Javanese particles that are commonplace in Indonesian usage answer well to characterizations of "interference." *Lho, kok, tá*, and others would count then as diacritics of Javanese dialects of Indonesian, "substratal" traces and linguistic marks of ethnicity. But this seems unsatisfactorily partial in light of the converse entry of Indonesian particles into otherwise native Javanese usage. Were it isolated, this latter process might be plausibly allied to what Thomason and Kaufman call "deep borrowing." Discourse particles could then be counted as what Myers-Scotton (1992) calls "system morphemes" which are unnoticed or, in her phrase, less "psychologically salient" because they derive significance from their distributional positions rather than semantic content (cf. Silverstein 1976). Such a development could be read, then, as complementing more striking, "shallower" patterns of lexical borrowing, considered later on.

Even ignoring the entry of Javanese into Indonesian, this seems unsatisfactory in two ways. First, these "deep borrowings" are not "filling in" gaps or supplementing repertoires of Javanese discourse particles. Instead, they match very closely the functions of "native" elements. Secondly, this particle usage goes on quite independently of patterns of lexical borrowing, and so seems to be "deep borrowing" which is independent of "shallow borrowings" of more "psychologically salient" material (Myers-Scotton 1992:44).

It seems too that the provenances of these Indonesian and Javanese elements have relatively little salience as markers of speakers' Javanese and Indonesian identities; they comprise rather an interactionally integrated and emergent repertoire of syncretic elements which can count as both, or neither, ethnic and national. In this way their seeming peripherality to the semantic content of speech can be seen as enabling their peripherality as diacritics of the interactional identities which speakers assume in and through their use. They make for a kind of practical naturalization of Indonesian, allowing that code to be brought into experience-near, Javanese modes of expression.

Borrowing and style complementary

The validity of universal distinctions between "borrowing" and "code switching" is a recurring topic in much discussion of language contact and mixture. Empirical and theoretical arguments on this issue have broader significance, in turn, for comparatively framed questions about relations between semantic systems, over and against sound and grammatical systems. These relations are partially revealed in the shaping of lexical items as they are transposed "out" of their "source" languages, and their structural adaptation "into" use of a "recipient" language. Thomason and Kaufman's (1988) distinction between "shallow" (i.e., lexical) and "deep" (i.e., structural) borrowing keys to the notion that lexical-referential material is relatively salient and isolable for appropriation across scenes of sociolinguistic contact. Romaine similarly places lexical elements higher than grammatical elements in her hierarchy of cross-linguistic borrowability (1995:64).

Of interest here are the interactional saliences of Indonesian lexical material which figures in otherwise Javanese talk. This general issue can be considered in light of specifics of structure touched on in chapter 3's sketch of the Javanese speech styles. At the same time, often rampant borrowing from Indonesian to Javanese is enabled by structural congruencies (Weinreich 1953:33) and minimal typological distance (Thomason and Kaufman 1988:72) between the two languages. Phonological and morphological similarities between them can count as infrastructural for the easy transposition of Indonesian material into Javanese, and so as enabling of its stylistic syncretization.

Broad similarities between Javanese and Indonesian sound inventories should be evident from the orthographies and transcriptions provided for both languages throughout this book (see the note on orthography and transcription). The single most obvious difference between their very similar vowel systems stems from the allophonic variation in (south-central dialects of) Javanese between low-central, unrounded a (also used in Indonesian) and low-back semi-rounded á, which appears in final open syllables and in penultimate open syllables preceding final open syllables with that vowel (e.g., *rásá*, "feeling"). Elsewhere the phoneme is realized as a (for instance, when the root like *rásá* is suffixed with the nominal/possessive marker *-(n)é*, as in *rasané*). In such morphophonemic environments, then, vocalic diacritics of lexemes' provenances are often neutralized, as is the case for *rasa*, which is a cognate shared by the two languages.

Consonantal systems of the two languages differ most obviously in that Javanese has two apico-alveolar stops, th and dh. Although dialects of Indonesian in Java may differ from others in numerous other respects – e.g., breathy voice and prenasalization of voiced consonants – these differences also lack dialectal salience in usage among native speakers of Javanese.

So too sound patterns of Javanese and Indonesian lexemes are generally similar enough that I can turn immediately here to grammatical aspects of Indonesian's lack of felt "foreignness." Convenient examples of the ready assimilation of Indonesian lexical roots into Javanese are forms which appear to violate the free morpheme constraint. In well-known research on English–Spanish code switching, Shana Poplack developed a continuum of integrability of elements across languages similar to Romaine's, and proposed a universal constraint on bilingual usage: "[c]odes may be switched after any constituent in discourse provided that constituent is not a bound morpheme" (Poplack 1980:585–86). (Bound morphemes include grammatical elements, like tense and plural markers in English, which always appear "bound" through affixation to their roots.) So, Poplack points out, an English root can be borrowed into hybrid adjective noun combinations like "*una buena* excuse" ("a good excuse"), but not into a verb formed with the gerundive morpheme *-iendo*, as in *eat*iendo* ("eating").

Research on other bilingual situations has turned up exceptions to this constraint, which lead Hill and Hill to suggest on the basis of syncretic Mexicano usage (1986:349) that the bound morpheme constraint is instead a useful diagnostic for distinguishing between "foreign" and "assimilated" lexemes: the latter are fully integrated into a language if their use does not violate it.

By this criterion, numerous Indonesian lexical items can be shown to be fully assimilated elements into Javanese, even if by other criteria they count as occasional, "nonce borrowings." Convenient examples here are a pair of Indonesian roots which appear in my corpus of recorded usage prefixed with the Javanese passive/object focus clitic *tak-*, "by me." The Indonesian root *gubris*, "to heed," appears in the phrase *takgubris*, "heeded by me," as does *runding*, "discuss," in the phrase *takrundingké*, "brought up for discussion by me." (This latter also includes the

Javanese transitive/causative suffix *-ké*, which is cognate and functionally comparable with Indonesian *-kan*.)

These are surely Indonesian roots which have not been fully assimilated into Javanese as loanwords: they are quite rare in Javanese usage I have recorded or observed; speakers evince little doubt that they count as Indonesian; neither appears in any Javanese dictionary I have consulted. Both nonetheless appear in morphosyntactic environments which violate the bound morpheme constraint. Their assimilability to this grammatical environment is enabled not just by their syntactic and morphological characteristics, but their sound shapes as well, which show no self-evident non-nativeness.

Javanese and Indonesian also share numerous, commonly used cognates. Although text 7.1 is provided for other purposes, its ninety-one tokens of cognate elements (listed in table 7.2) help illustrate this point. So too numerous Indonesian lexical elements, several of them in text 7.1, have become fully assimilated Javanese loanwords, as is evident from the fact that they regularly figure even in usage of old, monolingual Javanese villagers (e.g., *daerah*, "area," and *contoh*, "example").

Borrowing of Javanese elements into Indonesian speech is less widespread, but deserves to be briefly noted here. Some Javanese words now count as Indonesian, in Java and elsewhere (e.g., *ngelu*, "have a headache"; see text 7.1). So too the senses of some Javanese terms have come into conformance with their Indonesian cognates: Javanese *bánggá*, once used in the sense of "resist, revolt" (cf. Indonesian *bangkang*), now seems increasingly to mean "proud," like its Indonesian cognate *bangga*; on the other hand, the ascendance of Indonesian *resmi*, "official," has eliminated archaic, literary connotations of its literary Javanese (*kawi*) cognate.

Such overlaps and congruencies all enable the use of Indonesian lexical material in Javanese talk, and so too their assimilation to use of the Javanese speech styles. In the first place, these comparabilities across languages broadly resemble the morphological and phonological congruencies which link *ngoko* and *básá* usage and vocabularies. I pointed out in chapter 3 that speech style elements fall into two broadly distinct functional groups. Elements of the language's grammatical and deictic systems generally fall into three-member sets of *ngoko*, low *básá*, and high *básá*. Other elements of the Javanese lexicon are undistinguished in the style system, or are elements of simpler two-member, *ngoko/básá* sets. Figure 3.2 showed how structural differences between these three-member and two-member sets enabled their members to combine in high *básá* and several different low *básá* styles.

This broad difference – between deictic and grammatical elements on one hand, and referential elements on the other – is worth keeping in mind when considering heavily "mixed" usage like that which occurred during the interaction transcribed in text 7.1. This represents about three and a half minutes of talk between three teachers, all women, at a high school on Surakarta district's northern periphery, during a break between classes. For the previous five minutes or so, they had been chatting in lively, intimate *ngoko* about the trials and tribulations of menstruation.

The elements in this text can be divided into three broad groups. Transcribed in boldface are elements which cannot be categorically distinguished, at least in isolation, as Javanese or Indonesian: cognate lexical items, syncretic kin terms (discussed in chapter 6) and discourse particles (discussed earlier in this chapter). Distinctively Indonesian elements are transcribed in italics; identifiably Javanese elements are transcribed in "normal" roman typeface. The transcribed segment begins just as the topic has shifted slightly and Bu Sita, a forty-odd-year-old biology teacher, has been asked by her colleague, Bu Eni (about thirty) about the physiology of menstruation and reproduction. It concludes at the point when the interactional dynamic shifted with a male colleague's arrival. During the course of her explanation – punctuated by reactions, queries, and objections from her friends – Bu Sita has easy recourse to the same *ngoko* style she otherwise addresses to her friends in informal settings. But her topic leads her to also have extensive recourse to a technical Indonesian register of anatomy and biology.

Text 7.1

EN: Kuwi piyé **kok bu** *prosesnya itu gimana* **tá**?
S: *Proses mengembang* pá piyé?
ST: *Terjadi luka, terjadi luka.*
EN: **Lha kok** isá *mempengaruhi seluruh badan*?
S: **Ha** isá no, **lha** – *kontraksi* **kok.**
EN: *Kontraksi*?
S: *Kontraksi dinding rahim* **kok.**
Ngéné, geraké *kontraksi* ki ngéné
iki **terusan**==
EN: ==Ahh==
S: ==Dadi *kontraksi*
|dadi
EN: |Dadi iki *luka*
no,==
S: ==Dadi kuwi rak teluré **pecah,**
yá tá. **Kan** kuwi teluré sing *menempel* nèng kono kuwi **pecah** yá ta, ra *dibuahi* **kan** akhirnya akan **pecah** tá. **Pecah kan** terus – dadi káyá darah kenthel kuwi lho. Lha kuwi nèk mengelupas **lak** sakdhindhing rahimé mengelupas. Dadi **kan** terjadi – *luka*. Yá is kuwi dadi getih rahim barang kuwi, *terjadi luka*.
Ngko nèk wis *terjadi luka* **terus** – kuwi – jeneng – ápá jenengé – *proses* nyang mari kuwi,
lho|beberapa hari ngono.
EN: |Dadi ngéné terus **terus**

[1] EN: *How is that,* **bu**? *How about that process*?
S: *The development process* or what?
ST: *The wound happening, the wound happening.*
EN: *So how* can it *affect the entire body*?
[5] S: *Huh,* it can, **well** – *contractions,* **y'know**.
EN: *Contractions*?
S: *Contractions in the wall of the uterus,* **y'know**.
Like this, the *movement of contractions* like this, **continuously**.==
[10] EN: ==Ahh==
S: ==So the contraction
|becomes
EN: |So this is *damaged,*
like==
S: == So then the *egg* **breaks out**
[15] **right**? So the *egg* which *attached* there **breaks out, right,** [if] not *fertilized* **then** *finally* it **breaks**. **Breaks, then** – [it] becomes like that *thick blood,* y'know. Now if it peels off, tnen the *wall* of the *uterus peels off.*
So *happens – damage.* OK, then, it becomes blood
[20] from the *uterus, at the time there's damage.*
Later if *damage happens* **then** that it's – what's it called – the *process* of healing y'know, a |*few days* or so.
[25] EN: |So it's like this **continuously.**

S:	Dadi ngéné *kontraksi*. Mulá kabèh **rasan**é |iyá
EN:	|Tekan **ngelu** tekan **pegel** |tekan [1 or 2 unclear words]
S:	|O is **rasan**é ra karuan. Nyat *mempengaruhi aliran darah*
EN:	Jan **terus lemeeees** banget
S:	Ning áná sing ora lárá yá. Nèk aku kuduné – *pénak*é mung nèk turu==
EN:	==**kan** *mungkin anu* yá [1 or 2 words unintelligible] *sel* pirang-pirang yá
S:	Yá, ora no==
EN:	==*Sel* piyé
S:	Yá siji thok |áná
EN:	|**O** *satu* **tá**
ST:	|**O** siji thok
S:	Sing mateng ngono ki yá nyang *saluran* sing **siap** nèng, **siap** nèng nggon *lehernya*. *Leher* kuwi **tá**, kuwi **rak siap** *dibuahi* wis *masak*. Ngko nèk ra *dibuahi* **kan** nyemplung nèng nggon *rahim nempel* **terus pecah**, **terus** dadi *mens* kuwi. Ning nèk *terbuahi* **kan** *otomatis* yá ora isá *terjadi*| menèh.
EN:	|Takkira ki *sel-selnya itu banyak*.
E:	**Bedan**é *sel telur* ka|ro
S:	|Yá okèh ning *yang* **siap** *dibuahi* **biasan**é rak mung siji-siji. Nèk **pas** sing *siap dibuahi* ki ndhog loro **ndilalah** *terbuahi* kabèh mulá dadi **anak**	*kembar* sing **rupan**é persis kaé.
E:	|*kembar*
S:	**Hak-a**. Ning nèk wis *terjadi pembuahan* yá wis ora, wis ora *produksi telur* menèh. Nèk *terjadi pembuahan* ora *produksi telur*.
EN:	Kuwi *telur-telur* |kuwi
S:	|Wis ora *produksi* nèh, *telur* kuwi mandheg nèng nggon *rahim* **lha** karèk *proses pembesaran*.
E:	*Cárá dén*é *keguguran*?
S:	**Hak-a**. Yá ènèng sing *kegurgran*é, *mungkin menempelnya* **kurang kuat kan** ceblok. **Lha** *itu bisa*
EN:	**Lha soal***nya* sing nèng *luar*, *anu*==
E:	==**Lha** nèk kuwi *luar kandhungan* ki *istilah*é piyé **kok** kuwi?
S:	*Luar kandhungan* ki yá ra nèng nggon *anun*é, ora nèng – *jadi tidak berada di rahim*.
E:	*Tapi* **kok** *menurut* **Bu R** *tu itu bukan calon bayi atau bukan apa*==
S:	==ènèng, *luar negeri* yá ènèng *luar kandhungan*, sing *anu* nèng *luar kandhungan*.
E:	*Nggak* **kok**, *menurut* **Bu Ragil kok**, ápá ngono **lho**, *di luar kandhungan* ki *disebut* ápá ngono?
S:	Yá ènèng sing *sebut penyakit* ápá ngono yá ènèng. Ning *memang yang*, *yang besar di luar kandhungan* yá ènèng, **Conton**é káyá Amerika dhisik wis tau, **ibu** *yang* **anu**, ápá kuwi jenengé, *berkembangnya*==
E:	==**Lha** *itu trus berkembangnya*

S:	So it's like this, the *contractions*. That's why it all feels |so
EN:	|Gets all **headachy**, gets all **stiff** |gets
[30] S:	|Oh yeah, too much. In fact it affects the *flow of blood*.
EN:	Really **always feels** weak.
S:	But there are some who don't feel bad. Me, I have to – it's **comfortable** only lying down==
[35] EN:	==**Mightn't uh**, there [unintelligible] are so many *cells*, right
S:	Well no==
EN:	==*Cell* how?
S:	==Yeah, just |one
[40] EN:	|**Oh** one
ST:	|**Oh**, just one
S:	The ready one moves to the *tube* that's **ready** at, **ready** at its *neck*. *The neck*, **right**, it's **ready** *to be fertilized*, already *mature*. Later [45] if it's not *fertilized* it enters the *uterus*, **right** sticks, **then** *breaks*, **then** it becomes *menstruation*. But if it's *fertilized*, **then** *automatically* it can't *occur* |again.
EN:	|I thought *there* [50] *were many of those cells*.
E:	The **difference** between *egg cells* |and
S:	|Yeah a lot *but the ones* **ready** *to be fertilized usually* are only a few. If at that time those [55] **ready** *to be fertilized* are two eggs, and happen to be *fertilized* both then they become |twins who **look** just the same.
E:	|twins
S:	Yeah. But if there's *already conception* there's no, no *egg production* any more. [60] If there's *conception*, there's no *egg production*.
EN:	Those *eggs* |those
S:	|No more *production*, the *egg* stops in the *uterus*, **so** there remains [65] the *growth process*.
E:	What about its *dying*?
S:	Yeah. There are some their *death*, maybe their *attachment* **wasn't strong enough**, **so** they fall off. **Now** *that can happen*.
[70] EN:	**Well** the problem, those outside uh==
E:	==**So** if it's *outside* the *womb* what's the *term* for that?
S:	*Outside the womb*, there's no place for, uh, there isn't – *so it isn't in the uterus*.
[75] S:	*But according to* **Bu R** *it's not a fetus*, *or not*, *uhh*==
	==There are, *abroad* there are *outside the womb*, which, uh, are *outside the womb*.
[80]	No, according to Bu R, what's it like, uh, *y'know*, *outside the womb*, it's **called** what?
S:	Yes there are, *called a malady* or what, yeah there are. But certainly those, those, which [get] *big outside the womb* exist. An *example* like in America before there was [85] a **mother** *who*, **uh**, what's it called *development*==
E:	==**So** *the development of that baby*

```
         bayi itu piyé, kok di luar kandhungan            is how, how can it be outside the womb
S:       Yá isá no buktiné yá-an              [90] S:    Yeah, it can, the proof
E:       Piyé kok yá, aku kok==                    E:    How about it, yeah, I==
S:                        ==Nah kuwi prosesé          S:                    ==That, the process, I
         aku dhewé yá rung ngerti, ning buktiné yá isá    don't understand, but the proof is it can
         lahir kok, urip ngono kok yá. Luar negeri. Aku   be born, and live. Abroad. I
         wis tau mácá nggon majalah kuwi wis tau áná. [95] once read in a magazine, there once was.
         Prosesé piyé aku yá rung ngerti wong             The process I don't understand yet, since it was
         mung dicritaké ngono.                            only told about as a story, like that.
```

This unusual conjunction of topic and interactional dynamic throws into relief a broad complementarity which informs the large amounts of Indonesian referential material which appear in this otherwise Javanese interaction. This can be summarized crudely but effectively in table 7.1, which shows a broad correlation when 338 tokens are classified on one hand for provenance, Indonesian or Javanese, and on the other for linguistic function, lexical or non-lexical (grammatical, deictic, etc.).

Excluded from the table are convergent or cognate elements which compose about 38 percent of the text's tokens. Lists of the items so classified are provided in table 7.2.

Of some 138 referential, glossable forms – nominal, verbal, adjectival – more than three-quarters (109) are of Indonesian provenance. Fewer than half of these incorporate Indonesian affixes. On the other hand, 181 of the remaining 207 tokens of grammatical and deictic elements – demonstrative, personal, and anaphoric pronouns, clause markers, aspect markers, negatives, prepositions, and so on – are Javanese.

A quick perusal of text 7.1 will show these Indonesian elements to be fairly evenly distributed throughout Bu Sita's discussion, and that these are not spurious statistical reflections of islands of Indonesian lexical and grammatical elements in otherwise Javanese usage. Bu Sita's use of Indonesian as a technical register extends, for instance, to her preference for Indonesian *telur*, "egg" (seven tokens), and *darah*, "blood" (two tokens), over semantically comparable Javanese *ndhog* and *getih* (with one token each). So too Indonesian lexemes are wholly assimilated to Javanese grammatical environments, most obvious among these being suffixed with the *ngoko* nominal/possessive marker -*é* rather than its Indonesian analog -*nya*.

The broad complementarity is structurally analogous to that which characterizes "mixed," low *básá* Javanese style usage. Javanese grammatical and deictic elements in text 7.1 give that talk an identifiably *ngoko* structure and interactional feel, and so create little sense of stylistic discontinuity within an ongoing interactional flow. In this way un-native Indonesian lexical material can be seen as effectively syncretized to ongoing essentially Javanese interactional relations. As Bu Eni, who recorded this conversation, said while listening to it with me later,

Table 7.1. *Complementary Javanese/Indonesian usage*

	Function:	Lexical	Non-lexical
Provenance:	Indonesian	109 (79%)	26 (13%)
	Javanese	29 (21%)	181 (87%)
	Total	138	207

"there's a lot of Indonesian, but it feels very Javanese" (I: *banyak bahasa Indonesianya, tapi rasanya kok nJawani*).

Bilingual usage like this can be seen as binding Javanese and Indonesian material in a kind of figure–ground relation of simultaneity, as an Indonesian vehicle of reference enters into the linguistic modes of Javanese social biographies. Against the ground of coethnic conversation, such Indonesian material's un-native provenance makes it seem relatively transparent to or skewed with ongoing interpersonal dynamics; certainly the talk transcribed here carries the same feel of mutual engagement – marked by overlaps, latchings, affect-laden expression – which occurred in the entirely Javanese talk which immediately preceded it. There is little reason to think that with her Indonesian verbiage Bu Sita, the biology teacher, assumed a position of quasi-pedagogical authority. The seeming "naturalness" of this lexical usage can be taken as striking evidence of Indonesia(n)'s ongoing entrance into the intimacies of everyday interaction; its seeming "blindness to society" (recalling Gellner's phrase) can be seen as enabling its ability to inform without necessarily transforming interactional intimacies.

The future of language salad

Bahasa gadho-gadho's structural interstitialness makes it seem ephemeral and elusive for normative characterization – less a variety of speech than an emergent, interactionally grounded zone of "contact" – which may be the scene of enduring change in both languages. Such patterned transiencies of "mixed" talk may provide better grounds, then, for conjecturing on both languages' futures than do ideologically grounded predictions of language shift like those discussed in the introduction.

A broad inference is invited by the phonological and morphological similarities between the two languages which, I just suggested, facilitate the transposition of lexical material between them. These might be read as structural "preadaptations" which will facilitate Indonesian's ascendance over Javanese in the long run. Under this view, heavily "mixed" usage like that in text 7.1 is a harbinger of language shift in the Javanese–Indonesian collectivity at large.

Shifting languages

Table 7.2. List of elements in text 7.1

Convergent/ cognate	Lexical Indonesian	Non-lexical Indonesian	Non-lexical Javanese
a	barang	akan	aku
banyak	berada	berapa	áná 3
akhiré	berkembangnya 2	bisa	ápá 5, pá
barang	besar	bukan 2	banget
akhirnya	calon	di 3	dadi 8
berada	darah 2	gimana	déné
aliran	dibuahi 5	gitu	dhisik
Amerika	hari	itu 6	èněng 6
anak	istilahé	jadi 2	(i)ki 8
anu 3	kandhungan 8	nggak, tidak	is 2/wis 8
anuné	kontraksi 5	tapi	isá 3
badan	leher	tu	jan
bayi 2	lehernya	yang 4	ká
bedané	luar 9		kaé
biasané	luka 7		karèk
bu 3, ibu	masak	*Lexical Javanese*	karo
buktiné 2	memang	cárá	káyá
contoné	mempengaruhi 2	ceblok	kono
daerah	mengelupas 2	getih	kuwi 20
dinding	mengembang	jenengé 3	lak/rak 3
disebut 2	mens	kabèh 2	mau
enaké	menurut 2	karuan	menèh, nèh 2
geraké	mungkin 2	kenthel	mulá 2
ha 2	negeri	kirá	mung 2
hak-a 3	otomatis	kuduné	nèk 10
kan 9	pembesaran	lárá	nèng 8
(ke)gugur(an)é	pembuahan 2	lemes	ngéné 3
kembar	penyakit	loro	nggo
kok 8	persis	mácá	ngko 3
kuat	produksi 3	mandheg	ngono 5, no 4
kurang	proses 3	mari	ning 4
lha 6	prosesnya	mateng	nyang 2
lho 3	rahim 5	ndilalah	nyat
(me)nempel(nya)	rahimé	ndhog	okèh
ngelu	sakdhindhing	nggon 4	ora 8, ra 2
nyemplung	saluran	pénaké	pirang-pirang
pecah 5	satu	siji	piyé 5
pegel	sel 3	siji-siji	sing 10
rasane 2	sel-selnya	turu	sok
rupané	seluruh		tak-
tá 7	siap 5		tau
terus 8	telur 5		tekan 3
terusan	teluré 2		thok 2
	terbuahi 2		yá 17
	terjadi 7		yèn
	terjadinya		

But analogous structural phenomena have a different place in Thomason and Kaufman's comparative account, and in at least one other broadly similar multilingual situation. Thomason and Kaufman (1988) argue that heavy borrowing, lexical but perhaps also structural, can promote maintenance of a native language in the face of encroachment by another. They note as salient in this regard the multilingual situation in Kupwar, Maharashtra, India, described in a well-known article by Gumperz and Wilson (1971). Gumperz and Wilson show how local dialects of structurally distinct languages – Marathi, Urdu, and Kannada – have been shaped by long-standing processes of structural convergence. These have culminated in grammatical structures which are similar enough across the three languages to allow for intertranslation between them on a sequential morpheme-by-morpheme basis. As of the time of Gumperz and Wilson's research, at least, this appeared to be a situation of stable multilingualism.

Thomason and Kaufman (1988:86–88) judge such change to arise from conditions of "intense contact" and "moderate to heavy structural borrowing." Certainly the social forces engendering bilingual repertoires and communities in Java differ radically from those at work in Kupwar, where multilingualism arose from long-term contact between enduringly distinct ethnolinguistic communities, rather than between ethnic/native community and institutions of an unethnic nation-state. So too structural similarities between Javanese and Indonesian usage are a function of antecedent similarity, rather than sustained, reciprocal convergence through simplification.

But Thomason and Kaufman's description can be applied to the current scene of emerging Javanese Indonesian bilingualism. Stable patterns of multilingual use in Kupwar suggest that structural similarities between languages are neither necessary nor sufficient grounds for predicting patterns of language shift. The kinds of hybrid, syncretic Javanese–Indonesian usage described here, for instance, seem less conflictual than complementary: Indonesian lexical material can be structurally assimilated into Javanese talk, and so interactionally syncretized not to ethnically distinct but to stylistically familiar face-to-face experience. If those vocabularies count in fact as a contextually uninflected instrumentality – as a means for what modernists would call precise, efficient communication – then they seem as well suited to that function in otherwise Javanese usage as they do in Indonesian usage.

Viewed as syncretic elements, discourse particles and Indonesian lexical items together throw into question the usefulness of assumptions about categorical distinctness between autonomous, mutually exclusive Javanese and Indonesian codes. Such assumptions are an accepted part of standardist ideologies of modern national languages, and visions of language shift. But speakers' easy, situated recourse to elements of both codes in everyday talk seems to fit a rather different sense of conversation as a sphere of both Javanese and Indonesian interactional identities.

Ubiquitous "background phenomena" of discourse particle usage mute the felt difference between Javanese and Indonesian talk all the more effectively for their unobtrusiveness and peripherality to interactional awareness. Examples provided earlier show that they comprise a repertoire of speech elements indexically bound up with situat-ions of use, which correspondingly osmose across received institutional distinctions between the two languages. As an emergent, interactionally keyed matrix of terms, coavailable for use with either code, they appear to represent another syncretizing process which mutes the felt immediacy of difference between Indonesian and Javanese interaction.

Such diffuse "leakage" across categories can be read as an indirect consequence of these particles' peripherality to context-free characterization. Their indexical, non-referential, and so unglossable meanings, conative and expressive, are intrinsically and existentially bound to interactional senses of "we-ness," which they modulate. Their linguistic indexicality embeds them, in Bonnie Urciuoli's phrase, in "socially organized cultural experience" (1985:366), and makes them part of the "taken-for-granted intelligibility" (ibid.:367) of interaction.

This sketch of *bahasa gadho-gadho* is foreshortened, in that it ignores the aspects of "mixed usage" which involve code switching, taken up in chapter 10. In this way it counts as one kind of prefatory background for gauging code switchings' interactional saliences, over and against other kinds of "mixed," monolingual and bilingual usage. But other kinds of background are necessary, which I provide in chapters 8 and 9. They deal with dynamics of Javanese interactional process, and patterns of monolingual but multistylistic usage.

8
SPEECH MODELING

In his essay on language and hierarchy in Solo, James Siegel briefly notes the use of "high" and "low" Javanese in what he calls "indirect discourse," when "[t]he speaker will repeat something that has been said to him and his own reply" (1986:19). Siegel in passing alludes to this recurring conversational pattern en route to his broader ethnographic concerns: language and translation, the autonomy of self, and the anxieties of power. In his ethnography of Javanese shadow plays, Ward Keeler mentions "direct quotation" as the "recitation of a previous encounter [which] turns into something like a reenactment, each speaker quoted (supposedly) verbatim" (1987:257–58). He interprets such acts as evincing broader Javanese concerns with the assumability of voice and the dissimulation of a mediating presence.

With these two labels I take Siegel and Keeler to be alluding in different ways to the broader interactional dynamic I thematize here as "speech modeling." This chapter similarly sketches shifting interactional engagements which occur when speakers voice or model words which are somehow "not their own," and in so doing shift their stances to erstwhile addressees who temporarily become bystanding audiences. This practice is linked, in turn, with issues of style usage and style shifting taken up in chapters 9 and 10,[1] because speech modelings and speech style use are jointly presupposing of particular aspects of interactional self/other relations. In this respect, a sketch of speech modeling provides context for considering style shifting in chapter 9, and code switching in chapter 10. The striking immediacy of speech modelings in Javanese interaction (at least for a foreign observer) likewise throws into relief their general absence from monolingual Indonesian interaction among Javanese.

This sketch centers on six representative conversational texts, drawn from recordings of interaction in which speech modelings occurred, a few transient wrinkles in the fabric of everyday talk. But these raise broader questions of description and interpretation which I broach here. I consider the enabling, problematic ambiguities of conversation which, as the conversation is textualized, must become mirrors of my expository concerns in order to provide windows on Javanese interactional life.

Notions of practice and strategy, "mine" and "theirs," need to be scrutinized here along with the texts which they help to contextualize in my own very different sort of "report."

Modeled speech as reported speech

Speech modeling embodies the doubleness of "speech about speech" which is also "speech within speech," and which "derive[s] . . . in some respect at least from a source other than [the] actual speaker" (Volosinov 1986:16). For this reason it counts as part of the "problem of reported speech" which V. N. Volosinov showed to be focal for understanding language as a nexus of subjectivity and sociality, and the philosophical relevances of voicing. The distinctive double-voicing of reported speech has a structural correlate which Roman Jakobson made evident when he brought Volosinov's work to the attention of many non-Russian readers with his binarist taxonomy (Jakobson 1971 [1957]) of "duplex structures." There he schematized relations between messages (M) and codes (C) in such a way as to locate Volosinov's "problem of reported speech" within the class of "messages which encode other messages" (M/M, in Jakobson's two-by-two array).

Jakobson thus foregrounded the analyzability of "double-voiced" utterances into distinct, segmentable components. In formal registers of languages like English, for instance, an "encoding" segment can include a verb of speaking (*verbum dicendi*) predicated of an utterer (e.g., "Mary said . . ."), in a phrase which frames referentially the re-presented content, and perhaps form, of a reported act-utterance (" . . . (that) Bill was coming.").[2] Such encoding segments function metapragmatically (Silverstein 1976, 1993) as language use which referentially objectifies language use. So too they mediate between the *hic et nunc* of a context of reporting on one hand, and the disjoint, originary event of the act-utterance reported, on the other.

These segments of speech reportings – framing and framed, encoding and encoded – are thus asymmetrically related, insofar as the former regiments the latter (Silverstein 1993), stipulating and reproducing those of its characteristics which count as relevant within and with respect to a context of reporting. Speech can only be reported, then, as a partial re-presentation of an event which it partially rehearses, but always objectifies in reference.[3] Volosinov characterized this asymmetric, dynamic tension between reported and reporting speech as playing out in the "overtly analyzing tendencies" of "indirect reported speech" (1986:161) and the relatively imitative aspects of "direct reported speech," which confer relatively more re-presentational autonomy on its objects.

Javanese speech modelings resemble more closely "direct reported speech" (as Keeler's label suggests) because they are broadly imitative or "quotative" of the speech they represent. They bear some of the qualities of the verbal events which they (appear to) iconically signify, and to which they stand in "internal" relations of resemblance. But speech modelings differ crucially from indirect and direct reported speech in that they commonly lack overt, framing metapragmatic material, and so are not obligatorily bipartite in structure.[4]

To capture this difference, and show how speech modelings can represent speech without overtly regimenting it, I could use a rubric like "unframed direct reported speech." But besides being clumsy, this label frames these aspects of Javanese usage comparatively, and as comparatively unusual in relation to other languages. My concern here, on the other hand, is to try to foreground particular acts through their integral links to Javanese conversational life: the techniques which enable its accomplishment and construal; the interactional dynamics it creates and presupposes; the practical sense it embodies; the interactional strategies it may subserve.

As Siegel's and Keeler's remarks suggest, these can be radically imitative, minimally regimented acts of reported speech, presupposing of shifts in interactional relations between speech participants which may be striking for foreigners. My concern here is primarily with particulars of modelings which show how they are performed and construed in rapidly shifting interactional self/other relations.

A small performance: dialog modeling

Speech modeling might be most conspicuous and obviously artful as the basis for performance in hours-long Javanese shadow plays (*wayang kulit*). Keeler has traced relations between the perceived personal authority of puppeteers (*dhalang*) and their capacities as virtuoso speech modelers, who dissimulate their presence as performers by ventriloquating and animating leather puppets. Among the best-loved parts of *wayang* performances are humorous dialogs of the *dhagelan* genre between sometimes shrewd, sometimes hapless clowns. Text 8.1 is a transcription of such a dialog, which was animated and modeled by a speaker who hardly interpolated his "own" voice into the extended, two-part conversation he modeled.

But this *dhagelan* is extracted not from a shadow play performance. It occurred instead in a fairly casual conversation involving just three people. The speaker here, Pak Mus, is a fortyish teacher of religion in a high school in the area of Purwareja, south-central Java, who has been engaged in a theologically tinged conversation with a younger colleague Wid (W), during a break between classes. As will become clear in chapter

10, where more of the text of this conversation is presented as text 10.1, it had begun to take on a slightly contentious tone, and arrived at a chicken-and-egg sort of impasse when Pak Mus embarked on this impromptu performance to illustrate the false paradox he believes his conversational partner has embraced.

Text 8.1

M1: Yá pádhá waé umpamané Petruk [1] M1: Yeah it's like when Petruk and
    karo Garèng tuku wedhus, upámá   Garèng buy a goat, for instance
    a. [G] *Kang*, milih ngarep,   a. "*Kang*, I want the front,
    kowé lé mburi. Lha nyong   you get the back, ha, mine's better,
    sing gagah milih ngarep – [5]   I get the front
    ndhasé kok, áná sunguné,   with the head, there's horns,
    áná kupingé sing keplèh"==   and floppy ears"==
S: ==Nèk S: ==If
    manak   it has kids
M2:   M2:
    a.[P] Nyong mburiné **yá** *kang*? [10]   a. "I get the back end, right, *kang*?"
    b.[G] **Iyá**   b. "Yeah"
    c.[P] **Ha** ngko angger wedhusé   c. "Ha, later if the goat eats the
    dingon mangan tandurané   neighbor's plants,
    tangganè sing dituntut wedhusé   whose goat
    sápá? [15]   gets sued?"
    d. [G] **Yá** wedhusé nyong   d. "Yeah, mine"
    e. [P] **Lha** nèk manak?   e. "Well what if it has kids?"
    f. [G] Nèk manak, yá wedusmu,   f. "If it has kids, yeah, it's yours"
    Ha, tekan nggoné èrèt-èrètan kok   So they end up at home arguing
W: Lha iyá. [20] W: Right.
M3:   M3:
    a. [G] Nèk ngono takbelèh waé.   a. "Then I'll just slaughter it."
    b. [P] **Lha** belèh sing mburi mélu   b. "Slaughter it, and the back will
    mati.   die too."
    Tekan klurahan udreg-udregan   They end up at the *lurah*'s really
    ramé, wong niku mik upámá kok. [25]   fighting, well that's just a for instance.

I adopt a few notational conventions to foreground the transcribable elements of this speech which are indirectly enabling of such modelings of two-party conversations, in the absence of framing (metapragmatic) verbiage. Transcriptions of all conversational turns issuing from Pak Mus' mouth are marked by line-initial *M* and sequential Arabic numerals to facilitate reference. Each segment of M's speech which models a conversational turn taken by one of two antagonists – the clowns Garèng (G) and Petruk (P) – is indented and marked sequentially with a lower-case roman letter. I try to convey some sense of the "directness" of this modeled dialog by setting off English translations with quotation marks, and forgoing an identifying initial for each character as M ventriloquates his words.

After Wid's prior comment in the conversation, Pak Mus signaled his shift from conversation to performance at M1 by simply linking the names of his conversants-to-be with the topic of Wid's discussion. He then began (at line 3) to model conversation between Garèng and Petruk without bothering to specify that it is Garèng's utterance which he is modeling first. The transition from his contextualizing frame (*upámá* . . .) to modeled dialog was marked by the utterance initial vocative *kang* (short form of *kakang* "elder brother," discussed in chapter 6), which also appears as a closing parenthetical at the end of turn M2a. Rather than interpose "his own voice" to referentially specify the characters' identities, and so explicitly frame the utterances which he alternately ventriloquates, Pak Mus relied on utterance-internal conversational sequencers to cue transitions between Petruk's and Garèng's roles as speaker and addressee.

When Pak Mus' own speech partner S hastened (at line 8–9) to indicate that he had heard this one before, he does not say as much, but anticipatorily modeled the question from Petruk which Mus ensuingly models at line 17. This did not make Pak Mus feel constrained either to abort his performance or narratively reestablish its presupposed context (M2a, line 10). He continued modeling the dialog in syntactically and intonational marked question/answer pairs. Utterance opening interjections *ha* and *lha*, which mark connectedness to immediately preceding utterances (see chapter 7), punctuated transitions from 2b to 2c, 2d to 2e, 3a to 3b, and also from modeled speech at 2f to Pak Mus' own narration of the consequences of the argument (at lines 24–25).

Pak Mus closed his little performance by remarking again about the perceived relevance of the modeled dialog as an example of nonproductive argument. Otherwise, his "own" voice served only to narrate nonverbal consequences of the verbal actions of his two characters (at lines 19 and 24).

To carry off this extended performance, situated within an otherwise "ordinary" conversation, he had recurring recourse to devices – vocatives, intonation, discourse particles – which are indexically grounded in the interactional self/other relations they serve to mediate. These would be readily "analyzed out" in indirect reported speech, but in speech modelings these are "speech internal" cues which can transpose a modeled interactional sequence into a modeling context, and mark utterance sequencing with minimal narrative framing material. Thought of as a presentational technique, more or less skillfully deployed, speech modeling makes possible an autonomy and presentational immediacy for others' talk which is not unlike that created by shadow puppeteers, even if speakers lack a professional's performance skills.

If this text blurs the line between conversation and verbal art, this is because it brackets distinctions between talk in acts of address and acts of performance. It presupposes a shifting of interactional self/other relations such that a speaker animates another's words for an erstwhile addressee who then becomes an audience. Were "knock-knock" jokes performable in similar manner – signaled at their outset by uttering the phrase which gives the genre its name, and then animated by a single speaker in stereotyped exchange of questions/answer pairs – then speech modeling performances like that of Pak Mus would have a rough analog in English. But speech modelings are much more common in Javanese, and are usually much less overt.[5]

Modeling and interactional involvement

Text 8.2 presents a shorter, more negligible instance of speech modeling which I have extracted, along with a bit of surrounding verbiage, from the transcription of a long, meandering conversation between long-standing acquaintances. Involved were my thirtyish consultant who recorded it, Mbak Endhang (E), her neighbors – Mbok Atma (A) and Pak Atma, a villager couple in their mid-thirties and her longtime intimates – and Pak Wignyo (W), fiftyish kin to Pak Atma, whose purpose in visiting was unclear to Mbak Endhang. She told me that he, like her, seems to have just dropped in.

Text 8.2

W: Kandhani rong sasi ki [1] W: I'll tell you, two months I've been
   blánjá dhité dhéwé kok. [laughs]   living on my own money. [laughs]
A: Blánjá dhité dhéwé?   A: Living on your own money?
E: Lha biasané nggo dhité sápá?   E: Well usually whose money [do you live on]?
W: Dhité wong-wong kuwi, [5]   W: I'll tell you, two months I've been
   dhit turahan ngono adaté, rong   money left over, usually, two
   sasi ki blánjá nggo dhité   months now I'm spending my own
   dhéwé. [laughs] Mbokné ngantèk   money. [laughs] It's gotten so I
   ra takdhumi,   haven't given the wife anything,
   wa is== [10]   yeah well==
A: =="Saiki kowé ra takdhumi sik, A: =="I'm not giving you anything.
   préi sik, |mbokmu."   [I'm] not working now |mom."
W: |"Préi   W: |"Not
   sik" aku ngono.   working now," I [said] like that.

Wignyo had been talking about hard times in the livestock business, in which he works as a broker specializing in cows. At once exasperated and resigned, he half humorously said (lines 1–2) that he hadn't made a profit (i.e., has had to live on his own money, not other people's) for two months. Then he confessed (lines 8–9) with a rueful laugh that he hadn't even been able to contribute to household expenses.

This entire conversation, between persons of long acquaintance, was carried on in *ngoko*. Atma's utterance at line 11 appears to be a sympathetic response to Wignyo's narration of hard times; she modeled an utterance she imagined Wignyo might have addressed to his wife during the difficult period he has just described. Atma, self-evidently absent from that original event, claimed no knowledge of such an utterance from either direct first-hand observation, or an observer's report. Her modeling rather assimilated Wignyo's prior descriptive statement at lines 8–9 – addressed to herself, her husband, and Endhang – into an act of address transposed to the past referred to as "now" (*saiki*), and in which she models Wignyo's speaking position as "I" (*tak-*, "passive first person clitic") to his wife, as presupposed "you" (*kowé*). The pictorial (or iconic) quality of Atma's modeling may be clearest for non-native speakers through these indexically referential elements' meanings, which can only be construed by explicitly transposing the deictic grounds (Hanks 1990:217–22) for its participant roles to the previously narrated event.

To call this act "direct unframed quotation" or "direct unframed reported speech" seems misleading, insofar as each label tacitly and infelicitously presupposes that Atma's utterance is licensed by (and "reports on") her knowledge of an antecedent event, which she is modeling. In fact she had no clear evidence that it ever happened, and questions about her modeling as a reflection of reality are in fact beside the point. This is apparent from Wignyo's response. He tacitly accepted the appropriateness if not accuracy of Atma's modeled speech by modeling in turn (lines 13–14) a putative past utterance – his own, framed explicitly as such with the tag phrase *aku ngono*, literally, "I [did/said] like that" – which echoed exactly the part of Atma's previous model which was not based directly on the content of his own previous utterance.

Atma's utterance was, then, not so much a report of a past event as what can be called with Goffman (1974:504) a replaying, "something that listeners can empathetically insert themselves into, vicariously reexperiencing what took place." It enacted an experience which she imaginatively recovered from her addressee's narration, rather than reproducing something she observed; her audience, after all, was the only source of the information on which she based it. It may be that she was heightening and contributing to a sense of co-presence by empathetically and conspicuously placing herself, as speaker, in the interactional "here-and-now" of Wignyo's narrated "there-and-then." This is an instance of speech modeling, then, which did not dissimulate interactional presence so much as it heightened interactional engagement, and a sense of what Tannen (1994:25–26) calls involvement.

Prescriptive modeling: *mbasakaké*

Taken together, texts 8.1 and 8.2 illustrate the shifting interactional self/other relations which speech modeling can engender. They also show that modelings can take on variable saliences in relation to their interactional surrounds on one hand, and their "sources" (in Volosinov's sense) on the other. Because speech modelings are relatively unregimented by overt framing material, and derive significance from "internal" relations of resemblances to their sources, complex ambiguities can arise between the speech participant relations of modeler and audience on one hand, or speaker and addressee on the other.

These ambiguities arise at the point of juncture between interactional roles which Goffman (1974, 1981) distinguished as "author" and "animator," already broached in chapter 5. That these roles can be dissociated is very clear when talk is intendedly voiced not as a model *of* some antecedent act, but as source *for* some other utterance in the future. Such broadly modal modelings make speech an image of what will, could, or should be uttered at some future time, in some future context, by some speaker. When intended or construed as such by a co-present audience, modelings can take on a pedagogic or prescriptive tone, and as such presuppose a particular relationship between speaker/modeler and addressee/audience.

One such type of act, common enough in Javanese to be thought of as a named subtype of speech modeling, is called *mbasakaké*. This metapragmatic term can be translated, with Koentjaraningrat (1957:99), as "to speak the speech of the children." I have discussed it elsewhere (1988:160–62) with regard to pragmatically salient kin terms and personal pronouns. Normatively older, higher-status speakers use such interactionally crucial elements as a co-present person should or would, and in a manner broadly analogous to the ways one can refer in English to an adult as would a child whom one is addressing (e.g., asking a child "Where's mommy?" rather than "Where's your mommy/mother?").

An example is text 8.3, transcribed from a later point in the interaction between Mbak Endhang and Pak Iman which was presented earlier as text 2.1. Both were resting from work in their neighboring fields and chatting with Mas Nur, a twentyish man passing by with his young niece, L. L was addressed as *ndhuk*, a term of familiar address for younger women and girls. While Iman chatted with Nur – whom Endhang does not know and therefore addresses in *básá* at lines 8–9 – Endhang had been telling L (lines 1–2) to go look for a kind of edible grub called *gasir*. Pak Iman (at line 4) and Nur (at line 10) joined in.

Text 8.3

E:	Káná, golèk gasir sik káná.	[1]	E:	Over there, go look for *gasir* over there.
L:	E kéné okih==		L:	Hey, there's a lot here==
I:	==Gé gagé,		I:	==Quick,

	awakmu ka babi ka ngono thik	[5]		quick, your body like a pig's,
	golèk gasir aé.			why look for *gasir*.
L:	Iyá.		L:	Yeah [to I].
E:	Nggih niku lemuné, pakanané		E:	Yeah, she's fat from eating
	pohung niku.			cassava.
N:	"*Nggih mbah*" ngonoá	[10]	N:	"*Yes, grampa*," [say] it like that
	ndhuk.			**ndhuk**.

When Pak Iman affectionately ribbed L (lines 4–6), she responded with the familiar *iyá* rather than polite *nggih* (line 7). Uncle N stepped in to correct her by modeling the utterance she should have just addressed to the venerable Pak Iman, and so also the speech style and kin term she should address to him in the future. He punctuates this modeling with the *ngoko* demonstrative pronoun *ngono* "like that," suffixed with the modal, optative/imperative suffix -*á*, which overtly signals the prescriptive import of the utterance he has just modeled. N's avuncular utterance had clear import for L's future conduct: his social status as L's elder/superior was presupposed as he interposed himself in her proper interactional guise. An enduring status asymmetry, presupposed and made occasionally salient, again heightened rather than dissimulated the interactional salience of the speech modeler's identity as a speech prescriber.

A restricted but close analog of such usage in English might occur when a child makes a request of a parent (e.g., "Can I have some juice?") who immediately addresses to that child the bit of verbal politesse the child neglected to include (". . . please?") before responding "in his or her own voice." Though this presupposes similarly shiftable voicings and participant roles, it is likewise a more restricted interactional technique than is speech modeling in Javanese.

Expository and interactional strategies

The examples juxtaposed as texts 8.1–8.3 help to illustrate the centrifugal feel which speech modelings can lend to conversational dynamics, and which can be very striking for non-native speakers (like me) who are often hard-pressed to recognize or construe them. Unaccompanied by any overt signal of their "displaced" origins, speech modelings shift or decenter the relation of speech to modes of speakership. By performatively enacting a distinction between animator and author, they create slippage likewise between the roles of addressee and bystander (audience).

These three examples should also intimate something of the tacit, shared, interactional sensibility which grounds such transient speech modelings, part of practical competence in Javanese. In this narrow respect, speech modelings' taken-for-granted meaningfulness can be broadly analogized to the unstated yet transparent significances of recurring grammatical patternings. That tacit, shared meaningfulness is grounded in practical awarenesses of shiftable, indexical, part/whole relations between talk and context. To broach questions about the nature of this practical knowledge is to deal with the situated character of modelings' significances, and the operational strategies – classificatory, expository, and interpretive – which enable me to foreground them here through a series of abstracted, suitably textualized examples.

I have transcribed and juxtaposed texts 8.1–8.3 on the basis of this recurring, partial sameness they display, and which I have attributed to a broader, practical sense of Javanese conversational dynamics. This pattern is putatively recoverable from an indefinite number of other interactional moments, identifiable bits of "transient real time processes" (Gumperz 1982:vii) during which speakers' make their mouths available for words with sources other than themselves. To draw these few drops from an ocean of talk is thus to engage in a metapragmatic exercise which presupposes that each can be abstracted, via its textual surrogate, from its originary context. Each is therefore re-presented as a "self-contained entity . . . cut out from its surrounding context and analyzed in isolation" (Duranti and Goodwin 1992:9).

By selecting each such transcriptional bit, I take license to compensatorily narrate and metapragmatically regiment the act of which it is a trace with respect to its originary, "nonreadable surround or background" (Silverstein and Urban 1996:1). It may be obvious but is not trivial that, as author of such an encapsulating "co-text," I write with recourse to partial knowledge, and an eye to my own expository concerns. I consistently (or insistently) refer to these transcriptions as *texts* in order to foreground their multiply artefactual characters (see ibid.:2) as objects of my focalizing operations (Duranti and Goodwin 1992:10). These texts are thus mediating of relations between originary and expository contexts, and tacitly bring into convergence two distinct temporalities.

This circumstance can be read from the enabling ambiguities of conversation analytic questions of the form "Why that now?" (Bilmes 1985) and "Why this form now?" (Duranti 1994:172). Both queries derive motivating power from the doubled, shiftable senses accruing to the word "now." On one hand it foregrounds transient, originary, "real-time" instants which are scrutinized, via their traces, in inspectable recordings and transcriptions as "that" or "this form." On the other hand, those "nows" are reconstituted in "this" alien context, and assimilated to a virtual expository "here" and "now" of inspection and interpretation. This transposition of subjective, occasional experience ("there-and-then") into expository discourse ("here-and-now") presupposes the unity and coherence of texts like 8.1–8.3, during and after the "fact."

This double temporality likewise shapes construal of such texts as (past) vehicles and (present) evidence of speakers' originary intent. Read consecutively as verbal means to interactional ends, they are gathered under a profile of "motivational understanding," what the interpretive sociologist Schutz (1967a:27) called the "future-perfective mode" of temporal consciousness. In his view, a given instance of social conduct (say, an utterance which models speech) can be engaged in and construed as unitary and coherent because it has been anticipatorily imagined by its actor (speaker) as "a series of future events whose occurrences [the speaker] proposes to bring about" (ibid.) To construe conduct – *in situ*, or through talk's traces – is putatively to rehearse this operation, *post hoc*, by taking as interpretive grounds the "in-order-to" coherence one retrojects into it.

So focalizing operations which I adopt here confer a coherent, episodic appearance on such texts, and promote readings of them as traces of strategies which speakers pro-jected – beginning, continuing, ending – prior to their implementation (see Schutz 1967a:87–91). This expository strategy, in turn, makes it easy to read conversational texts with recurring, operational recourse to assumptions about the purposeful, strategic orientations of talk's originators and performers. The upshot is an appeal to "strategy" and "intent" which can be both explanatory and heuristic.

Before pursuing methodological implications of this issue, I want to show how its practical consequences can obtrude when considering texts of talk which resist easy assimilation to such a categorically strategic, agentive profile. Consider in this regard text 8.4.

Text 8.4

A: Mánggá.	[1]	A:	Come in.
W: Inggih. [enters the room and sits down next to me on a sofa]		W:	Yes.
A: Saking tindak pundi?		A:	Where are you coming from?
W: Saking kantor tilpun.		W:	From the telephone office.
A: Lajeng dos pundi?	[5]	A:	So how about it?
W: Nuwun inggih "Panjenengan kulá aturi ngisèni formulir, sampun rampung, lajeng punfotokopi rangkep kalih lajeng Ka Té Pé, rangkep tigá."	[10]	W:	Well "You I ask to fill out the forms, when they are done, then copy them, two copies then the identification card, three copies."

This transcribes a bit of talk which happened at the very beginning of a conversation I recorded during a visit with a distinguished male member of Solo's courtly elite, Pak Agus. (So it also is convenient evidence that speech modeling is common in elite as well as non-elite interaction.) We had been chatting for about twenty minutes in polished, high *básá* when another visitor appeared on the veranda, at the open door to the guest room where we were seated. The new arrival was Pak Wig, a man of about fifty whom I had met before at Pak Agus' house, and who had been under Pak Agus' command in the Indonesian army during the revolution. He had since maintained close ties with Pak Agus, often undertaking chores like that around which the ensuing conversation developed. The transcription of Pak Wig's speech begins at just the point where his voice was loud enough to be recordable and transcribable, after he quietly uttered the formulaic greeting *kulá nuwun*, and entered the room.

Pak Wig had undertaken, I inferred from the conversation, to act as Pak Agus' agent in his dealings with the telephone company aimed at procuring another extension. In response to Pak Agus' elliptical query about his trip to the office, Pak Wig offered a polite prefatory phrase (*nuwun inggih*) which in no way signaled that he was about to model speech which was putatively addressed to him ("you," *panjenengan*, line 7) by the office employee with whom he dealt. There is no point of thematic connectability between this modeling, which occurred at the very outset of the interaction, and some broader interactional project which could be imputed *post hoc* to Pak Wig; he was "simply" responding to Pak Agus' open-ended query.

Such acts resist interpretation as overtly intentful – "why that speech modeling (rather than report or narrative) now" – because of a lack of contextual information for linking conduct to context via some imputed intent. Speech modelings like that represented by text 8.4 offer only weak, artefactual readings of "intent," and do not differ in principle from those represented in texts 8.1–8.3. This became gradually evident to me through my recurring efforts to elicit "explanations" or "interpretations" when I presented recordings and transcriptions of speech modelings to Javanese speakers. I failed to develop accounts which those speakers would either accept or correct. I suggested to Endhang, for instance, who recorded the interaction reproduced in text 8.2, that Mbok Atma was trying to empathize with Pak Wignyo. She evinced little sense of either agreement or disagreement, nor was she able to describe what sense of interactional difference would have arisen had Mbok Atma framed (directly or indirectly) the words she modeled as Wignyo might have said them to his wife. (In fact, she was hard put to imagine any such alternate phrasing which would be plausible.)

She and two other speakers I queried similarly evinced little agreement or disagreement when, after playing them the recording from which text 8.4 is extracted, I suggested that Pak Wig's modeling helped him avoid any impression that he, Pak Wig, was responsible for these onerous requirements. This suggestion, and my request for alternative phrasings they might imagine, seemed simply beside the point. I was unable to hit upon or develop a useful vocabulary of "intent" (J: *karep*, I: *maksud*) or "meaning" (J: *teges*, I: *arti* or *makna*) for developing plausible retrospective understandings or interpretations of such modelings.

Whether speakers to whom I proffered broadly instrumental readings of such examples demurred, politely accepted, or politely rejected them, none evinced real agreement or engagement. Consultants commonly declined to try to explicate texts of shifts they did not observe first hand, but were hardly more forthcoming for shifts which they did observe or, for that matter, which they themselves performed. They rarely rejected interpretations which I proffered, but neither did they accept them in anything more than lukewarm fashion. Nor was I successful in proffering a range of alternate interpretations of the significances of such speech modelings – the forced choice technique of "indirect conversation analysis" used by Gumperz (1982:72) – to gain access to speakers' "unconscious knowledge."

This problem is not just expository or operational. It is symptomatic of the intrinsic doubleness which accrues to these texts as representations of verbal events in an alien context. The problems I had in developing explanatory or exegetical accounts of the texts set out above are symptomatic of the lack of salience of my generic rubric, "speech modeling," for Javanese. They suggest that such a notion be understood as part of my strategy for addressing a recurring point or mode of difference between Javanese and (minimally) English ways of speaking. Since mechanical replications of talk can only be opaque, I am obliged to make them intelligible *vis-à-vis* concerns quite different from those who produced them originally. This is the conflicted problematic of "interest in interest," which requires "recognizing the interests of someone else without conflating them with what one already knows and already is interested in oneself" (Siegel 1986:10).

Speech modeling as practice and strategy

When texts like 8.4 resist explication in terms of "motivational understanding" as verbal means to extrinsic ends, their coherence and isolability can seem to be artefactual of expository projects in which they figure. They provide reason for foregrounding the heuristics of this text-based expository project, and for avoiding overeasy recourse to underqualified notions of "strategy" or "intent," which can reveal too little when they are applied to too much.

The rubric "speech modeling" can be considered minimally as a means for foregrounding recurring, partial samenesses in talk, which count as examples of a recurring, interactional dimension of Javanese talk: part of the collectively shared "knowing how" about talk's multiple, indexical (perhaps but not necessarily referential) links to context. Such texts can be thought of as traces of acts showing a language-and-culture specific sensibility to talk's shiftable footings: the "alignment[s] we take up to ourselves and others present as expressed in the way we manage the production or reception of an utterance" (Goffman 1981:128).

In this way "speech modeling" counts as a rubric for bringing patterned, non-referential, non-grammatical dimensions of language use into convergence with the subjective, occasional, situated concretenesses of use. Instances of this practice can in turn be read as differentially susceptible to interpretation as motivated, "strategic," or strongly "intentful." Such understandings of strategy and intent are situationally grounded, like the instances of practice they serve to evaluate.

Consider in this regard, and in contrast to text 8.4, another text of speech modeling which fits much better a strongly agentive profile. The recording from which text 8.5 is taken had a strongly strategic feel for me during my first review of it, and also for the man who was present at and recorded the event for me. It is drawn from a much longer discussion among members of a family, five men and two women, about the ticklish business of land inheritance. (*Ngoko* verbiage is in italics; bású is in roman type; a few Indonesian borrowings are in boldface.)

Text 8.5

R:	*Carané maju bareng nyang klurahan,*	[1]	R:	The way to do it is to go together to the lurah's office.
	"Pak lurah, gandheng sabin meniká taksih naminé simbah, tasih naminé tiyang sepah kulá rumiyin, lha sameniká kulá **keluarga** badhé kulá pecah. Lha kulá nyuwun pandangan kalih pak lurah dos pundi. Ning, menawi kulá gadhah pemanggih. Kulá nyuwun **keterangan, biaya**nipun antawis pinten reginipun. Lha **biaya**, mangké badhé kulá dolaken sawah meniká. Kulá anggé **mbiayai** meniká."	[5] [10] [15]		"Pak Lurah, as this land is still in mother's name, still in the name of my parents from before, now I and my **family** want to break it up. So I ask for advice from you how to do it. But I have an idea. I ask for **information**, the **cost** roughly will be how much. So for **payment** later I'll sell off some land. I'll use that **to pay** for it."

They along with their spouses had gathered for their regular meeting at their mother's house as members of a kind of rotating credit association (*arisan*). At the previous meeting the mother had made it known that she wished to pass on her rights to farmland to her children before she died, in part to be sure that the process engendered no bad feelings. But she had left up to them decisions about how to divide the land and deal with daunting bureaucratic hurdles involved in transferring title from one to seven owners.

The lead discussant in all of this conversation had been her fourth-eldest child, a man of about forty whom I call Pak Ratna here. Some fifteen years younger than his eldest sibling, Pak Ratna was nonetheless qualified by his education – highest of the group, as a graduate of high school – and by his occupation as the only white-collar worker in the family. The four other men were all farmers, the youngest of whom also worked part-time as a security guard in a large market in Solo. Pak Ratna exchanged *ngoko* with all of his siblings and with his mother. Having agreed to participate in a lottery for sections of the land to be bequeathed to them, the group has shifted discussion to the mechanics of transferring title.

It is not difficult to impute intentfulness to Pak Ratna's way of presenting his approach to the problem of financing: modeling an act of *básá* address to the village head, rather than addressing its substance "directly" to his siblings in *ngoko*. My consultant – an in-law with an interest but no influence in the process – noted spontaneously to me that Pak Ratna saw himself as the head of the group, and agreed that my suggestions of two intentions (*karep*) which might inform this act of speech modeling were plausible.

On one hand, because he modeled rather than reported (or predicted) some person's future action, Pak Ratna left referentially indefinite the identity of the spokesperson (animator) who would represent the group at the village head's office. There was mention first of a joint visit (*maju bareng*), but no term referential of the person who might actually speak for them. But since, as my consultant noted, Pak Ratna's *básá* is strongest, he was qualified interactionally by skills he modeled here to act as the group's delegate in dealing with the authorities. So he was able indirectly to presuppose himself as future animator of words being modeled here, a performative act of asking – *Lha kulá nyuwun pandangan kalih pak lurah dos pundi*, "So I ask for advice from you how to do it" – at lines 8–9, and simultaneously exemplifying his fitness to reanimate them later as the group's representative in address of the *lurah*.

On the other hand, Pak Ratna's strategy of selling a part of the land to pay for changes in title to the rest was presented to the siblings as modeled speech to the authorities, as an already ratified decision to which the village head can agree. Pak Ratna thus modeled as a *fait accompli* the decision he wishes (not in vain, as it turned out) his collective addressee would reach, with respect to substance and spokesmanship alike.

Where such relatively strong lines of instrumental inference are available, act-utterances invite construal (via their traces) as specifically strategic relative to extrinsic aspects of their originary circumstances. Speech modelings like Pak Ratna's in this respect take on the appearance of being extrinsically motivated "deployments" of linguistic resources, or as micro-rhetorical techniques within an interactional episode. They are then retrospectively reconstituted as pro-jected means to social ends which are evident *post hoc*.

So texts like 8.5 suggest that some speech modelings can be interpreted as relatively strategic by virtue of their "implicational 'reach' backward and forward within the event" (Irvine 1996:141). Such events allow (or require) construal as "strongly" agentive, because they offer interpretive links to circumstances beyond the immediately preceding and succeeding dynamics in which they are existentially and so "self-evidently" situated. To the extent that it can be read as the extension of some larger, extrinsically identifiable project, a modeling like Pak Ratna's contrasts with that of the conversation by Pak Mus in text 8.1, or Pak Wid's words to his wife by Mbok Agus in text 8.2, or Mas Nur's interactionally keyed act of *mbasakaké* in text 8.3. Insofar as modelings like Pak Ratna's appear integral to the larger social projects which they interactionally mediate, they have the appearance of strategically framed, socially consequential outcomes of interaction in which they figured.

Such a relatively agentive reading imputes to speakers a "real-time," future-perfective strategizing process, but needs at the same time to be seen as doubly relative or artefactual. On one hand, it contrasts with non-agentive readings of more motivationally "opaque" texts like those presented earlier, which resist framings in terms of social projects and purposes. On the other hand, it subsists on interpretive recourse to collateral knowledge about the broader situation in which the modeling occurred, knowledge which can be highly partial and distinct from that of speech participants.

Focalizing operations and the comparative perspectives they enable make necessary some such contrast between strongly and weakly strategic/intentful acts, and presuppose recognition of the interpretive indeterminacy which can exist between them. To consider a speech modeling, via its text, as weakly or artefactually strategic is to have expository recourse to a sense of difference in conversational attunement or sensibility – the potential of mouths to be open to "voices" other than their owners' – which can be broadly called "cultural."

Considered as enabling means in this interpretive project, notions of "strategy," "intent," and so on can be set in productive, operational opposition to a broader rubric of speech modelings as practice: tacit, shared attunements to indexical relations of talk and context. The contrast thus established may open up a space for recognizing what Paul

Ricoeur calls "the specific plurivocity [of] . . . the meaning of human action . . . [as] a limited field of possible constructions" (1982:213). It does this by allowing for principled comparisons between texts of talk which can be made evidence of patterned similarities in interactional dynamics, but which can also be more and less plausibly read as vehicles of originary, recoverable strategic intent.

Speech modeling, authorship, and narrative

The possibility of strongly strategic readings of speech modeling arises from the broad, underlying doubleness created between modeled and modeling voices, enacted and enacting speech contexts, and participant relations between speech partners, past and present. This counterpoint makes it possible for modeled speech, unlike reported speech, to disclose ("here-and-now") what is in no overt way claimed about an originary "there-and-then." In this respect, readings of modeling as intentful or strategic are invited by and inferrable from different kinds of "leakage" between modeling and modeled contexts.

A final illustration of these complexities is text 8.6, which shows speech modeling in the sort of broadly autobiographical narrative which Siegel and Keeler both mention. Text 8.6 is drawn from a much longer conversation which Mbak Endhang recorded during a visit to the house of another of her neighbors. The speaker here is a poor widow and distant relative whom Endhang addresses (and I henceforth refer to) as Lik Praya. (*Lik*, short form of the kin term *mboklik*, lit. "parent's younger sister," is touched on in chapter 6.) Endhang and Lik Praya had been ruminating about the behavior of another neighbor who they (and, it seems, most others in the neighborhood) agree has been generally unpleasant and sometimes outrageous in his unthinking speech and careless conduct. This man had estranged himself from Lik Praya through encounters like the one she relates to Endhang.

Lik Praya, herself childless, had long fondly looked after some of the needs of this neighbor's children. But he had recently instructed them to avoid her and her house for reasons she still did not understand. Just before the part of the conversation transcribed below, Lik Praya had spoken of how, earlier in the month, she had dropped everything at his request to travel forty minutes by bus to a hospital in Solo to help look after his youngest, a girl seriously ill with fever. But he showed little appreciation for her help, taking her presence so much for granted as to neglect to ask her whether she was hungry or thirsty during the better part of a day and a night she was there.

Praya had held forth on this person's general irresponsibility before narrating how she got to the hospital and then, in the talk presented in text 8.6, how she had nothing to eat or drink. She recounts meeting another villager there, a young woman named Jumi, whom she invited to accompany her outside the hospital grounds to find something to eat. This encounter is modeled as conversation with Jumi in the hospital, then with an anonymous foodstall worker, and finally back in the hospital with Endhang's father, who happened to be at the hospital as well. Praya modeled distinct dialogs with minimal use of "external" framing devices, and so displayed without claiming verisimilitude for her words. As such, it seems a straightforward alternative to a narrative voice. But it also had implicational reach which makes it construable as relatively strategic *vis-à-vis* the larger topic of prior conversation, because it discloses (without asserting) Lik Praya's moral sensibility.

Text 8.6

P1: He nggèmbol dhit wolung éwu kok.
Ha ápá yá nèk ungguhná ki yá kolu nèk wong barang nunggu bocah kaya ngono kuwi, kolu?
Aku metu mak blesèd ngajak Jumi.

a. [P] **Mi** gèk kéné ki ngulu idu wé saking lé salib garing **ndhuk**, **Mi**.
b. [J] Ènten nápá **mbokdhé**?
c. [P] Yá aku terná nyang njábá golèkná wédang ning panas karo anu, pangan ning panas.
d. [J] Nggih nggá **mbokdhé** tekan ndalan.
E: Kowé pethuk Jumi tá?
P2: Lha Jumi lak nunggu adhiné neng káná tá, lé manak kaé,
a. [J] Nggih **mbokdhé** nggá. Lha njutan
b. [P] Nggon kono ki njutan
c. [P] **Mas**, mangdoli bakso anu nyatus sèket men nggih **mas** loro.
d. [J] Kulá mboten mawon lho **mbokgedhé**, kulá mboten.
e. [P] Ngajak wong ki tanggung jawab. Ning bayar aku ngko. Aku yá ngono tá, njutan ndang anu trus mangan wong loro, karaké

[1] P1: I had eight thousand rupiah. Now, for instance, do you lose your appetite when you're looking after a kid like that, lose your appetite?
[5] I went out, and invited Jumi.

a. **Mi**, I'm swallowing my spit from being so dry, **ndhuk**, **Mi**.
[10] b. What do you want to do, **mbokdhé**?
c. Yeah, come with me outside, look for something hot to drink along with, uh, some food
[15] which is hot.
d. Yes, let's go, **mbokdhé**, out to the road.
E: You met Jumi?
P2: Well Jumi was looking after her younger sister, there, giving birth,
[20]
a. Yes, **mbokdhé**, let's go So then,
b. Let's go there then
[25] c. **Mas**, sell us bakso, **150** rupiah worth, **mas**, two servings.
d. Not for me, **mbokgedhé**, not me.
[30] e. Invite someone and you're responsible. I'm the one who'll pay. I [said] like that, then, uh, then we both ate, the *karak* was

	sèket, baksoné telung atus, dadiné	[35]		fifty, the *bakso* was three hundred, so I
	ntèk telung atus sèket tá.			was out three fifty, right?
f.	[P] Wah wis ra sah ngelak ki		f.	OK, so now [we're] not hungry
	Mi, ayo **Mi**, ayo bali é.			**Mi**, let's go **Mi**, let's go back.
g.	[J] Nggá **mbokdhé**.		g.	OK, **mbokdhé**.
	Lha kowé ro pakdhé Sindu rak	[40]		Now you and pakdhé Sindu asked me,
	tékon tá, kowé rak nèng tretepan tá.			right, you were under the eaves.
h.	[S] Ka ngendi **Ya**?		h.	Where from, **Ya**?
i.	[P] Kas mlenthoké weteng		i.	From filling my belly,
	pakdhé, géné ntèk telungatus			**pakdhé**. [I'm] out three hundred
	sèket wong loro é mlenthu.	[45]		fifty for two people, we're full.
	rak ngono tá aku, terus			I [said] like that, right,
	pakdhé Sindu.			so then pakdhé Sindu
j.	[S] Ah aku ki gur ndé dhit		j.	Ah, I've only got
	limang atus ki,			five hundred
	rak ngono tá.	[50]		he said like that.
E:	Mlenthokké weteng		E:	Fill your belly.
P3:			P3:	
a.	[S] Aku gur ndé dhit limang atus		a.	I've only got five hundred,
	ki ngko nèk ra jarangé			later if I don't have some hot water,
	kentèkan piyé, telung atos niku			how about it, I use three hundred
	mangnggé jajan ning telung atus,	[55]		for a snack, three hundred,
	jágáné jarang mengké			a glass of something hot is
	rong atus. Yá is,			two hundred. Oh well,
	ngko-ngko é.			I'll worry about it later.
	Pakdhé Sindu rak ngono tá. Terus			That's what Pak Sindu [said]. So
	aku ki lèhku mikir yá	[60]		me, I'm thinking
b.	"lèk wengiá, lèk wengiá,		b.	"let it be night, let it be night,
	lèk wengiá"			let it be night"
	gur ngono aé, **ndhuk**. Mbásá wis			just like that, **ndhuk**. When it got
	wengi			to be night
c.	"lèk padhangá lèk padhangá"	[65]	c.	"let it get bright, let it get bright"
	krungu jago kluruk.			'til I heard the cock crow.

In ten of Praya's modelings appear vocative and parenthetical uses of proper names (Mi, Yá) or kin terms (*mas, mbokdhé, mbokgedhé, pakdhé*) which help identify speakers and addressees in the modeled conversation. But in one instance, at line 25, the opening vocative *Mas* identified not just a new interlocutor (the foodstall keeper) but also signaled that at the time of this utterance, Jumi and Praya had left the hospital grounds and found a place to eat. Praya also routinely relied on intonational contours and syntactic markers of question–answer routines.

A single narrative sequencing element (*njutan*, roughly "then") appeared just three times (between reported speeches 2a and 2b, 2b and 2c, 2e and 2f) in Lik Praya's speech, marking passage of time between the reported speech events. Turn 2e was also followed by one of just two narrated contextualizations for reported speech (line 33); the other was at line 40, where Lik Praya reminded Endhang that she and her father were at the hospital when Lik Praya returned from her foray with Jumi.

Explicit narrative framers were similarly sparse: one occurred as part of the narration following turn P2e; two served to set off Lik Praya's utterance in P2i from Sindu's in P2j, and the last likewise identified Sindu as utterer of P3a.

As a recounting of events, experiences, and talk, Lik Praya's portrayal may seem incomplete. She narrated meeting Jumi but not their parting; the foodstall was not even mentioned, let alone described as to type or location; the conversation between Jumi and Lik Praya, as modeled, was quite bare, and invites the inference that Lik Praya had heavily edited her rendition. But in two respects she has linked the modeled and modeling contexts in ways which can be construed as parts of an interactionally strategic performance, relative to Endhang.

One has to do with the styles of these modeling/modeled utterances: to Jumi, her familiar junior, Lik Praya apparently used plain *ngoko* and straightforward imperatives. But she showed (without claiming) that Jumi addresses her with polite low *básá*, along with the respectful kin term *mbokgedhé* (or its shorter alternant *mbokdhé*). Within Praya's and Endhang's interaction, this modeling can (but need not) be construed as evidence of Praya's intent to disclose that this other status relation exists. This is a specific instance, then, of the multiple construability of usage which Keeler alludes to as displaying a speaker's felt "need to dissimulate an interpretive, mediating presence" (1987:257). But it correlatively presupposes an interpretive presence on the part of an addressee.

At the same time, there is thematic resonance between the conversation which Praya models and the antecedent conversation between her and Endhang, which gave rise to it. This is the theme of responsibility for others. Although Lik Praya peripheralizes a great deal of what presumably passed between her and Jumi, her talk to Jumi modeled at P2e – which also happens to be the most explicitly identified with respect to sequence, identity of speaker, and context – served to display the same point. Praya modeled her ordering of two bowls of *bakso* (a kind of soup) and Jumi's demurral, implicitly because she didn't want to pay for it. At this point (line 30) Lik Praya modeled her own speech:

> "*Ngajak wong ki tanggung jawab. Ning bayar aku ngko.*"
> *Aku yá ngono tá . . .*
>
> "Invite someone and you're responsible. I'm the one who'll pay."
> I [said] like that . . .

Praya thus juxtaposed a modeling of her own past address to Jumi with prior commentary, in the interactional "present," to one neighbor about another. In this way she can be seen as tacitly affirming her criticisms of him in contrast with the example of her own demonstrable (not merely reportable) sensitivity.

If this is in fact the moral of Praya's story, it emerges from the double connectedness, thematic and existential, between her interaction with an addressee/audience (Endhang) on one hand, and a prior speech partner (Jumi) on the other. To read this fleeting self-representation as bearing on enduring, morally fraught understandings of social responsibility, I impute to Lik Praya here authorship of a "social text" presented to Endhang. To recover this reading from a text of Praya's talk is to interpret it as a relatively strongly strategic modeling, an instance of conversational practice with specific, recoverable links of intent to its conversational surround.

Voice and interactional dynamic

Together, these six short texts illustrate a challenge for non-native speakers who encounter in Javanese speech modeling a form of language difference arising not from structure or semantics, but voicing and dynamic. Non-Javanese who lack practical attunement to such rapid, transient shifts in conversational participant relations (like me at least) can easily miss them in the *hic et nunc* of interaction, and construe them better in retrospect, through their textual traces.

I have tried to present particular speech modelings in a way which intimates this sense of interpretive remove, and concern for procedures without which, as Siegel notes, transcriptions of usage can only be transferred without being assimilated, appearing less Javanese than simply alien. Similar problems arise in text-based descriptions of style shifting in chapter 9, and code switching in chapter 10.

This sketch of speech modeling, as part of an account of Javanese conversational dynamics, shows style shiftings as more or less overtly grounded in recoverable interactional strategies. It also provides a kind of negative, contrastive preface for the kinds of Indonesian usage discussed in chapter 10, where speech modeling can be seen as an unobtrusive "background phenomenon" which is missing in Indonesian usage. In this respect Indonesian usage resembles more closely English and other languages, in which reported speech is overtly regimented when it is reported.

Keeler has suggested that in modelings "[t]he speaker as narrator disappears," and so engages in a mundane sort of "self-dissimulation" (1987:258) which, he suggests, serves as grounds for valid interpretation. So too, following Keeler, these modelings can be seen as resonating not just with artful shadow plays, but the sorts of authority ventriloquated in power-laden dissimulations of self in public speakering, discussed in chapter 5. Under such a broad ethnographic purview, speech modeling can be considered interpretively as a descriptive rubric which resonates with broader dimensions of "rhetorical motive" (ibid.) and prenational political culture.

In his book's last pages, Siegel notes that recurring recourse to "paraphrases" of what one hears involves the hazard that "one leaves out the possibility of recording what one does not recognize" (1986:332). This may be part of the reason why the speech levels, more than speech modeling, are focal in his discussion of translatability and authority. Without recorded traces of speech – "actual words, pauses, hesitations, and so on" (ibid.) – instances of patterns like speech modeling, which are intrinsically independent of style shiftings, appear only fleetingly and (as it were) at the corner of one's eye. By providing texts drawn from physical recordings, I have tried here to develop some sense of the textures of Javanese verbal life in which such acts figure. The goal has been a multiply qualified sketch of speech modelings relative to the practical sense of conversational life in which they are tacitly grounded. So too, as one broad aspect of Javanese conversational practice, speech modeling shapes and is informed by the kinds of speech style shifting which I sketch in chapter 9.

9
SHIFTING STYLES AND MODELING THOUGHT

In chapter 3, *ngoko* and *básá* were sketched first as a "basic" and a stylistically "augmentary" way of speaking, and then as aesthetically unequal social competences, unevenly distributed across lines of territorial hierarchy. Both sorts of difference, structural and social, make it easy to think of "switching between these [sub]codes in Javanese" as "tantamount to code switching between different languages" (Romaine 1995:321). Under a comparative profile, then, multistylistic Javanese usage can be treated as a special subcase of bilingual usage, and therefore like that involving Javanese and Indonesian which I sketch in the next chapter.

But *ngoko* and *básá* are also integrally related through their groundings in interactional self/other relations between native speakers of a single language. So multistylistic usage needs to be considered first with an eye to the kinds of dynamic participant roles sketched in chapter 8. I sketch style shifting here, then, relative to *básá*'s pragmatic markedness, over and against *ngoko*, for a "thou-orientation." This keys to what I called in chapter 3 the generic appellative function of *básá* (recalling Bühler's terminology), making its use presupposing of a stance to a co-present addressee which is not necessarily presupposed by use of *ngoko*.

For this chapter's text-oriented sketch, this relation can be rephrased in dramatistic terms: *básá* usage "systematically undermines the possibility of conveying – at least with any ease – certain matters that are handily conveyed" (Goffman 1974:533) in *ngoko*. *Básá*'s presupposed orientation to an interactional other "undermines" its appropriateness for talk which tacitly brackets or is performed in disregard of co-present others. Pragmatically unmarked *ngoko*, on the other hand, can serve to utter such "thinkings out loud" without overt orientation to some co-present addressee.

Javanese has designations for these latter acts which presuppose such shifts to a soliloquizing stance. *Ngunandiká* and *ngudarásá* are intransitive verbs whose meanings Wolff and Poedjosoedarmo characterize as "quotations ... from one's own thoughts" (1982:69), or "quoted feelings" (ibid.:70–79). As their recourse to "thoughts" and "feelings" suggests, such acts of *ngunandiká* can exteriorize or manifest interior states which are cognitively and affectively grounded. For the sake of convenience I use the briefer designation "modeled thought" to cover the wide range of usage illustrated below, and consider later their usefully awkward phrase "quoted feeling."

Ngunandiká often but not always effects a shift from *básá* to *ngoko*, as one shifts interactional stance "away" from some respected addressee. But *ngunandiká* can equally well occur in otherwise *ngoko* talk, and can be marked by the other sorts of contextualization cues which likewise figure in the speech modelings sketched in chapter 8. With or without style shifts, acts of *ngunandiká* and speech modeling similarly transform participant roles by according to erstwhile addressees the temporary role of bystander or audience. In this chapter I present examples to show the place of "modeled thought" and "modeled speech" in Javanese conversational practice, with and without shifts between speech styles.

The texts I present of such usage raise the same issues of expository and interpretive strategies which I discussed in chapter 8. If anything, issues of intent and interpretation are more pointed when one gauges the potentially strategic character of such soliloquizing speech, and looks for interpretive links between what is "on the surface" of such conduct, as Wolff and Poedjosoedarmo put it, and what might "really [have been] aimed at" (1982:70).

Shifting styles and addressees

When dealing with two or more persons to whom one addresses different speech styles, shifts between those styles are presupposed by and can mark shifts in a speaker's orientation to one or the other. In these situations speech styles effectively impose an obligatory, pragmatic distinction between those who are co-present as talk's addressee and its ratified, bystanding observer(s). Examples of such presupposed style shifts were provided in some of the examples of speech modelings in chapter 8. In text 8.3, for instance, such a shift was focal for the uncle to ventriloquate his niece's properly polite utterance to her respected elder: he shifted from *ngoko* in address of her to the *básá* she should speak to her elder, and then back to *ngoko*. Similarly, text 8.5 showed a speaker "naturally" shifting from *ngoko* address of his siblings to a *básá* modeling of properly polite speech to a village functionary.

When modeling conversation between persons who asymmetrically exchange *ngoko* and *básá*, style shifts can likewise indirectly signal shifts in identity of speaker and addressee for the speech modeled. An example is Lik Praya's modeling of her conversation with Jumi in text 8.6. There, style shifts counted as artefacts of her relation to Jumi, and so helped (like the conversational sequencers discussed earlier) to mark points of transition between the speaking roles being modeled: Jumi as *básá* speaker, and Praya as *ngoko* speaker.

Because such shifts in style are of a piece with broader shifts in participant roles, they are grounded in the same sense of conversational practice which informs speech modeling in general. A convenient way to illustrate interactional convergence between shifts in style and shifts in footing, through speech modeling and "thought modeling," is usage like that in text 9.1. In this minor bit of interaction occurred style shifts which marked and mediated multiple shifts in participant roles: some shifted with the speaker's orientation to two co-present persons, as addressee and bystander; others were bound up with her addresseeless performances of feelings and thoughts.

The speaker is Mbok Prapti (P), a villager in her mid-forties who works as a midwife (J, I: *dhukun bayi*). She has long known both Pak Sandhi (S) and his daughter Eni (E), who dropped in for a visit on their way back from the major regional market north of Surakarta. Prapti familiarly addresses Eni, some twenty years her junior, in *ngoko* and with the intimate kin term *ndhuk*; to Pak Sandhi, some twenty years her senior and an object of respect, Prapti uses low but entirely suitable *básá* with the respectful kin term *mas*. Because Prapti addresses different speech styles to her interlocutors, she shifts between *ngoko* and *básá* as her attention shifts between them. She is speaking of problems with her unfaithful husband, who is doing little to disguise his visits to the house of a neighbor.

Text 9.1

[to Sandhi]
Nèk kulá, mboten semerep
ngoten men. Dados nggih mpun
sok kulá niku sok nèk ajeng . . .
nèk lé lénang mboten ènten niku
rak ajeng márá niku.
Nèk tangi, rindhik-rindhik niká,
mengké ngancing lawang nggih
rindhik-rindhik.
    [to Eni]
*Mapan turu rindhik ngèn ra ngerti
aku* **ndhuk**.
  [P] Kowé kimu ká ngendi R?
  [R] Ká ngendi?
  [P] Lha yá ká ngendi kowé ki
      mau?
  [R] Ra ká ngendi-ndi, genah ká

[1] Me, I don't know about it,
just leave it like that. So sometimes
I'm sometimes if I'm going . . .
if my husband's not there, he's
[5] going to go there, right?
When he gets up, quietly,
later latches the door,
quietly.

Lies down quietly, so that I don't
[10] *know,* **ndhuk**.
Where were you just now R?
Where?
Yeah, where were you just
now?
[15] Nowhere, just in

kebon!
[P]　Oh ká kebon!
aku yá ngéné iki.
[to Sandhi]
Ning menggahnèn kulá niku, **mas**
ájá, ájá jenengé kulá niku, ning
kulá éman niku si bocah lénang
siji lan sijiné. Mbok kulá niku
diná-diná nangkep uwong njoh
mas. Ning kulá éman niku mung
siji lan sijiné. *Ngko aku jenengé*
étuk jásá karo wong okèh ngko
terus aku èntuk èlèk karo
cahé lénang sijiné.
Lha nggih tá niku?

　　　　　　the yard.
　　　　　　Oh, the yard.
　　　　　　I [said] *like that.*

　　　　　　But as for me, **mas**
[20]　don't, don't, it's like for me,
　　　　　　I feel sorry for the boy and
　　　　　　his sister. I could,
　　　　　　any day, catch him, I could,
　　　　　　mas. I only feel sorry for
[25]　the boy and his sister. *Later I'll be*
　　　　　　well regarded by most people,
　　　　　　[but] *I'll do badly by the*
　　　　　　boy and his sister.
　　　　　　Now isn't that right?

Most of the narrative in the conversation was in *básá* (transcribed in roman typeface) addressed to Pak Sandhi, whom Prapti explicitly identified as her addressee with parenthetical use of the vocative *mas* at lines 19 and 24. But she also turned to Eni (whom she mentioned as *ndhuk* at line 10) with *ngoko* words (in italic typeface) at lines 9–10 and again at 18 before reverting to address of Sandhi in *básá*.

The *ngoko* talk in lines 11–17 was not addressed to Eni; rather, it modeled her prior conversation with her husband for Eni and Sandhi alike. Prapti performatively replayed this talk with her husband, marked as R, with minimal recourse to external framing devices. Conversational turns were demarcated as question/answer pairs solely through parentheticals and intonation; only after modeling her own, final retort to her husband (line 17) did Prapti use a punctuating, framing phrase – "I [said] like that" (at line 18) – which, being *ngoko*, marked her orientation to Eni as primary addressee.

Prapti then turned (line 19) back to Pak Sandhi to explain her dilemma. But later she shifted twice more between *básá* and *ngoko* in the course of explaining her dilemma: calling her husband to public account would jeopardize the security and happiness of her children (literally, "the one and the other," *siji lan sijiné*). Prapti presented her problem narratively in *básá*, and then performatively in *ngoko* with two instances of modeled thought, or *ngunandiká*.

The first, fleeting style shift (line 20) replayed her feelings of apprehension in dealing with this situation. She said and repeated the *ngoko* word *ájá* – which has distinct high and low *básá* alternants *sampun* and *ampun* (J. Errington 1988:213–16) – and which in this context could be clumsily called a negative optative and glossed as "may it not happen that . . ." But then she fell silent for a fraction of a second and, shifting back to *básá*, explained to Sandhi the reasons for the apprehensiveness she had just exteriorized.

The second shift occurs at line 25 with the beginning of the longer utterance "Later I'll be well regarded by most people . . ." Eni told me that she recalled no physical indication of a shift in attention to her, as addressee, when Prapti shifted to *ngoko* here. Rather, Prapti seemed to Eni to model (*niru*) or replay a line of thought for Sandhi, as is evident from the final *básá* phrase – *Lha nggih tá niku?*, "Now isn't that right?" – which presupposed Sandhi as addressee. She thus invited Sandhi (primarily) and Eni (in passing) to confirm the validity of her already completed line of thought. This modeling can be read as rehearsing what Irvine calls (1996:152) a shadow conversation which Prapti had already held with herself, and was now replaying for Sandhi's approval; she rehearsed a conclusion reached and decision made for her respected elder's re-view and, she hoped, approval.

Modeling thought

The style shifts at lines 9 and 19 of this text mediate interactionally situated shifts in orientation to addressees, and as such are distinct from the performed "thinkings out loud" or "quoted feelings" (recalling Wolff and Poedjosoedarmo's phrases) of *ngunandiká* which occur at lines 20 and 25–28. These latter style shifts subserve modelings of "unaddressed" language, which happen to occur in the course of otherwise *básá* rather than *ngoko* talk. In this respect Prapti's replaying of her thoughts and concerns is worth comparing with the last bit of text 8.6, when Lik Praya "replayed" her state of discomfort and tedium during the hospital visit which she had just narrated:

Text 8.6 excerpt

Terus aku ki lèhku mikir yá	[1]	So me, I'm thinking,
"lèk wengiá, lèk wengiá,		"let it be night, let it be night,
lèk wengiá"		let it be night"
gur ngono aé, **ndhuk**. Mbásá wis wengi		just like that, **ndhuk**. When it got to be night
"lèk padhangá lèk padhangá."	[5]	"let it get bright, let it get bright"

These thought modelings, overtly framed as such with the intransitive, active verb *mikir* "think," occurred in Praya's *ngoko* address of Endhang, and with no shift in styles. It shows that modelings of subjective states and internal thoughts are not all driven by or exude the sense of urgency which Prapti evinced in the talk presented as text 9.1. They can serve, for instance, to model states of subjective awareness of occasion-relevant knowledge or norms, as text 9.2 illustrates.

Text 9.2

E:	Lha sakniki niku kalih bángsá wong ngoten-ngoten niku, nèk kulá sakniki nápá-nápá angur meneng kok **lik**.	[1]	E:	Nowadays with that kind of person like that, as for me now whatever [happens] I shut up, **lik**.	
	Ora kenèng gluwah-gluwèh.	[5]		[One] can't shoot one's mouth off.	
S:	Wah wong kuwi alam adat thik piyé.		S:	What's he doing acting like that.	
E:	Nggih ngerti, kulá niku ngerti. Nápá-nápá mung meneng.		E:	[I] know, I know. whatever, I just stay quiet.	
S:	Wong kuwi yá salah lé muni.	[10]	S:	He spoke wrongly.	
T:	Lé muni gur anggeré metu.		T:	He talks just to say something.	
E:	Barang káyá ngono kok disindhir niku lho, wong muni niku nggih kená mawon ning lak kudu mpan papan.	[15]	E:	Something like that, he's making fun of it, if you want to say something that's fine, but it has to be the right place and time.	
	Pokoké kulá niku roh *yá is meneng.*			The main thing, if I see something *yeah, that's it, stay quiet.*	

This is drawn from talk between a young man named Edy (E) and his older neighbors about dealings with the police on Java's crowded roads. Edy had been telling his respected interlocutors, in low *básá*, about a jitney bus driver he saw bring trouble on himself with careless talk within earshot of a policeman. Edy interspersed two brief *ngoko* modelings of his thoughts and reactions. The first (at line 5) was marked by the opening *ngoko* word *ora* (vs. polite *mboten*, "no, not"). The other (at line 17) consists of the performed utterance *yá is meneng*, which could be translated as "yeah, stay quiet." It replayed a thought which Edy had at the time. Edy's first modeled reaction resonated with his interlocutors's feelings. They agreed that inadvisable words got the driver what he deserved. But the second thought modeling, of a general moral to the particular story, is not specific to the incident as such.

Such modelings are unremarkable facts of Javanese conversational life, in which speakers can disclose what they do not claim. Like speech modelings, they can be internally mute as to their fit with the interactional dynamics in which they are situated. When they involve shifts from *básá* to *ngoko*, they are stylistic correlates of this broader shift in engagement: on one hand with "experience-near" modelings, and on the other their relatively formal, stylistically mediated orientations to addressed interactional others.

Consider in this regard text 9.3, recorded by Pak Hari (H), a villager of about forty during a chat with an elderly friend to whom he habitually uses low *básá*. When the conversation turned to difficulties between Hari and a neighbor, he shifted to *ngoko* (in italics, at line 3) to model his feelings and thoughts about the conflict which is his topic.

Text 9.3

Ha pripun kulá niku,	[1]	Well, how about it, as for me,
pamané sing terus terang lho niku,		for instance, to be honest, right,
mbok ènèngá wongé ki aku yá		if that guy's around, I'm
wani waé.		willing.
Kados bayané mriki niku, sing	[5]	Like the *bayan* here, what's
genah, anggeré dilapuri niku		for sure, if he's reported to
mlengos. Sebabé		he ignores it. The reason,
mbuh		*dunno*,
kulá mboten ngerti.		I don't know.

At line 8, to profess ignorance as to why the *lurah*'s local representative will not involve himself in the dispute, Hari uttered the *ngoko* interjection (*mbuh*) as an index of his subjective, immediate psychological state of ignorance (see J. Errington 1988:217). (Compare colloquial English "duh," or a shrugging of the shoulders.) As a maximally subjective expression of ignorance, it fits the state it exhibits. Hari then described the state he had just enacted, shifting back to *básá* to make the descriptive statement *kulá mboten ngerti*, glossable literally as "I not know."

Speech modelings can occur in multiple embeddings, which themselves deserve considerable space and attention. But text 9.4 will suffice as a fairly easily explicated example of the multiply situated or layered perspectives which are routinely presupposed by modelings. Before making this utterance the speaker, Pak Waya (W), had been listening sympathetically to a hard-luck story from another man in a meeting of a mysticism (*kebatinan*) group called Sumarah, described in more detail below. When his interlocutor queried Waya about his own feelings of outrage at the mistreatment he has just narrated, Waya opened his response in appropriately polite *básá*, but interjected a brief remark in *ngoko*.

Text 9.4

Lha mung ngaten,	Well, just like that,
lha nyat yá ora karu-karuan,	*"This is really outrageous"*
menawi kulá mboten.	as for me, no.

This *ngoko* utterance (in italics) neither disclosed Waya's current state of mind, nor rehearsed an experience from his own past. Rather, it projectively or empathetically modeled a subjective state he gathered had been experienced by his interlocutor, inferred from the manner and content of the narrative just addressed to him. Waya transposed his own speakership, as it were, to his addressee's subjective position. He modeled an affect-laden state/utterance for and "in place of" his addressee, and with minimal contextualization. A prefatory *básá* framing phrase identified the just-narrated situation as topic, against which he figured the ensuing *ngoko* modeling. Though addresseeless in one respect, it counted as a kind of empathetic preface to the advice Waya goes on to proffer to his addressee, presented as text 10.6 in the next chapter.

Situated in this interactional dynamic, Waya engaged in *ngunandiká* in a manner recalling Mbok Atma's modeling (in text 8.2) of words her own interlocutor, Wignyo, might have addressed to his wife. Both acts likewise evince sensitivity to and empathy for interlocutors' difficulties. But where Atma modeled an event which might have happened, and would have been at least potentially observable, Waya modeled a state of mind or subjective stance which he can only infer from his speech partner's narration.

Usage like that in text 9.4 suggests one part of the range of rhetorical uses which shifting interactional footings can serve: how they emerge through and are subserved by *ngoko* and *básá*'s generic meanings. In this way *ngunandiká*, as a recurring conversational pattern, can be seen as grounded in the same shiftable conditions of speakership and addresseehood which ground speech modeling as well.

Interactional and interpretive strategies

This chapter's text-centered strategy, focalizing transcripts as instances of a recurring conversational practice, involves the ambiguities of expository and interactional strategy which I broached in chapter 8. Here again texts are made to illustrate recurring, partial samenesses in social process, that is, moments when shifting speech styles mediate interactional self/other relations between speakers/modelers and addressees/audiences. These texts have been similarly excised with operational recourse to broad, enabling assumptions about their unity and coherence as traces of intentful conduct, and about their origins in pro-jective, means–ends, agentive stances to interactional context.

This general assumption likewise enables Wolff and Poedjosoedarmo's brief characterization of an example of *ngunandiká*. Under the rubric "non-directed speech" they present the text given below as 9.5, during which "the speaker offers her guest something to drink in *madya* [i.e., low *básá*] and then remarks as if to herself in *ngoko* (italicized here) that she does not have anything to offer to eat (but in fact she is apologizing)" (1982:71).[1]

Text 9.5

Nggá, dèn, mangké unjukan táyá bening mingang. [laughter]	Here, drink your glass of water, honey
Ha ra áná nyamikané kok ya?	(*Why, there's nothing to go with it!*)

In this way the act represented by text 9.5 is framed narratively relative to its originary context, and interpretively with recourse to an imputed disjunction between act and intention.[2] By attributing what Schutz calls an "in order to" motive to the speaker whose act they recorded, they license its excision, via their text, from that originary context and in the unmarked, timeless present. Their co-text narratively encapsulates this interactional setting, and interpretively attributes to it – and, by implication, all *ngunandiká* – a categorically purposeful aspect as the mobilization and manipulation of verbal resources in the service of extrinsic, recoverable social projects.

But "quoted feeling," Wolff and Poedjosoedarmo's own gloss for *ngunandiká*, itself provides reason for querying enabling assumptions about the categorically strategic or agentive character of such usage. "Quotation," as indicated in chapter 8, is a notion which tacitly but generally presupposes asymmetric relations between distinct, quoted and quoting acts and contexts of talk. "Feeling," on the other hand, generally alludes to transient, affective, im-mediate experience which need take neither verbal nor other ex-pressive form.

To the extent that "quotation" presupposes the objectification of speech, it lacks fit with acts of *ngunandiká* which have at least the guise of "spontaneous," im-mediate indexes of subjective feelings and states. So too it elides any sense of difference between speakership as an agentive, interested position, and as interactionally situated self-presentation. Consider again in this regard the acts of *ngunandiká* uttered by Mbok Prapti in text 9.1. The second of her modelings, I suggested, "replayed" her own past thoughts, and so can fairly be thought of as "quoting" a prior state of mind. But her prior fleeting utterance, twice, of *ájá*, "may it not happen that," at line 20 seems significantly different. It is at least as easily read as an affect-laden, im-mediate expression of her subjective state in the *hic et nunc* of interaction, as she once again pondered her oppressive double bind. Then this fleeting bit of talk does not seem just to "quote" strategically a distinct subjective state she experienced in the past; rather, it arose from and indexed her present, im-mediate, subjective state.

The English word "blurt" might fit such bits of talk better if it did not connote an unsanctioned failure of self-control. But it usefully captures such talk's potential expressive feel, and its construability less as means to an interactional end than an exuded subjective state. Read in this way, diagnostically and "in terms of the actor's past experiences" (Schutz 1967a:91), such utterances can be traced in quasi-causal manner to antecedent conditions, rather than projective strategic stances. Talk in textual guise thus takes on a double readability, relative to antecedent states as well as other-oriented projects. So too style shiftings' variably strategic character, like those of speech modelings described in chapter 8, can be considered to have different degrees of "implicational reach" into their originary surrounds.

Consider in this regard text 9.6, which I recorded while chatting with another elderly member of the Solonese elite, Pak Sus. It was apparent early in our relationship, which had by the time of this conversation extended over four moderately lengthy encounters, that Pak Sus felt his seniority and status offset my educated foreignness in the interactional scheme of things. He felt constrained to address me most of the time in refined *básá*, but deployed the rather old-fashioned, somewhat condescending, intimate second-person pronoun *sampéyan* (see chapter 3). By a technique I have described elsewhere (1988:162) he early on extracted my use to him of the highly deferential first-person pronoun *dalem*.

His sense of superior status carried over to his tendency, as early as our second meeting, to speak a great deal in *ngoko*, and to reserve *básá* for moments when I and my presence became topically salient. As his discussion shifted away from matters related directly to me, so too his conversational style became increasingly familiar, evincing (in my opinion) a condescension which became less and less mitigated as our acquaintance grew. This was not an uncommon mode of usage, in my experience, with older Surakartan *priyayi*. It seems to be a kind of interactional license which self-assured elders can take with younger, somewhat intimate persons. Ordinarily it has little further import, but in this case I believe it served a larger project which Pak Sus brought to our interaction. During this interchange, as in our previous meetings, Pak Sus repeatedly invited and tried to induce me to begin studying shadow puppetry (*wayang*) under his tutelage. Text 9.6 begins with my first move in this conversation to sidestep his recruiting efforts.

When addressing questions to me (lines 3 and 29), and figuring me topically in his remarks (as at lines 24–25) he shifted to *básá* (in roman type). Elsewhere in this passage, and much of his other talk, *ngoko* (in italics) predominated. (A few Indonesian borrowings of no further interest here are in boldface.)

It is relevant to such occasions that, were any such teacher/student relation to be established, Pak Sus would address me wholly in *ngoko*, while continuing to receive high *básá* in return. So too it is not coincidental that he transiently adopted this guise while nonetheless avoiding "direct" address of me with the *ngoko* second-person pronoun *kowé* (as at line 14) rather than *sampéyan* (lines 3 and 25). By verging on but not committing himself to categorically *ngoko* address to me, Pak Sus made his style of address subserve the same long-term interests which are apparent in its content. To shift to a fairly measured, formal variety of *ngoko* and "model" himself as a teacher, he did not just accord me the

Text 9.6

J:	Menawi sinau pedhalangan mboten kiyat.	[1]	J: As for studying puppetry, [I'm] not up to it.
S:	Sampéyan?		S: You?
J:	Rumaos dalem dereng kiyat.		J: I don't feel up to it.
S:	Anu, **garis besar**ipun mawon. Garis besaripun. Jeneng dhalang meniká, bau cerita. Cerita thok. *Sinajaná ora ngerti swaraning gamelan tabuhan, ora ngerti gendhingé. Ning bau caritané* meniká, *yá kuwi dhalang. Kowé isá nyaritakké lelakon, isiné, caritané wayang sing nganggo wulangan, minangka dadi* **pendikikan**. *Ngerti tabuhané ning ora bisá caritané sing,* **mengenai pendidikan**, *nul. Wong dolanan, wongdolanan wayang, ditabuh, ning ora teges*. Dus bakunipun, upaminipun sampéyan *isá caritá kabèh, énak dirungokké kená dianggo tuladan, wis dadi dhalang.* Sampun mudheng, dèrèng?	[5] [10] [15] [20] [25]	S: Umm – just the **broad lines**. The **broad lines**. The word "dhalang" means "carry the story." Just the story. Even if one doesn't know about the accompaniment, doesn't know the songs. But to carry the story, now, that's a dhalang. You can tell the story, its contents, a shadow play story for teaching, so that it can be **educational**. Know the music but can't do the story which is, **about education**, it's nothing. A person plays, a person plays with puppets, with music, but it's meaningless. So basically, for instance you can do the story, it's easy to listen to, can be used as a lesson, [one is] a puppeteer. Understand yet, or not?

role of audience. He was able to mobilize ambiguities (as he saw it) in our participant roles, and to map onto this interactional process another long-term relation, nudging things in the direction of a different future biography for our social relation.

Because acts of modeling can disclose what their utterers do not claim for them, I can only impute this strategy to Pak Sus and his style shift, on the basis of collateral information and contextual inference. Were I somehow in a position to query Pak Sus about this usage, he could plausibly and perhaps genuinely disaffirm my reading. But in textual form – dislocated from his state of mind when he spoke these words, and informed by my recollections of the history of our relationship – his words are plausibly inscribed with such an agentive, "in order to" stance, and with broadly social strategic intent.

This example, like Wolff and Poedjosoedarmo's in text 9.5, offers itself for strategic reading because of its implicational reach into the biography of a social relation. As such, both texts contrast significantly with style shiftings like that in text 9.7. This transient bit of verbal/interactional turbulence, which took up some twenty-five seconds in an interactional event lasting almost two hours, is a bit of interactional there-and-then which resists easy intentionalist appropriation in an expository here-and-now. In the following transcript, *ngoko* segments are italicized, Indonesian is in boldface, and all others are in normatively presupposed high *básá*.

Text 9.7

T:	Meniká kantun wonten panjenengan nggih tá?	[1]
W:	Nggih.	
T:	*Piyé yá iki mengko?*	
W:	**Seni** meniká kados ngaten [sound of a motorcycle starting] *Iki lho* **sudah selesai**. *Tujuné mung metu, terus anyel.* Upami mboten medal rumiyin – kasèp. Sampun késah. Lha meniká rak késah tá?	[5] [10]
J:	Selak menápá tá?	
W:	Mboten mangertos. Lha kados ngaten, *Mulané ora takarani arep lungá tá.* Lha meniká kulá mboten mangertos.	[15]

T:	But you've been left behind right?
W:	Yes.
T:	*So how about it?*
W:	**This art** is like that. *Well here,* [he's] **already finished**. *He wants to get out, all angry.* If he didn't leave right away – too late. He's gone. He's already left now, right?
J:	What's he late for?
W:	I don't know. Well like that, *At the beginning I didn't think he would leave.* I don't understand.

This was recorded by another researcher in Solo, David Howe, whom I and James Peacock had accompanied to a weekly meeting of thirty or so members of the large, Solo-based mysticism group called Sumarah, devoted to meditation and spiritual cultivation.[3] (The doctrine and the operational style of this group only broadly resemble those of Pangestu, mentioned in chapter 2.) Seated on chairs in the crowded front room of the modest house of one of the group's members, these students of "the art of living" (I: *seni hidup*) came to be taught and advised by Pak Waya, whose years of meditation, extrasensory abilities, and interpersonal skill made him a popular teacher and adviser (J: *pamong*). (Text 9.4 was taken from a later remark by Pak Waya during this same meeting.)

During these meetings, attendants would ask Pak Waya to meditatively monitor their interior states, and then offer advice on spiritual and social problems they faced in everyday life. Pak Waya brought a fluid, eloquent conversational style to these encounters, alternately tactful and direct. Seated in the front row at this particular meeting, facing Pak Waya and slightly to his right, was a man younger than most other attendants, who were forty and older. But he was dressed like them, in the manner of students and white-collar workers. Though not a regular attendant, this young man had prior acquaintance with Pak Waya and had come this day (it became apparent) at the behest of his mother, who was sitting next to him.

He was there to ask for help with problems studying for national college entrance exams. Early on in the meeting, this young man queried Pak Waya about his problem. As their conversation developed, Pak Waya intuited an unstated part of the young man's problem: he was being distracted from his studies by a complicated, three-sided affair of the heart. Pak Waya's surmise, once uttered, elicited terse confirmation from his interlocutor, who appeared stunned at having been unexpectedly found out (J: *konangan*). Following an awkward, perhaps forcedly humorous bit of conversation – amid murmurings of others present, his mother's expression of wounded surprise at having been kept in the dark, and Pak Waya's ongoing queries – the young man breached a basic rule of Javanese etiquette. He abruptly rose, exited the house with no word of parting or request to be excused, hopped on his motorcycle, and took off.

Sitting at Pak Waya's left, as he commonly did at these meetings, was Pak Tipta, a regular attendant perhaps sixty-five years old to Pak Waya's fifty. He and Pak Waya normally exchanged high if not terribly formal *básá*. As the young man disappeared into the kitchen, Pak Tipta invited comment from Pak Waya on the abrupt ending to this unexpected event. This is the point where text 9.7 begins.

It contains three style shifts. Pak Tipta's first, leading question in *básá* elicited a noncommittal *básá* response from Pak Waya. So Pak Tipta asked again, seemingly more pointedly, in *ngoko* (line 4). Pak Waya's second *básá* response was suddenly interrupted by the din of the young man's motorcycle being kicked to life in the driveway, just outside the window at Pak Waya's back. As his discomfited former interlocutor pulled away, Pak Waya, his face turned to the window behind him, uttered a two-word *ngoko* phrase (line 6, "Well here . . .") then two words of Indonesian ("already finished") and then an observation in *ngoko* ("He wants to get out . . ."). Then he shifted back to *básá*. To my own *básá* follow-up question (line 12), posed hesitantly from the seat to his right, Pak Waya responded in the high *básá* he and I exchanged. But inserted into his talk was a brief *ngoko* segment (lines 15–16, "At the beginning I didn't think he would leave"). At this point another attendant asked for Pak Waya's attention, and the meeting began to resume its usual pace and moved in less unexpected directions.

This flurry of shifts, as the stylistic face of a passing interactional turbulence, is difficult to construe *post hoc*. It involves contingencies which resist retrospective description, and it lacks a self-evident point of closure of the sort which makes part/whole readings possible. In the absence of a recoverable internal dynamic, only weak surmises can be made about the reactive or intentful character of each shift. The first can be considered with an eye to the question which preceded it, and the social biography of Pak Tipta's and Pak Waya's relation, which offers several possible readings. Perhaps Pak Tipta was briefly "modeling thought," that is, thinking out loud without addressing someone whom he wished to avoid putting on the spot. Or perhaps his shift evinced the immediacy of his interest in these goings on, and his desire for a comparably straightforward, down-to-earth answer. Or maybe he was trying to deflate the passing awkwardness – perhaps more acute in the presence of foreign guests – with a mild stylistic joke, seeking to punctuate an unfortunate interlude.

I suggested these and other possibilities to Javanese whom I asked to peruse the larger transcription from which this text was drawn; I thus effectively asked for their help in gauging what Ricoeur would call the "specific plurivocity" of this text. Their reactions, much like those to speech modelings discussed in chapter 8, were generally flat and nonplused. No proffered interpretation was rejected as implausible; none was, by the same token, clearly preferable. I do not believe that this was due to felt lack of adequate collateral information – certainly none asked for any – but a more basic lack of fit between my assumptions and forced-choice queries on one hand, and the interactional sensibility which informs this Javanese practice, and their *post hoc* evaluations of this instance of it, on the other.

Pak Waya's brief shift at lines 6–7, where he responds in surprise to the loud noise coming suddenly from outside, raises other interpretive problems. It might have been caused by a condition of startlement, a momentary removal from an other-orientation caused by his being abruptly "overthrown as an interactant" (Goffman 1974:358). If Pak Waya then appears to have briefly "lost it" or "flooded out," his verbal demeanor was wavering and im-mediately indexical of his internal state. This reading of what Schutz (1967a:91) calls a "because-motive" connects one past event with another anterior to it, through which the speaking "self" becomes subject to factors beyond its "own" purview and control.

But it is unclear how this reading could be extended to Pak Waya's immediate shift to Indonesian ("already finished"), then to *ngoko* ("He wants to get out") and then to *básá*. And it is suspect if only because the person who engaged in this behavior, Pak Waya himself, did not affirm it. He agreed when I asked him some time later if he had been startled (J: *kagèt*), but seemed less sure that his interjection was a function of that startlement. When speakers themselves decline to author-ize construals of their actions with appeal to a vocabulary of intent, that notion itself needs to be relativized to *post hoc* strategies of interpretation, rather than *hic et nunc* processes of interaction.

Interactional styles and identities

Javanese who reviewed recordings and transcriptions of speech at my behest were frequently disinclined to impute strategies to speakers (including themselves). I do not believe that this was for lack of insight into interaction, or of understanding of my aims in querying them. I believe that my broadly interpretive questions, animated by assumptions about talk's intentful character, worked against the grain of their practical assumptions about interaction generally, and that which I recorded, transcribed, and showed them particularly. Relevant in this regard is Keeler's note that speech modeling resonates with what he calls a Javanese "need to dissimulate an interpretive, mediating presence" in speech (1987:257–58). The "internal" qualities of these acts enable their presentational autonomy, and so derive rhetorical power from their ostensibly non-mediated character as re-presentations.

Recordings and transcriptions of talk which I presented to them did not manifest a similar presentational autonomy, and so my mediating efforts here, as translator and interpreter more broadly, are necessary. My failure to enlist Javanese as "full" collaborators or surrogates in this project stemmed, I believe, from a felt lack of fit between those texts and my vocabulary of intent or agency.

This is quite different from saying that Javanese do not understand speech to be vehicular of intent or instrumental in interactional projects. Notions of projective intent are minimally relevant for reading strong implicational reach from texts into their originary surrounds. But rather than deploying explanatory notions of intent under a categorically agentive profile of speakership, I have tried to relativize them to culturally variable assumptions about speech within broader understandings of conversational practice.

Some such relativization is needed, for instance, to show a broad fit between *ngoko/básá* style shifting on one hand, and practices of speech modeling on the other. If interaction is shaped by such a language- and culture-specific sense of talk's relation to interactional identities, then multistylistic *ngoko/básá* usage resists direct assimilation to abstract, comparative, and culture-independent models of code switching. It needs to be read instead as being informed by shared, practical senses of shiftable, part/whole relations between talk and participant roles, which are beyond knowledge of "code" of Javanese *per se*.

Relativized to the interactional dynamics sketched in chapter 8, *ngoko* and *básá* usage has been sketched here as a modulator of interactional counterpoint, as mediating the fluid space of Javanese "thee/me" relations. This is one reason I write here of "shifts" rather than "switches" between speech styles. "Shifts" can be intentful or non-intentful, actions which are performed or which happen. The notion also helps show how monolingual, multistylistic usage lacks fit with appeals to "code switching" which are abstract enough to make such acts seem, in Goffman's words, "too mechanical and too easy" (1981:155). So too it helps develop cultural context for chapter 10's sketch of bilingual code switching as one linguistic facet of Indonesia(n)'s entry into Javanese (conversational) lifeworlds.

10
JAVANESE–INDONESIAN CODE SWITCHING

Javanese–Indonesian code switching can be sketched here in two broadly different ways. From a comparative angle, developed with recourse to broad classificatory criteria, I foreground its commonalities with bilingual usage in other, disparate languages and sociohistorical circumstances. An obvious starting point for this general classificatory approach to multistylistic Javanese and un-native Indonesian interaction is John Gumperz's highly influential, portable account of code switching as a species of "discourse strategy."

But Javanese–Indonesian code switching, besides being transient moments in shared social biographies, can also count as among the most intimate points of entry for Indonesian-ness, via Indonesian, into everyday Javanese life. To frame particulars of bilingual usage in these more situated ways, I work here to sketch Javanese–Indonesian code switching relative to a national ideology on one hand, and native conversational practice on the other.

These paired projects can be conveniently broached through a pair of pronominal metaphors. One, at the heart of John Gumperz's approach, is the in-group/out-group, native/non-native, "we/they" distinction which informs his framings of code switchings, irrespective of otherwise huge differences between their originary social circumstances and interactional contexts. By centering this quick review of his classificatory approach on this trope I can also reconsider un-native Indonesian's lack of a "they" from a comparative perspective.

The other pronominal distinction, developed indirectly in prior chapters, is tripartite and helps here to develop a more relativized account. In chapter 3 I sketched *ngoko* and *básá* in an interactionally situated opposition, likening them to styles of "I" and "you." This trope figured in chapters 8 and 9 in descriptions of speech modeling and style shifting as other-oriented self-expression. In chapter 4, I sketched Indonesian's social history and ideologically informed value as a de-situated "it-code," a "third-person" instrument of context-free reference. This resonated with the flattening of Indonesian pronominal repertoires (touched on in chapter 6) and syncretic Indonesian lexical usage in

Javanese interaction (described in chapter 7). Put together, these pronominal distinctions yield an interactionally grounded set of distinctions for describing multistylistic and bilingual usage – "subcode switching" and "code switching" – relative to Javanese conversational practice on one hand and Indonesian language ideology on the other.

Comparative strategies

John Gumperz's important classificatory paradigm for code switching, part of a broader interactionalist account of language, centers on a broad distinction between native "we" and non-native "they" codes. The underlying logic of this core metalinguistic trope is worth considering here, then, with an eye to Indonesian's status as the "they" code which has no "they" there. It is worth noting in this regard how Gumperz's metaphor exploits those pronouns' grammatical plurality and indexical referentiality to bring otherwise broadly distinct sociohistorical and interactional descriptive spheres into convergence. As terms referential of pluralities of persons, "we" and "they" tacitly serve Gumperz as rubrics for the macrosocial conditions which shape lines of collective linguistic and social difference; because those referential meanings are also indexically grounded in use, they can simultaneously serve as rubrics for verbal particulars in the microsphere of "real-time" talk.

In his broad comparative sketch Gumperz can allude only in passing to the diversity of sociohistorical circumstances which have engendered bilingualism. But he is able to characterize what he regards as prototypical social milieux for bilingual communities and interaction. However different otherwise, these situations involve "cohesive minority groups" which have come to participate in the broader social networks of "modern urbanizing regions" (Gumperz 1982:64). Constellations of institutional and macrosocial pressures (political, economic, etc.) in this way make interaction across lines of sociolinguistic difference both needful and possible, and thus engender bilingualism as a correlate of divisions between "our" minority in-group and "their" majority out-group.

In this way, a distinction between "we" and "they" serves to transpose particulars of historical change, within and between social *collectivities*, to the relatively abstract domain of grammatical *plurality*. This is a shift of considerable power, which abstracts away from sociohistorical diversity through the unitary idiom of grammar; it enables a simple referential opposition between "one" and "more than one" to be superposed on and subsume heterogeneous particulars of social difference, and constructions of social otherness.

At the same time, "we" and "they" are personal pronouns which are meaningful because their uses are grounded in interaction. In the sphere of "real-time" face-to-face relations they have indexical referential meanings, which shift with the contexts in which they are existentially embedded (Jakobson 1971). The importance of their interactional grounding for Gumperz's expository purposes has a symptom in a crucial narrowing of sense which his metalinguistic usage requires. In "ordinary" (English) usage, the general meaning of "we" (along with "us" and "ours") is indefinite as to whether the addressee spoken *to* is included in the plurality of persons spoken *of*. But in his discussion of sociolinguistically distinct communities, Gumperz's metalinguistic use of "we" must be construed in the narrower, inclusive sense which presupposes the addressee (interactional other) as member of the group including (minimally) the speaker. In this context "we" is doubly inclusive: with respect to sameness of community identity, and a shared interactional grounding for referential identity. The former grounds "our" sense of sharedness over against "them" and "their" language; the latter subsists in the transient mutuality of intersubjective relations, what counts as "our" talk with and for each other.

Gumperz brilliantly mobilizes this accessible trope to bring institutional and interactional dimensions of bilingual usage into convergence. But he also extends it still further, into the intrasubjective domain of interactional awareness. Gumperz characterizes "we" groups as interactionally tight, closed communities, grounded in members' "shared communicative experience" and practical mastery of "unverbalized context bound presuppositions" (1982:71). These shared, tacit understandings inform the tacit mutuality of communication in a "we" code among "us." Mastery of a "they" code, on the other hand, involves mastery also of relatively explicit, context-free norms which inform use of that out-group language.

In this way too, then, a "we/they" distinction serves to ground a comparative account of "bilingual *experience*" in a broad account of social history, linking differences between collectivities ("us" and "them") to "our" shared sense of "separation between in- and out-group ['their'] *standards*" (Gumperz 1982:65, emphases added). His argument here recalls the class-linked distinctions between elaborated and restricted codes developed by Bernstein, and tacitly invoked by Gellner to distinguish premodern/prenational and modern/national languages.

In all these respects, the absence of a native-speaking Indonesian "they" appears socially significant. "Standards" for speaking that language, for instance, can only be referred to historically contingent institutions which ground it, and the politically salient ideology which legitimizes that language as one among other institutions of the nation-state. In the absence of an extrinsically identifiable out-group, these sociohistorical and overtly ideological groundings take on the saliences which I discussed in chapter 4 with recourse to the ungendered, singular third-person category of "it."

Just as Indonesian lacks fit with notions of a "they" code, the Javanese speech styles appear to elude classification within a unitarily framed understanding of "we" code, grounded in closed networks of interaction in a (non-minority) community. The territorial logic of high and low *básá*'s unequal distribution, which I sketched in chapter 3, would seem to require some sort of subethnic "we/they" distinction. Since speech style use appears to vary territorially in what Brown and Gilman (1960) call group styles, it is seemingly grounded in other, culturally and politically salient understandings of community, status, and participant roles. Javanese "we-ness" thus seems a sociohistorically and interactionally slippery idea. Still, the "we/they" pronominal trope suggests the suitably relativized, three-way analog I develop later in a sketch of Javanese–Indonesian code switching.

Functional classifications

Gumperz's expository strategy for presenting and classifying bilingual usage appeals to what he variously calls the functions, meanings, and situated effects of code switchings. With these notions he brings together maximally broad classificatory criteria with examples which are presented as "brief exchanges . . . just long enough to provide a basis for context bound interpretation" (Gumperz 1982:75). Of interest here are broad differences which distinguish five of his classificatory rubrics from his sixth and final rubric.

Gumperz's five functional classifications depend on correlations between aspects of message form – points of juncture and difference between codes used – and various types of independently identifiable features in context. These latter include switches in speakers' orientations to addressees, authorship of words which a speaker animates (in Goffman's sense, discussed in chapters 8 and 9), the speaker's conative or expressive orientation (as discussed in chapter 7), and so on. These categories all tacitly refer to existential links between aspects of form and context, and so count as indexically but not referentially significant aspects of talk.

Peter Auer has observed in this vein that code switchings' meanings can be read as significant by virtue of the facts of difference they create, which are in turn iconic of some other differences thus presupposed or created in context: "the mere fact of (usually abruptly) changing one (or more than one) formal characteristic of the interaction may be enough to prompt an inference about why such a thing has happened . . . The only 'meaning' the cue has is (to paraphrase Jakobson's definition of the phoneme) to 'indicate otherness'" (Auer 1995:124).

I indirectly anticipated these five rubrics in earlier discussion of monolingual Javanese and bilingual Javanese Indonesian usage. Gumperz's universal category of "quotation," for instance, can be applied to instances of Javanese practices of speech modeling; phenomena of what he calls "addressee specification" were broached in chapter 9's discussion of style shifting; "reiteration" and "message qualification" are rubrics which can be applied to numerous instances of modelings of thought and internal states; so too his category of "interjections" appears to overlap with the kinds of syncretic discourse particle usage discussed in chapter 7. Below are four examples which similarly illustrate how four of Gumperz's functional classifications can be applied to instances of code switching between *ngoko* Javanese (roman characters) and Indonesian (italics). All are drawn from text 10.1, which I present and discuss later, and which can be consulted as fuller context for each example set out here. (I include line numbers in that text for each example; other similarly illustrative examples in text 10.1 are at lines 85–86, 108–09, 116–18, 138–40, and 161–64.)

1. Quotation:
   Ha nèk wong *pembunuhan perampokan* kaé ápá yá, "wah aku arep matèni wong" kelingan *"Wah ada Tuhan"* ha ora mungkin no.

   Ha, if [one] – *murder, robbery*,[1] and such – well, "I'm going to kill someone," [one] remembers *"Oh, there is a God,"* well it's not *possible*. (63–65)

2. Addressee specification (in an otherwise *ngoko* conversation, the speaker addresses a former bystander):
   Gimana Pak Mul?
   How about it, Pak Mul? (68)

3. Reiteration:
   Hukumé nèk arep amal ora sah nyolong, pádhá waé kok. *Tetap tidak boleh.*

   The law [is] if [one] wants to be charitable, [one] needn't steal, [it's] just the same. *One still can't.* (175–77)

4. Message qualification:
   Nèk saiki upamané ngéné, *satu contoh ya,* ki wong ndésá ki *kan* mlarat kabèh, lha ndilalah aku ki rádá mletik pikirané.

   Well now, for instance like this, *an example right,* here villagers are all poor right, so it happens I'm rather clever at thinking. (156–58)

Examples like 1 and 4 also show how contrasts between Javanese and Indonesian code elements can map onto independent contrasts between constituents of speech. I noted earlier that in both languages, syntactic configurations commonly key to the contextual saliences of "old" and "new" information which is conveyed in "topic" and "comment" phrases, respectively. Code switchings commonly occur at these points of juncture, and so generically augment the kinds of contrasts between informational relevance of phrases which are otherwise marked by use of anaphoric pronouns, intonation, and so on. This can likewise be seen in code switchings from *ngoko* (in roman) to Indonesian (in italics) in example 5 and Indonesian to *ngoko* (like example 6). (Compare Gumperz 1982:79.)

    5. Aku ki *diciptakan dari Tuhan.*
       I [was] *created from God.* (57–58)

    6. *Nah itu bagaimana?* Maling aguna kan ngono? Ha kuwi.
       So how about that? A good thief is like that, *right?* There.
       (168–69)

Javanese speakers to whom I presented isolated examples like 1–6 above, either in recordings or transcription, had few substantive responses to my queries as to "why" or with "what intention" these code switchings were carried out. Their reactions, much like those to my queries about speech modelings mentioned in chapter 8 and 9, were terse, *pro forma*, and largely unenthusiastic agreement to suggestions that they might "draw attention to" (I: *menarik perhatian*) or "stress" (I: *menekankan*) something.

Gumperz has approached similarly opaque examples with a "contrastive" strategy, that is, by eliciting from speakers characterizations of such code switchings in counterposition to their hypothetical "mirror images." This tactic I found too artificial to be useful in my interviews for Javanese and, as indicated in earlier chapters, I had little success with the "forced-choice" technique of proffering different possible "readings" of examples for speakers to judge between as more or less plausible. Speakers were as disinclined to make such evaluations of code switchings as they were of speech modelings like those sketched in chapter 8, or style shiftings mentioned in chapter 9. I believe that by plying an alien elicitation frame (Frake 1980) I ran the danger of presupposing too much of what I sought to discover, and ran too strongly against the cultural grain of Javanese ways of construing talk's meanings.

When speakers are hard-put to correlate a change in speech form with some extrinsic aspect of context, then code switchings' "meaningfulness" is difficult to relate to the situations of their production and construal. Gumperz analogizes such elusiveness to the "meaning" of formal grammatical patternings like use of the future tense in English (to cite Gumperz's example, 1982:62). But a lack of recurringly patterned form, function, and context makes for broader operational and methodological problems, which Suzanne Romaine has pointed out. A real danger of circular reasoning arises when "the meanings postulated for code switching are of such a degree of abstraction [that] they are unlikely to be accessible to . . . introspection" (Romaine 1995:175). Certainly considerable abstraction is presupposed by any universal "we/they" opposition which licenses comparison across otherwise disparate instances of use, interactional contexts, and social milieux.

Textual interpretations

Gumperz indicates that his final category, "personalization vs. objectivization," differs from the others primarily in its lack of distinctness. It is a rubric for gathering "merely rough labels" for a "large class of stylistic and semantic phenomena," and so also for a "relatively large" number of examples (Gumperz 1982:83). Significances of these instances of code switching are "more difficult to specify in purely descriptive terms" (ibid.:80), and lead Gumperz to develop example-specific, interpretive, situated inflections of the we/they distinction: "warning/personal appeal; casual remark/personal feeling; decision based on convenience/decision based on annoyance; personal opinion/generally known fact" (ibid.:93–94).

Such contrasts rest not on correlations between message form and extrinsic features of context, but on provisional *post hoc* construals of what switchings might be "seen as suggesting" or "imply[ing]" about "interactional tone" (ibid.:95). The circumspectness of much discussion under this rubric befits Gumperz's broader allusion to these examples as "*metaphoric extensions*" (emphasis added) of the we/they code opposition. In the absence of presupposed features of context to which they can be indexically and quasi-conventionally related, code switchings like these cannot be seen as standing to their "meanings" in code-like relations like those between "words and referents" (ibid.:95).[2] Instead, they must be approached as tiny social texts with "meanings" which are open only to interpretive construal, in the discursive present, with an eye to their larger, originary, interactional surrounds.

Such readings rest more obviously and crucially, then, on the richness of the originary contexts, as co-presented with examples. A minimalist presentational strategy yields disproportionately broad construals, which therefore seem more clearly artefactual of the focalizing strategies which serve Gumperz's expository project. In this way the breadth of the "personalization vs. objectivization" rubric seems symptomatic of more general assumptions enabling of this classificatory approach. It shows another point where such a comparatively oriented strategy lacks purchase on the biographical, cultural, and sociohistorical particulars from which oppositions ("we/they" and "personal/objective") are abstracted.

For some descriptive purposes, and in some bilingual situations, this may be a necessary and enabling strategy. But the social origins of Javanese Indonesian bilingualism point to the usefulness of a more relativized approach to (Javanese–Indonesian) code switching. On one hand, it needs to be considered relative to native conversational practices, especially the kinds of *ngoko* speech modeling which recurringly serve to figure "first-person" ("personalized") points of view. On the other hand, un-native Indonesian can be considered as the institutionally and ideologically privileged instrumentality for "third-person" ("objectivized") acts of reference and predication. (Gumperz can be read as tacitly licensing this latter linkage with his own allusion, via Bernstein, to the relatively context-free nature of "they" code usage.)

So too, the context dependence of some readings of code switching leads me to try to introduce considerably more information about interactional dynamics and originary contexts, as with texts provided in earlier chapters. To avoid flattened accounts of overisolated examples here, I draw first on the longish transcription of interaction presented as text 10.1.

Text 10.1 is convenient for broaching Javanese–Indonesian code switching because it includes almost no *básá*, and so allows for an initial focus just on switchings between *ngoko* (in italics) and Indonesian (in boldface). It also helps to illustrate some of the difficulties which syncretic usage, discussed in chapter 7, can make for classification and transcription. This is because code switching is structurally constrained by samenesses and differences between the patternings of the languages in question. As Romaine points out, "[t]here is an inverse relationship between the degree of similarity between any two languages in contact, which will have the effect of maximizing the potential sites for code switches, and the extent to which code switching and borrowing can be distinguished" (1995:151).

Structural congruencies between Javanese and Indonesian, coupled with their numerous cognate and emerging syncretic elements – discussed in chapter 7 – can make it difficult to distinguish code switching from borrowing; so too it often occurs, as Woolard shows for the closely related languages Castilian and Catalan, that "it is sometimes possible to know that a code switch has taken place but quite literally not to be able to identify where it began" (1988:61). When it is impossible to demarcate points of difference between two languages, it is correspondingly difficult to distinguish which might count as the "base" or "matrix" language for a switch from one into the other. (See in this regard Clyne's discussion

[1987] of Dutch and English usage, which includes similar "bilingual homophones.") These I transcribe in what follows in roman type.

This problem's practical, orthographic aspect can be illustrated with the transcription presented as 7 below. (Numbers in parentheses after examples in this section correspond to line numbers in text 10.1. I transcribe syncretic/convergent elements in a distinct typeface, even if this misleadingly implies that they somehow count as a distinct class for speakers in interaction.)

    7. Nèk anu, **kan ajaran boleh**?
       As for uh, *isn't the teaching that* [one] *may*? (8)

The first phrase consists of the *ngoko* topicalizer *nèk* and the syncretic discourse marker *anu*, equally available in Indonesian or Javanese to mark hesitation or uncertainty. The second phrase, separated from the first by a brief silence, opens with the discourse marker *kan*, of Indonesian provenance but, as shown in chapter 7, now also an alternative to *rak* in otherwise Javanese usage. The utterance concludes with the fully Indonesian *ajaran boleh*. When syncretic discourse markers are juxtaposed in this manner, it can be difficult to identify a point of transition between codes.

More troublesome can be repetitions of parts of prior utterances, like example 8. At line 83 in text 10.1, Wid, who was the primary audience for the bit of dialog presented as text 8.1, has used the Indonesian word *tersesat* to describe a hypothetical Muslim who is faithful but misguided. His interlocutor (M) requested clarification for use of that word, uttering the otherwise *ngoko* utterance which I reproduce here along with Wid's reply.

    8. M: Karepé *tersesat* piyé kok?   What d'you mean, "*lost*"?
       W: *Tersesat* ki *jalan*   "*Lost*" is [taking a] way
           yang tidak benar.   which is not right. (86–87)

Wid's reply is entirely in Indonesian save for the *ngoko* deictic *ki*, which marks the end of the phrase containing the Indonesian word *tersesat* as his topic, carried over from the preceding utterance. Were one unaware that Wid was repeating that word metapragmatically, as the topic of his own utterance, this use of Javanese *ki* might seem isolated and perhaps anomalous. But in context it can be read instead as marking a point of juncture between *ngoko* and Indonesian phrases, the former of which contains an interactionally conditioned use of Indonesian.

Borrowings like this could be set off typographically from the Indonesian material which figures in code switchings. But examples like 8 suggest that this could intimate too strongly a feeling of categorical difference between borrowings and code switchings. So I have adopted a minimalist strategy for transcribing text 10.1. (One brief aside in *básá*, made to an erstwhile bystander in the ongoing discussion, I write in boldface.)

Contestation and code switching

Text 10.1 presents about two minutes of a longer chat involving four male teachers relaxing between classes at their high school near the southwest Central Javanese city of Purwareja (see map 2). Pak Mus, about forty, teaches religion, which has just emerged as a topic in what had been a desultory *ngoko* conversation. Pak Wid, his interlocutor, is an Indonesian teacher in his mid-twenties. They know each other well enough not just to exchange *ngoko* Javanese, but for the elder to address his junior with the very familiar second-person pronoun *kowé* (line 14).

Aside from Danu's brief entrance (marked D) at lines 18–30, he and another teacher count as an audience for the increasingly focused engagement between Wid and Mus on theology and morality, which began at about the point where text 10.1 begins. Wid is looking for points of morally permissible slippage between the motives for and effects of social acts. He proffers a series of somewhat fanciful scenarios which Mus rebuts, as at the beginning of text 10.1, by asserting that one cannot live dissolutely and then gain salvation simply by appealing for God's forgiveness just before dying. Mus reacts to Wid's conjectures (at lines 9, 31, 62, 106) sometimes indulgently or dismissively, and once contestively as he seeks to block and correct what he views as misguided efforts to blur religiously sanctioned lines between the sinful (*haram*) and the permissible (*halal*).

I choose this text in part because it contains an overt, situated evaluation of the prior interaction by one of its participants. This evaluation both provided a clue to and shaped the ensuing interaction. At line 14, after instructing Wid on the error on which his first scenario is founded, Mus instructs him in Javanese: *Kowé já ngéyèl tá* (Don't be stubborn, OK?). *Ngéyèl* is a Javanese metapragmatic term glossable roughly as "to persist in a demonstrably weak argument or false opinion." It is notable that at this point direct interaction between Wid and Mus temporarily broke off: Wid turned to the former bystander, Danu, with another of his hypothetical scenarios (lines 18–30). But at that point Mus interposed himself as speech partner again to counter Wid's conclusion.

If Mus' instruction at line 14 signaled his general interactional stance, and shaped the ensuing feel of talk for both parties, it also provides a clue for reviewing particular bits of code switching with an eye to the larger interactional contour. It both names and shapes what Gumperz alludes to as the "tone" of conversation, and the ways "bilingual

Text 10.1

M:	**Jadi sepanjang usia, ndak boleh tu, potong-potong** mumpung agèk nom saiki dosa sik, suk kono nèk wis tuwå mertobat, |**tidak bisa**==	[1]	M:	**So all** [one's] **life** [one] **mayn't** [do] **that, cut corners,** "Since [I'm] young now [I] can sin, later when [I'm] old, [I'll] repent," |[one] **can't**==
	|*Nah itu* == *Ning*			|ah ==**But**
W:	**kan ya boleh** tá pak?	[5]	W:	[you] **may, mayn't** [you] *pak*?
M:	*Nèk oleh ki, luwèh-luwèh, ning aku ra ngolèhké. Karepmu dhéwé.*		M:	If it's allowed, that's up to you, but I don't. Whatever you want.
	[4 secs. of laughter, unintelligible talk by others]			
W:	*Nèk* anu, **kan** |**ajaran boleh**?==		W:	As for uh, |isn't **the teaching**==
M:	|*Yå ora* ==*Ora oleh*		M:	|*No* ==one mayn't
	|ong	[10]		|Well, well "**Repent** |**before**
	|**Boleh.** Wong, wong "**Bertobatlah** |**sebelum**			|Why
	|Lho			
	kamu mati."			**you die.**"
M:	*Kowé ja ngèyèl tá?*		M:	Don't be stubborn, OK?
W:	**Ya boleh.** Nggih, Pak Mul? [general laughter]	[15]	W:	Right, Pak Mul?
Mul:	*Piyé-piyé?*		Mul:	What? What?
M:	*Kandhani ra olèh.*		M:	[I'm] telling [you], [you] can't.
W:	[to D]: *Ngéné awaké dhéwé ki nèk kepengin sugih.*		W:	Like this. Someone wants to get rich.
D:	Haq-a.	[20]	D:	Uh-huh.
W:	*Imané kita copot* |terus **korupsi** *sik.*==		W:	**We lose** *faith* |then [are] corrupt *next.*==
D:	|mmm ==**Korupsi**		D:	|mm ==Corrupt.
	terus?			then?
W:	*Dhité didepositokan atas nama orang lain,* ha ngko trus **diakukan** *aé.*		W:	The money **is** deposited under another name, and then [one] **confesses.**
D:	Terus karepé piyé?	[25]	D:	So what's the point?
W:	Terus, kosik, terus mlebu pakunjaran tá, mlebu pakunjaran ki, ngko nèk wis metu saka		W:	So, hold on, so go to prison, OK, goes to prison, later comes out of

Text 10.1 (contd)

	pakunjaran kita beriman lagi kan wis olèh		W:	prison and becomes faithful again, then gets the
	deposito.			deposit.
M:	|Wong, masuk penjara itu tidak berarti dèdèl	[30]	M:	|Well, going to prison doesn't mean losing
	iman, ya?			faith, right?
W:	Em, tidak apa? |Ora dedel imane?		W:	Uh, doesn't what? |Doesn't lose his faith?
M:	|iman		M:	|Faith
W:	Lha apa?	[35]	W:	Well then, what?
M:	Ya tetep orang beriman kuwi		M:	Ya still a person of faith, that.
W:	Tapi hanya lima puluh persen.		W:	But only fifty percent.
M:	Ha ya ora.		M:	Hah, of course not.
W:	Tidak mungkin kalau orang yang beriman itu		W:	It's impossible for a person of faith to become
	akan menjadi seorang pembunuh.			a murderer.
M:	Orang yang beriman itu bisa berbuat dosa, tapi	[40]	M:	A person of faith doesn't – they sin, but the sin
	dosa itu tidak merusak iman.			doesn't ruin their faith.
W:	Satu contoh?		W:	An example?
M:	Dosa |itu		M:	The |sin
W:	|Kasih contoh?		W:	|Well yeah, an example, how about it?
M:	Dosa itu menimbulkan siksa.	[45]	M:	The sin causes suffering.
W:	Lha ya satu contoh piyé?		W:	Yeah, well, an example, how about it?
M:	Itu, ya, perbuatan dosa itu tidak merusak iman.		M:	That is, committing sin doesn't ruin faith.
	[approx. 1 second silence]			
W:	Saiki definisiné iman sik piyé pak?		W:	So what's a definition of "iman" first, pak?
M:	"Iman" itu keyakinan terhadap, keyakinan dan,	[50]	M:	"Iman" is faith in, faith and, uh, an
	uh, satu sikap batin yang, meyakini terhadap			internal attitude which affirms
	Allah dan |membenarkan apa-apa yang			Allah and |supports whatever
W:	|Ya		W:	|Ya
M:	yang diajarkan pada para nabi dan rasul.		M:	by the prophets and teachers.
W:	Ya. Pokoké nèk sing jenengé wong, wong	[55]	W:	Yeah, but the main thing, as for what's called
	membunuh orang iki ki ora ngerti,			killing someone, [then one] doesn't understand,
	ora kélingan nèk "aku ki diciptakan dari			doesn't remember that "I [was] created from

M: *Tuhan"==*
W: *==Nèk wong perang, lha |ápá yá*
                                           |Ora, ora
   perang.
[60] M: **Wong mbunuh, mau membunuh.**
W: Ha *nèk wong* **pembunuhan perampokan** *kaé ápá yá*, "*wah aku arep matèni wong*" *kelingan* "Wah, **ada Tuhan**" ha *ora mungkin no.*
M: *Nèk* perampokan itu membuktikan bahwa ada yang batal. Tidak berarti berdosa itu.
[65] W: *Gimana* Pak Mul?
[laughter, several voices, unintelligible for about two seconds]
A: Seperti Pak Mansur.
W: *Ya Rasullulah ya.*
M: Pokoknya namanya pelajaran
[70]   agama itu mengatur perbuatan. Perbuatan yang sama, tapi nilainya selain itu terdapat pada |agama.
W: |Pada agama.
M: Tidak pada agama juga ada, pada hukum.
[75] W: Kalau begitu orang yang masih |beriman
M: |Itu
   perbuatannya sama, tapi nilainya==
W: ==Tidak sama==
[80] M: ==Tidak sama.
W: Berarti kalau orang yang tersesat itu juga masih beriman.
M: Betul. Tersesat yang bagaimana? *Karepé tersesat piyé kok?*
[85]

M: *God=="*
W: *==When there's war, well |what about*
                                           |No, not
   war.
M: **Someone kills, is going to kill.**
W: Ha, if [one] – **murder, robbery**, *and such* – well, "I'm going to kill someone," [one] remembers "Oh, **there is a God**," well **it's not possible**.
M: As for robbery, that proves that something has failed. It doesn't mean it's sinful.
W: How about it, Pak Mul?

A: *Like* Mansur.
W: Oh, Lord.
M: The main thing is, what's called religious instruction orders behavior. The same deed, but its value aside from that is found in |religion.
W: |in religion.
M: Others not due to religion also exist, to law.
W: In that case a person who is still |faithful
M: |There an
action is the same but its evaluation==
W: ==*Is not the same*==
M: ==*Not the same.*
W: That means if one is lost, one also [can be] still of the faith.
M: True. "Lost" how? *What d'you mean, "lost"?*

Text 10.1 (contd)
W: **Tersesat ki jalan yang tidak benar** [umpamané malimá.
W: *"Lost" is* [taking a] *way which is not right,* for |instance the five "ma."
M: |Contoné?
M: |An example?
W: Umpamané contoné ma-limá.
W: For instance, an example is the five "ma."
[90] D: **Judi itu berdosa, berdosa.**
[90] D: **Gambling is sinful, sinful.**
W: **Itu imannya==**
W: There the faith==
M: ==**Imannya tidak tetap**==
M: ==*the faith isn't firm*==
W: ==**Tetap**
W: ==*Firm*
M: **Tetapi kalau sudah menyembah sesuatu selain yang harus disembah itu sudah lepas imannya.**
M: **But if one has worshipped something which shouldn't be worshipped, then the faith is lost.**
[95] W: Lepas imané?
[95] W: The faith is abandoned?
M: Yá mangkaná wau lampahirá Raden Gathutkácá.
M: Yes, thus the fate of Sir Gathutkaca.
W: E, anenggih negari pundi tá kang kaéká adi kuásá purwá.
W: Uh, indeed that 'and which was most powerful of old.
[100] M: Ditudùhi angelé ki tetep.
[100] M: [You're] shown the difficulty is still there.
W: Ngerti ra karepé?
W: Understand or not, the point?
M: Nyong ra ngerti.
M: I don't understand.
W: Nèk kimau ngaji.
W: Well, like before, about praying.
M: Ngajiné piyé?
M: Praying how?
[105] M: **Perbuatanya sama, tapi nilai perbuatanya itu berbeda.** Pádhá-pádhá, pádhá-pádhá mangan sing di pangan pádhá déné segá, ning **hukumnya berbeda**, **beras** colongan **beras** lé tuku. Lé tuku nganggo dhuwit, lé golèk nganggo nyambut-gawé nganti kemringet.
[105] M: **The act is the same, but the evaluation of the act is different.** The same, eat the same, what's eaten is rice, but **the law is different, rice** stolen [and] **rice** bought. The bought is with money gotten by working 'til you sweat.
[laughter]
[110] W: Karo lé golèk dhuwit nganggo ngrampok ngono halal ndi pak?
[110] W: Compared with getting money by robbery like that, which is permitted, pak?
M: Ya ájá halalé. Nèk kuwi
M: Yeah, don't [talk about] "permitted." As for the

		Javanese	English
W:		sing ngrampok genah haram *kok*.	one who robbed, of course it's forbidden, right.
W:	[115]	Kuwi anu *kuwi dhuwité kan wis*, wis **berujud uang** tá, *ning* **dia makannya tidak berujud uang**, *ning ora* halal? Halal tá kuwi.	That, uh, the money is already, already **in the form of money**, right, but **what he eats isn't in the form of money**, right? But it's not permitted? Permitted, right, that.
M:		Wis. Upamané hurung landhung	Forget it. Supposing one isn't too quick.
W:	[120]	Hurung landhung, halal ra kuwi?	Not too quick? Permitted or not?
M:		Saiki ra ánâ wong muni mangan dhuwit ki ra ánâ yá tá.	Now no one's going to talk about eating money, not anyone.
W:		Aku ngrampok==	I rob==
M:	[125]	==Patrape dhuwit kuwi kena kanggo tuku segá	==[will say] the money can be used to buy rice.
W:	[130]	Ning kan **asal-usulé se** – **nasi itu** kan **tidak dari rampokan**, ning sákâ mergá ngrampok dhit, terus nggo tuku sega ning – kan ora halal tá, halal tá?	But isn't its **origin one** – **that rice isn't from theft**, but because it's from stealing money, then for buying rice but – it isn't permitted, huh? Permitted, right?
M:		Karepé segané halal?	[You] mean the rice is permitted?
W:		Haq-a, segané halal tá.	Uh-huh, the rice is permitted.
M:		Kuwi yá nèk cárâ, **wongé ngarani dhéwé**.	That's how the one [who did it] calls it.
W:	[135]	Halal tá pak. Terus aku, aku nyolong dhit akèh==	Permitted, right pak. So I, I steal a lot of money==
M:		==Ha yá wong dhuwit ki jané ya ápá tá |kuwi	==Whoa, well the money actually |what?
W:	[140]	|Nyolong dhit akèh trus taknggo tuku segá kanggo **keluarganya, keluarganya bagaimana**?	|Steal a lot of money, then I use it to buy rice for **the family, the family, how about that?**
M:		Nyolong dhuwit= =dhuwité nggo tuku segá==	Steals money= =money for buying rice==
W:		==Yá== ==go makani anak bojo.	==Yeah== ==for feeding children and wife
M:		Segané kuwi kalal. Nek cárâ Pak Wid,	That rice is permitted. By Pak Wid's method,

Text 10.1 (*contd*)

	Iho. *Soalé lé dicolong kuwi dhuwit, segané tuku.*	that is. *The problem is what he stole was money, the rice was bought.*
[145]	[laughter]	
W:	**Logikané** kan ngono. *Yá tá?*	[The] **logic** of it is like that, right. *Right, huh?*
	Halal tá?	Permitted, huh?
M:	*Ora.*	No.
W:	*Ora?! Lho.*	*No?!* Huh.
[150]	[laughter]	
D:	**Tapi kan akibat dari suatu proses**==	**But isn't it the result of a process**==
M:	==*Apa,*	==*Well,*
	segala sesuatu yang datang muncul dari sesuatu yang dikaramkan menjadi karam, meskipun pada dasarnya halal.	*everything which arrives or arises from something which is forbidden is forbidden, even if it is at base permitted.*
W:	*Nèk saiki upamané ngéné,* **satu contoh** *ya, ki wong ndesá ki kan mlarat kabèh, lha ndilalah aku ki rádá mletik pikirané.*	Well now, for instance like this, **an example right**, here villagers are all poor right, so it happens I'm *rather clever at thinking.*
	Wadhuh gayané.	Oh, what style.
M:	*Ya.*	Right.
W:	*Aku, terus,* **mengadakan perampogan** *nèng daerah Bandung ra taktuduhké lha itu kan* **saya** *kan* **mendapatkan uang banyak ning untuk menghidupi**==	So I **stage a robbery** in the area of Bandung, don't tell anyone, so then don't, don't **I get a lot of money but for supporting**==
M:	==*Wong-|wong*	==*The |people*
W:	|*Orang-*	|*People*
[165]	*orang satu dhusun itu agar tidak kelaparan.*	*in that village, so they won't starve.*
	Nah itu bagaimana? Maling aguna kan ngono?	So how about that? A good thief is like that, right?
	Ha kuwi.	There.
M:	*Lha sápá kae? Pádhá karo critá* **seribu satu malam** *kaé ápá jenengé, sing dadi maling?*	Now who's that? Same as the story [from] **the thousand and one nights,** what's the name, who became a thief?
[170]		

W: Ha wis ayo, kuwi hukumé ápá iki?
   Hukumé piyé pak?
M: Hukumé nèk arep amal
   ora sah nyolong, pádhá waé kok.
   Tetap tidak boleh.
W: Pádhá waé.

W: OK now, how about it, for that what's the law?
   How about the law, pak?
[175] M: The law [is] if [one] wants to be charitable,
   [one] needn't steal, [it's] just the same.
   One still can't.
W: Just the same.

participants see and use" language (Auer 1995:117). In this regard broad shifts in sequencing, together with broad shapes of code switching themselves, provide context for construing its particular instances.

The interaction's first, heavily Javanese part (roughly, 1–30) gave way to switchings between Javanese and Indonesian (40–70) and then to predominantly Indonesian discourse (70–97). After that there occur a few *ngoko* exchanges (98–105), and then a return to highly mixed usage which continued up to the end of the text (after which their talk continued for another minute or so).

Listening to this recording and reading its transcription with Danu led me to a general inference which he was willing to confirm: that Wid's easy-going, conjectural way of talking did not accord well with the doctrinal reactions it elicited from Mus. Wid "seemed not to want," in Danu's (Indonesian) words, "to be taught" (*kayaknya ndak mau digurui*, lit. "acted like a teacher to"). This is not a stance which can be gleaned from any particularly obtrusive bit of usage to which I or Danu could point; rather it emerged in – or, in retrospect, was inscribed into – the broader sequence as a whole.

No individual switching between *ngoko* and Indonesian, considered in isolation, can be read as focally marking this sense of conflict, or provide clear evidence for imputing such conscious intent to either participant's act of switching. Differences and samenesses in code use, within and across turns, seem to carry a more diffuse sense of agonism and collaboration: Wid's casual, conjectural stance fits his *ngoko* usage, while Mus has recourse to the language of laws and cases, Indonesian.

Such a broad reading can be applied to particular instances of use, but only developed out of perusal of the text as a whole. It can be extended in this way to the sequencing of talk at different points in the interaction: how Wid and Mus collaborate and conflict over who should take which participant role, speaker or addressee. The first bit of largely *ngoko* interaction is choppy because of several attempted and successful interruptions, as well as several contestatory back-channel cues. The Indonesian interaction in the middle portions, in contrast, appears to be smoothly sequenced (roughly, 40–54 and 71–85) as Mus' measured assertions elicit Wid's back-channel cues of assent, acknowledgements of his right to continue speaking, and confirmatory echoes of the final words of some of Mus' assertions. (Such usage resonates with a common pedagogical technique, at least in Java, which may have informed Danu's remark on its overall feel. See in this regard Siegel 1986:138–43.)

From this broader, interactionally situated point of view, acts of borrowing can appear to be as freighted as code switchings. Consider for instance Wid's definitional query, posed to Mus at line 49:

Saiki *definisiné* iman sik piyé pak?
So what's a *definition* of "iman" first, pak?

Definisi is not just conspicuously Indonesian, but quite transparently a borrowing from English. When I observed to Danu that it obtruded (*janggal*) in this bit of *ngoko* usage for me, he agreed. It might be read in isolation, in the manner of text 7.1, as the figuring of an elevated register of Indonesian in otherwise *ngoko* interaction. But in this context it augments a sense of interactional opposition (not intimacy) which would have been muted by a wholesale shift to Indonesian.

The "correctness" of these interpretive observations, as applied to any particular utterance, is less at issue here than the broader, text-oriented stance which such observations presuppose. It keys neither to particular, isolable contextual correlates of particular code switchings, nor to discrete strategies of which any particular code switching might have been the vehicle. Rather, it assumes that usage in general, and code switchings in particular, are grounded in diffuse, transient, intersubjective stances which shape and are shaped in the biography of interaction, and which can only be recovered interpretively from talk's cumulative traces. These dynamics move "through" particular utterances as much as they are punctually shifted by them; so code switchings need to be open to readings with respect to the broader temporal processes – before, after, and during them – from which they are adduced for study. In this way code switchings are available for interpretive construal in the manner of the textualized speech modelings and style shiftings sketched in chapters 8 and 9.

Ngoko and Indonesian, modeling and "objectivization"

A notion of "personalization" can be relativized to the Javanese ways of modeling subjective states, thoughts, and feelings sketched in chapters 8 and 9. Because *ngoko* is presupposed for such modelings in monolingual Javanese usage, over and against interactionally other-oriented *bása*, it is worth considering switches from Indonesian to *ngoko* which might exhibit analogous patterns. Consider in this light the first utterance in text 10.1, which begins and ends in Indonesian with an intervening switch to *ngoko*:

9. *Jadi sepanjang usia* [1] *So all* [one's] *life* [one]
   ndak boleh tu, *potong-potong*,   mayn't [do] *that, cut corners*,
   mumpung agèk nom saiki   "Since [I'm] young now
   dosa sik, suk kono nèk   [I] can sin, later when
   wis tuwá mertobat,   [5] [I'm] old, [I'll] repent,"
   tidak bisa.   [one] *can't*.

Because Javanese is highly elliptical (permitting of zero anaphora), I am obliged to choose personal pronouns for my English translations which have no direct counterparts in the original. I choose third-person pronouns to translate the Indonesian, and first-person pronouns for the Javanese translation, to show how this switch can be read as a modeling of thought which concomitantly shifts participant relations.

This usage maps very well onto the interactional dynamics of native style shifting sketched in chapter 9, and the practices of speech modeling sketched in chapter 8. It shows that alternations between *ngoko* and some non-*ngoko* speech variety, Indonesian or Javanese, can presuppose and create analogous shifts in footing, as a speaker's stance shifts "away" from address of an erstwhile addressee. Such bilingual code switching thus appears, then, to be shaped by an antecedent, native sense of conversational practice, which Mus tacitly exploited to model a subjective state in *ngoko* within an otherwise Indonesian act of address. Danu acceded to my reading of the *ngoko* portion of this utterance as being like other instances of modeled thought in monolingual usage he and I had considered together. His observation was that it was as if Mus here was "imitating" or rehearsing a subjective thought process (I: *niru pikiran*).

Consider in this light text 10.2, drawn from a recording of a meeting of the village youth group which was discussed in chapter 6. Text 10.2 is taken from a recording of talk during a meeting two weeks later in the production process, as the director discussed staging and blocking. He is explaining to the young woman who is playing the hero's mother how to direct her eyes as she calls to her son, Teja, somewhere off-stage. Here, as in most of his dealings with members of the group, he uses Indonesian. That this is not a function of formality is apparent from his address of this young woman with the relatively familiar Indonesian *kamu* (at line 13), rather than a kin term, as well as with the pedagogical, anonymizing *anda* at line 17. But he switches to *ngoko* (italics, at line 6) to model what he has been discussing: first with recourse to his own physical location (the distance to Maryati), then with his eyes looking in that direction (line 9: "that much, that much, that much . . . ") and finally (line 14) with the thoughts which will occur to members of the audience.

He performatively models in *ngoko* the immediate perception and process of inference which will follow from observers' attention to his physical location and directed gaze. This correlation between features of language use and extrinsic contextual features could be captured with a more abstract, comparative, functional rubric, but no such rubric would afford room for the native sense of practice which informs this perspectival transposition.

Text 10.2

Supaya diingat ya, bahwa ada pengaruh perasaan ketika memanggil Teja, itu seakan-akan di situ ada Teja yang duduk, ketika manggil "Já Já! Já Já!" Ha ini jaraknya *tekan nggoné Maryati*. Tapi ketika mata saya melihat ke sana *sakmono, sakmono, sakmono*. "Já Já!" jadi jauh Já ini. Ha jadi yang menèntukan jaraknya si Teja itu kamu harus hati-hati di mana kamu meletakkan mata kamu ya. *Iki mau jané ki wis nèng kéné iki, ha nèk nèng kéné yá ngápá tá kok diceluk ngono lho.* Ya anda boleh di mana saja, walaupun Yanto itu cuma di-, di-...	[1] [5] [10] [15]	Remember, yeah, that there's an influence on the feeling when [you] call Teja, it's as if over there is Teja sitting down, when you call "Ja Ja! Ja Ja!" So, the distance *to where Maryati* [is]. But when my eyes look in that direction *that much, that much, that much*. "Ja Ja!," so he's far away. So what fixes the distance to Teja, you have to be careful where you fix your eyes, right. *Here just now, he's already here, so if he's here why is he being called like that.* You can do it wherever, although Yanto is only...

I described Indonesian in chapter 4 as having institutional authority overtly grounded in the state apparatus, and a sense of legitimacy grounded in a broader, nationalist ideology of development. Together, I suggested, these helped to make it a privileged vehicle of detached, "third-person" reference and predication. Its use in text 10.1 can be construed as authoritative in both respects: on one hand presupposing its speaker's position as an educated professional, and on the other the validity of its discourse independently of the situation in which it is deployed by that speaker.

Most convenient as evidence of Indonesian's relative salience for referentially focused talk are its metalinguistic uses, which reify language itself as an object of reference. So, for instance, at line 50 in text 10.1, Mus responds to Wid's *ngoko* request for a "definition" (I: *definisi*) of a cognate Javanese and Indonesian term (*iman*, roughly, "faith") with a careful, circumspect gloss in Indonesian. (That the word *iman* figures here in an objectifying, metalinguistic mention, is indicated orthographically with double quotation marks.)

"*Iman*" itu keyakinan terhadap, keyakinan dan, uh, satu sikap batin yang, meyakini terhadap Allah dan membenarkan apa-apa yang...

"Iman" is faith in, faith and, uh, an internal attitude which affirms Allah, and supports whatever...

When Wid refers to the *type* of act called murder at line 56, rather than a specific instance of it, he similarly has recourse to an Indonesian designation for that class of actions (lit. "kill [a] person") rather than its Javanese equivalent (*matèni wong*) in an otherwise Javanese utterance.

> Yá. Pokoké nèk sing jenengé wong, wong,
> *membunuh orang iki* ki ora ngerti...
> Yeah, but the main thing, as for what's called
> *killing someone*, [then one] doesn't understand...

His use of *definisi*, noted above, can be read similarly.

At the end of text 10.1 (lines 175–76) Mus similarly responds to Wid's last example first in Javanese and then in Indonesian.

> Hukumé nèk arep amal ora sah nyolong, pádhá waé kok.
> *Tetap tidak boleh.*
> The law [is] if [one] wants to be charitable, [one] needn't
> steal, [it's] just the same. *One still can't.*

This "capping" of his reaction can be read in multiple ways, and so as functionally overdetermined. It serves to qualify his message (as Gumperz puts it) and to reiterate his main point. It derives positional authority from the pedagogical stance which it suggests as a depersonalized observation on the relation between law and instance, recalling what Gellner calls "like treatment of like cases" (1983:20).

Such switchings to an objective guise can subserve personal interests; their disengaged quality can simultaneously shape broader interactional dynamics. Consider in this regard text 10.3, which continues the discussion of the physiology of reproduction transcribed in text 9.1. At the point in that interaction when Sita concluded her disquisition, she responded to Eni's followup question in a way which, Eni told me when we reviewed the recording, startled her a bit. After Sita mentioned that people with reproductive troubles can go to a gynecologist – she performs an Indonesian modeling of address to that doctor at line 3 – Eni asked (at line 6) which spouse would go. Sita's joking rejoinder (starting at line 7) – that Eni, who is unmarried, has no need to know and seems peculiar in asking – fell flat. Eni replied in full Indonesian (line 11).

Text 10.3

S: *Konsultasi dokter ahli kandhungan*
 aé terus nèk ngono kuwi carané,
 kapan siap dibuahi dok, dadi,
 ning angèl lho, nèk mensné,
 mensné ora ajeg, kuwi angèl.
E: Sing nglakoni...
S: Yá nglakoni wis ndé bojo kok,
 nèk rung ndé bojo,
 nèk rung ndé bojo yá ra isá
 ngomong. Kowé ki yá anèh kok.

[1] S: *Just consult with a gynecologist*,
 that's what should happen,
 when will I be fertile, Doc? so,
 but it's hard when the period,
[5] the period isn't regular, that's hard.
 E: The one who does it...
 S: The one who does it has a spouse.
 [if you] don't have a spouse,
 don't have a spouse, [you've] got
[10] nothing to say. You're strange.

E:	Lho saya kan perlu tahu.	E:	Why, I need to know, right?
S:	Ning *kamu juga perlu tahu* wong wis tuwá wis dewásá ngono yá perlu tahu	S:	But *you also need to know* [you're] old, already adult, yeah, [you] need to know.
ST:	Silahkan konsultasi pada guru biologi, silahkan, silahkan		Please consult with the biology teacher, please, please go ahead.

Eni was a bit nonplused when she listened to the recording of this interaction with me, and at a bit of a loss to clarify it for me. "Anyone," she said to me, in careful Indonesian, "should understand" (*Siapapun mesti ngerti*) that she, as an adult, should know about such things; using Indonesian, she suggested, helped make that "clear" (*terang*).

Her *post hoc* explanation suggests that Indonesian was immediately salient for her assertion of a self-evident, objectively true state of affairs. But her usage can also be construed as accomplishing a shift in footing, a microrhetorical deployment of the language of objectivity which dissociates her, as topic, from a self-justifying statement. Indonesian's objectivity helps here, then, to effect a minor shift in intersubjective relations.

Such examples suggest the contingencies which interactional dynamics of "third-person" Indonesian usage can create when figured against subjective, "first-person" *ngoko* stances. Consider in this regard the usage set out earlier as example 5, which demonstrated alternations between Indonesian and Javanese at points of juncture between topic and comment phrases. It actually appears at lines 57–58 in text 10.1. (*Ngoko* talk is in roman typeface; Indonesian in italics.)

> ora kélingan nèk "aku ki *diciptakan dari Tuhan.*"
> doesn't remember that "I [was] *created by God.*"

That this utterance includes modeled thought – demarcated by the Javanese complementizer *nèk* – is evident from the fact that the deictic first-person pronoun *aku* refers not to Wid as speaker *per se*, but as conjectural would-be murderer whose state of mind he is performatively representing.

But this is a modeling of thought which includes Indonesian material: the code switched phrase following the topic phrase final deictic *ki*. Under a minimalist comparative profile, no recourse need be made to such circumstances to note the simple, semiotic salience of "different code, different message segment." But once recognized as part of a modeling of an internal state, it appears to have a different rhetorical sense, informed by a Javanese-speaking sensibility.

Consider this same utterance in light of Wid's utterance at line 63 of text 10.1, where he engages in another modeling of thought, and again switches from *ngoko* to Indonesian. But this switch occurs between two juxtaposed modelings marked by the Javanese framing word *kelingan*, glossable as "to remember, to become aware." *Wah*, which marks the beginning of each modeling, is a syncretic psychoostensive which marks mild surprise.

| . . . "wah aku arep matèni wong" kelingan "*Wah, ada Tuhan*" ha ora *mungkin* no. | "I'm going to kill someone," [one] remembers "*Oh, there is a God,*" well it's not *possible*. |

This switch between codes seems to model two thematically opposed states of mind, and creates a thematically relevant sense of their disjunction. *Ngoko*, the "first-person" language, serves to model an im-mediate, affect-laden state of overwhelming anti-social desire; Indonesian, the "third-person" language, marks a state of awareness of a transcendent moral truth. In this way a generic counterpoint, shaped by native conversational practice, resonates with the disjoint subjective states each modeling presupposes. Such a parallel can likewise be read back into Wid's immediately prior code switching, which analogously models first a subjective position (*aku ki* . . .) and then awareness, self-predicatively marked, of transcendent origin (. . . *diciptakan dari Tuhan*).

Whether or not these are "overreadings" of tiny bits of casual usage, they demonstrate that a larger interactional dynamic can crucially inform bilingual code switchings, and that Indonesian code use is shaped by Javanese senses of conversational practice. Even these few examples of code switching and speech modeling can be seen as bringing language ideology and conversational practice into convergence in the contingencies of talk. That code switchings from Indonesian into *ngoko* should serve to model internal states may be unsurprising; but it turns out that the shifts in the reverse direction allow Indonesian to figure in that subjective sphere as well.

A "we/they" distinction may lack purchase on Javanese–Indonesian usage, but a "personal/objective" distinction, suitably relativized to native conversational practice and national language ideology, helps to make sense of code switching in both situated and comparative ways. But I prefer the interactionally grounded trope of "first-" and "third-person" here to frame examples of un-native Indonesian which model subjective states.

Bilingual, multistylistic usage

To develop this sense of counterpoint between Javanese and Indonesian, I have held in abeyance questions about interaction between Indonesian and *básá*, the speech genre for polite address of the "second person." With an eye to the kinds of *ngoko/básá* dynamics described in chapter 9, this third element of a tripartite pronominal trope helps sketch distinctively polite bilingual usage. The following examples illustrate a few ways in which all three varieties together can inflect speaking perspectives within broader interactional dynamics, and for broader projects.

The recording from which text 10.4 is taken served also in chapter 6 as a source for evidence of the "flattening" of Indonesian pronominal repertoires in Javanese interaction. This is some gossip, recorded by Ari (A) between himself and his older neighbor Cipta (C), with whom he usually exchanges *básá* (as at this text's beginning). They are talking about the daughter of a mutual acquaintance who had recently become a nun, a decision Ari is seeking to diagnose. *Básá*, as Ari's interactional ground, is transcribed in roman typeface; Indonesian is in italics; *ngoko* is in boldface.

Text 10.4

A: Mboten kok, klepat ndelik. Padhané kulá dolan mriká, nápá Marna ngandangké montor **ngono we, yá wis** *tidak berani menampakken diri.*
C: Kok ngoten nggih. Mboten==
A: ==anu nggih goleki lho mas. Mboten kok mesthi "brooken hard," *tapi melihat anu,* kulá nèk ndelok mimiké, kok nèk tegesé sok suatu waktu pas bing nyongé onten niká, kulá delok iman Supingné nong ngoten niku . . . *patah hati!* **Kuwi mesthiné káyá geting karo wong lanang.**
C: **O iyá, geting** *berarti semua* **wong lanang.**
A: *Sebab saya menilai, tidak kok* tegesé ngrèmèhké nggih, *tapi umumnya orang yang masuk suster yang seratus persen tumbuh dari hati nuraninya karena dia hanya betul-betul akan mengabdikan dirinya ke dalam proyek kemanusiaan, sesuai dengan panggilan agamanya, itu ya kira-kira lima persèn,* **hem, ora ku ngènyèk no ora ning,** *dalam pengalaman saya lho* **aku wis tau nganti nyang Sálátigá káná, kono lak okèh daérah ngono kuwi. Kuwi umumé** *bekas patah cinta* **kuwi.**
C: *Jadi termasuk biara-biara* **kuwi.**

[1] A: No, she hides. It's the same, I drop by there, Marna's just fixing his car, **even like that** [she's]
[5] *not willing to show herself.*
C: How about that. It's not==
A: ==Uh, [if] you search, *mas*. It's not for sure a "broken heart" *but seeing,*
[10] uh, when I see, uh, I mean, if some time her boyfriend was there, I saw Suping, her boyfriend, like that . . . a *broken heart!* **So she must**
[15] **hate men.**
C: **Yeah, hates** *meaning all* **men.**
A: *Because* [as] *I see it, it's not,* to belittle them, right, *but*
[20] *generally women who become nuns one hundred percent from their innermost hearts, because she only, truly will devote herself to*
[25] *humanitarian projects, according to her religious calling, that's maybe five percent,* **uh, I'm not mocking, no, but,** *in my experience,* right, **I've been**
[30] *to Salatiga,* **there's lots in that area. Most of them** *have had their hearts broken.*
C: *So they go into a nunnery* **there.**

As Ari's talk becomes disquisitional it also becomes more Indonesian, which can be seen as bringing speech variety into line with speech activity: "evaluating" (cf. his own Indonesian word *menilai*, line 18) the situation in dispassionate terms. But he switches back to *ngoko* to briefly narrate his own personal experience – the time he himself spent in the heavily Catholic area around Salatiga (lines 29–32) – on which his general conclusions are grounded. So too he switches to *ngoko* briefly to bear witness (28) to his own lack of maliciousness in making this judgement.

In this counterpoint between impersonal and personal perspectives – on his topic itself on one hand, and an attitude to it on the other – Ari's normative *básá* orientation to the person he is addressing can be temporarily bracketed. Such usage can be seen as rhetorically informed by the three perspectives alluded to earlier, and as generically weighted for the three functions of language (conative, expressive, referential) distinguished by Bühler. *Básá* provides the interactional-other orientation for his talk, against which he can figure a kind of split between objective (third-person) Indonesian and subjective (first-person) *ngoko* perspectives as they are topically relevant.

A similar, perhaps more richly implemented (micro)rhetorical deployment of resources can be read from text 10.5, which transcribes talk by Pak Waya just before the awkward bit of interaction transcribed as text 9.7. There had been a bit of casual sideplay about a severe accident on the always hazardous roads around Surakarta, which led him to discuss the need to "feel the feelings of others" in everyday life. He did this by describing his own way of driving his motor scooter. His interactional attention was at first on an older intimate whom he ordinarily addresses in *ngoko* (roman type, lines 1–3), but then he turned to me, immediately to his right, to speak in fairly high *básá* (in italics). This interactional transition is marked by a brief switch to Indonesian (boldface) which, like several in text 8.1, occurs at a phrase marker (the *ngoko* deictic *kuwi*) and serves to foreground the topic of his following remarks: keeping someone (like his foreigner interlocutor) from getting too nervous as a passenger on a motor scooter.

Text 10.5

W: Mangkakná wong nyopir janjané sing apik supáyá sing nunggang kuwi **mempunyai rasa tenteram. Ini apa? Supaya yang naik itu, sopirnya itu supaya menjaga perasaan yang naik itu, merasa tenteram.** *Menawi kulá, banter mangkakná tiyang sepuh menawi kaliyan kulá, ajrih kálá wau. Ning kulá ngertos. Kulá mawi anu, menawi, anu, menawi wonten* **jalan**

[1] Whereas when driving, actually, what's good [is] so that the rider **has a feeling of being relaxed. What is this? So the one riding –**
[5] **so that the driver cares for the rider's feelings, [so] feels relaxed.** *As for me, going fast when an old person, if* [she/he] *is with me,* [feeling] *afraid. But*
[10] *I understand. I use, uh, if, uh, if there's a* **road**

sempit trus saya rindikken pelan-pelan ora ndak-dakné, **nanti kalau jalan sudah lurus, di sini sawah-sawah lebar, ta?** Itu banter ndak tahu. Kalau di sini sudah meningkat jalannya. Karena, di samping itu tidak terpengaruh oleh, *meniká wit-witan menawi* **itu** cedhak rak "wut, wut, wut"? Mesthi **perasaan** "Tibané kok banter tá." *Ning menawi wonten lapang mboten ngertos banter.*	which is narrow then I slow it down little by little, not suddenly, **later the road's straight, here there's** [15] **rice fields, it's open, right?** It's fast, [but they] **don't know.** If we've already speeded up. Because, aside from that, they're not influenced by, *this,* [20] *trees, if* **they** [are] close, isn't it [like] "wut, wut, wut?" The **feeling** [is] "Suddenly [we're going] fast." *But in an open area they don't realize* [it's] *fast.*

From this text can be read a thematic and generic counterpoint somewhat like that adduced earlier: between Javanese narration of personal experience and Indonesian setting out of conclusions or consequences which follow. He describes the way he himself drives and the subjective sensations of speed in Javanese (lines 7–10), but shifts thematic focus and interactional attention away from his addressee (me) to thematic exposition, brought to a close by a restatement of the general conclusion in *básá* (lines 23–24). Pak Waya likewise has recourse to *ngoko* when, as part of his explanation, he models a hypothetical sensation of moving quickly past trees close to the road (line 21), and a passenger's feeling (line 22), modeled in *ngoko*, that they are moving quite fast.

This passage, like transcriptions of much of Pak Waya's other talk, can be read as a transient, microrhetorical code switching. As such, uses of *ngoko* after line 2 count not as spontaneous occasions of "personal" language of the self, but as figurings of a transposable, decontextualizable subjective state within an otherwise Indonesian (boldface) and *básá* (italic) narrative. *Ngoko* serves, then, to model reactions to the sensation of trees going by (line 21), and the feeling of surprise at going fast (lines 22–23), framed as performances rather than Pak Waya's own immediate subjective, immediate experience. *Ngoko* stands as Indonesian's complement in enactments of feelings and descriptions of a state of affairs.

Examples of similarly nuanced usage could easily be multiplied, to show different interactional inflections of the perspectival weightings which bilingual, multistylistic usage can lend to speech. I conclude with just one, which helps to show an open-ended indeterminacy which imbrications of speech genres and interactional dynamics can have. Text 10.6 is drawn from still another, later point in the same meeting. At this point Pak Waya has just listened to a lengthy recounting of one participant's outrageous treatment at the hands of her superior in the governmental bureaucracy.

Text 10.6

Lha mung ngaten, **lha nyat yá ora karu-karuan**, menawi kulá mboten. *Begini saja – baiknya* janjané ngaten malah yèn kulá lho, ngaten mawon, *saya* niku lho. *Kalau saya itu mesthi merasa benar. Saudara juga merasa benar. Apakah saudara itu percaya pada Tuhan tidak? Saya juga percaya pada Tuhan tidak. Coba mari – kita itu mengencerkan sesuatu. Jangan percaya dulu; tapi saya mohon apakah tuduhan itu benar atau tidak.*	[1] [5] [10]	Well just like that, "*Wow* **really** [this is] **outrageous**" – as for me, no. *It's like this – better* actually like this rather for me, right, like this, [for] *me*, right? *Me, I certainly feel in the right. You also feel in the right. Do you believe in God or not? Do I also believe in God or not? Let's try, let's us try to think it out. Don't take it on faith*; *but I ask respectfully if the accusation is true or not.*

Pak Waya begins his response in the informal high *básá* (roman) he exchanged with most of those attending these meetings. Here he uses it very briefly, and only to frame his empathetic modeling, in *ngoko* (boldface), of the state he infers his interlocutor to be experiencing from the narrative he has just heard. In the first person, he figures his addressee's standpoint before reverting to *básá* to referentially contrast his own stance (lines 2–3). Then he models, in Indonesian, an alternative way of thinking by addressing his interlocutor not with the *básá* first person *kulá* as at line 4, but with Indonesian *saya* (line 5): a speaking/thinking position he further topicalizes with the low *básá* deictic *niku*.

He then models the line of thought, if not an act of address, which he advises his interlocutor to adopt, entirely in Indonesian (lines 6–14). This is a stance his addressee (as *saya*, "I") might take to her oppressor, addressable – in thought, if not in actuality – as *saudara* (formal Indonesian). Though Pak Waya models a first-person perspective, it figures in this interaction as belonging to his addressee; when he uses polite *básá* to address "his own" addressee "directly," he does so to referentially clarify his own, first-person perspective on the matter at hand. With impersonal Indonesian he models the stance of reasoned distance which is desirable, here and now, in his addressee's difficult circumstance.

In the unfolding biography of face-to-face relations, such talk appears to emerge from converging feelings, thoughts, and interactional projects. But from an "external," long-term perspective, it represents the most intimate dimension of Indonesian's broader entry, along with Indonesian-ness, into Javanese lifeworlds. If speaking Indonesian is an aspect of being Indonesian, then such usage suggests how the language's ideologically grounded, un-native values are gaining situational salience in emerging patterns of bilingual, interactional self/other relations. That assimilation can be seen not so much to be neutralizing Indonesian's institutionally shaped associations as an assimilation or syncretization of them to antecedent projects and understandings of conversational practice. Its "third-person" perspective turns out to be figurable within characteristically Javanese interactional self/other dynamics, and to take on a variety of contingent saliences in those dynamics. Multiply relativized to Javanese interactional projects and identities, Indonesian can be seen less as an instrument of a state system, and more as part of the fabric of everyday, conversational lifeworlds.

11
SHIFTING PERSPECTIVES

Even as Indonesia suffers in the throes of unforeseen economic collapse in 1998, its long-term program of national development deserves attention from anyone seeking to understand the survival of development's "imaginary" into the "post-development era" (Escobar 1992, 1995). From almost any angle of vision *pembangunan* offers a paradoxical appearance. Agents and beneficiaries of the New Order support it assiduously, yet worry about its pernicious side effects; domestic critics read it as thin pretext for coercive state action, but must also acknowledge its real salience for "ordinary" Indonesians' visions of the future and their efforts to make sense of social change in everyday life.

Foreign critics must also recognize this conflicted imaginary's pivotal place on shifting Indonesian landscapes, and in numerous local engagements with far-reaching, translocal change. Outsiders may be quicker to read self-interest into the development rhetoric deployed by a paternalistic, often corrupt state. But if they deny authenticity to any version of development, they can only accord most "ordinary" Indonesians the status of dupes, victims of false consciousness. To insist on the derivativeness of Indonesian development's and nationalism's discourse (Chatterjee 1985) is to deny Indonesian-ness authenticity as a ground for criticizing the state in the name of the nation.

Little reflexivity is required, in turn, to read such external, critical stances as versions of older West/Rest distinctions, reworked for new geopolitical circumstances. "Development" began to come under critical scrutiny as postcolonial nations began to show real signs of "development"; "nationalism" has come for some to seem a fiction just as "new" nations show signs of coming of age. (See in this regard remarks by Hobsbawm, noted by Anderson 1991:xii.) When the nation is seen as a waning Western phenomenon, then nation-like social formations elsewhere in the world, including Indonesia, are effectively removed from the vanguard of world history.

Reflection on development's secular teleology recurringly engenders such conflictedness, and so provides good reasons (as Escobar suggests) for considering it less abstractly and more modestly through its situated, particular realizations. I have tried to develop one such description in this book, by framing Javanese Indonesian talk within the microclimactic of social life which is ongoingly shaped by macrosocial forces. This has meant bracketing some of the enabling assumptions of epochalist, developmentalist visions of language shift, which I briefly review below. It has also involved readings of transcribed talk, suitably textualized, with an eye to the enabling and constraining presence of "development's imaginary" in interactional life. This interpretive project similarly diverges from more analytic, comparatively oriented approaches to bilingual conversation.

Interactional syncretisms

Functionalist visions of language shift (like Yoshimichi's specifically, or Gellner's more generally) are epochalist, like the developmentalist teleologies of which they are a piece. They presuppose that, although all once spoke Javanese and none Indonesian, the fact that now some speak both foretells the day all will speak Indonesian and none Javanese. These broad assumptions enable teleological accounts of the particulars of syncretic and mixed language use which are not problematically interstitial between language codes, but transient reflexes of ongoing social transformations and "contact" as Indonesian displaces Javanese.

By this line of reasoning, the kinds of distinctively ethnic features of Indonesian usage I sketched in chapters 6 and 7 are destined to become either un-ethnic or extinct in some future version of the "good and true Indonesian" (I: *bahasa Indonesia yang baik dan benar*) which is being promoted by a prescriptivist pedagogical industry. This process will culminate in Indonesian usage which no longer shows the "lack of maturity" of which "salad language" is, in some eyes, symptomatic (Buchori 1994).

Bilingual code switching can similarly be framed as epiphenomenal in this ongoing sociolinguistic transition. Alternatively, if code switching is not to be read as portending monolingual Indonesian-ness, it can be taken as a soon-to-be-stable, regular aspect of usage in a Javanese Indonesian community no longer "too young and culturally unstable to have developed shared norms of language choice" (Auer 1995:127). Standard Indonesian usage in everyday life might then converge with newly ceremonial high *básá* in a state of stable bilingual diglossia (cf. Fishman 1967; Ferguson 1959; J. Errington 1991). In either way, teleologically framed linguistic particulars appear as minor ripples on the surface of a shifting sociolinguistic tide, as microphenomena deriving from but not themselves shaping long-term developmentalist macroforces.

My own description has not been framed as an empirically better prediction of Java's linguistic future. Instead, I have directed attention to situated social process, and tried to avoid glossing over immediacies of interactional experience in favor of such cumulative, long-term social change. To describe language in development's microclimactic, I have worked to center aspects of talk which seem peripheral or contingent with respect to broadly institutional forces. To frame these minor, negligible transiencies I have made a double qualification of received notions of language as code.

On one hand, I have foregrounded patterned aspects of usage – discourse particles, speech modeling, style shifting, kin term and personal pronoun use – which are typically peripheral or elusive for structure-focused descriptions of autonomous linguistic systems. On the other hand, I have tried to explicate the ideological saliences of reference- and code-focused views of language in the ideology of development. Ernest Gellner's writings were useful in this respect for explicating tacit, ideological links between Indonesian's status as an autonomous language code and a form of national identity, between knowing and being (or "doing being") Indonesian.

When applied to the "case" of Indonesian language development, Gellner's broad argument resonates strongly with Michael Silverstein's account of "the historical emergence of codification" and a "culture of standardization." In a much more critical vein, Silverstein foregrounds tacit "adherence to the idea that there exists a functionally differentiated norm for using [a standard] 'language' denotationally (to represent or describe things)" (1996:285). Gellner's functionalist *cum* positivist claims for the privileged status of standard national languages hinges on this same point, as did my own explication of a New Order "imaginary of language in development." Standardist conceptions of language like Gellner's can be seen, then, as articulating a point of convergence between (state) ideology and (functionalist) social theory, where "[political] actors' desires" map well with "[academic] observers' epistemology" (Handler 1988:15).

My alternative focus, on language as mediator of interactional process and self/other relations, led me to partially bracket structurally informed questions about speech elements' provenances. I have countenanced the significant possibility that interactionally crucial speech elements might not admit of the usual sorts of classification into one of two categorically distinct, autonomous systems.

Kin terms, as pragmatically salient means (J. Errington 1988) for marking and mediating interactional status relations, are interactionally crucial but also elude easy classification as either Indonesian or Javanese. They can count as both, or neither (in south-central Java, at least), because their situated significances for self/other status relations are grounded more in emerging modes of territoriality (urban/rural, elite/non-elite).

Discourse markers on the other hand are non-referential, transient indexes of subjective interactional stances and states. They elude easy characterization in the categorical, context-free idiom of code, and so for different reasons are peripheral as diacritics of the ethnicity or nationality of speaker and speech. In chapter 7 I suggested that their osmotic character can be seen as part of an emergent repertoire of syncretic elements. Because they are subjective and occasional in significance, their use is skewed with respect to interactional awareness of talk's Indonesian-ness or Javanese-ness. Syncretic discourse marker usage is indexically grounded in talk, but non-referential and seemingly peripheral in speakers' interactional awarenesses of talk's meanings; syncretic kin term use is grounded in self/other relations but also in shifting, territorially grounded understandings of community and authority. So each sphere of use can be seen as a syncretic aspect of interactional identities, emerging (as it were) right under everyone's noses.

Over and against both stands the conspicuously "mixed" usage of lexical elements of one language with grammatical material from the other. The label *bahasa gadho-gadho* ("language salad") keys crucially, it seems, to the appearance of lexical material of one language (usually Indonesian) in the other (Javanese), whether that lexical material is combined with grammatical material of the same provenance (so, "code switching") or not ("borrowing"). In chapter 7 I suggested that even talk with strikingly heavy patterns of Indonesian borrowing can be seen as interactionally syncretized into the Javanese face-to-face dynamics which speech style use marks and mediates. This is because Indonesian lexical material is then tacitly assimilated to the same secondary role which Javanese lexical elements play as stylistic diacritics of modes of address. Considered (like Javanese lexicons) as a structurally secondary aspect of style usage, Indonesian lexical usage like that in text 7.1 can be seen as peripheral to the felt stylistic intimacy of *ngoko* use in interaction. So borrowings can be seen as contrasting in interactionally significant ways with code switchings, as suggested by the transition from usage presented as text 7.1 to that in text 10.3.

I have described these three dimensions of Javanese Indonesian as being skewed with received understandings of languages as autonomous systems, and of speech as use of one or another such system. In different ways, each descriptive sphere fits a broader sketch of the differential interactional relevances which code elements can have as emblems of collective social identities. This sketch centers interactional dynamics rather than structured codes, and keys to syncretic moments in talk which bring codes into both/and relations of simultaneity, rather than either/or, binarist relations of disjunction. These simultaneities emerge in experiential immediacies of consociateship, when relevances of collective social difference (ethnic vs. national) can be bracketed. Such syncretisms point to limits of what can be an ideology as well as a "myth of the discreteness of linguistic systems" (Gardner-Chloros 1995).

Pronominal tropes, pronominal usage, and conversational practice

If categorically structuralist accounts of language systems lack fit with talk's syncretic aspects, they likewise make it easy to bracket sociosymbolic values which those systems tacitly derive from their institutional grounds. Much linguistic description of the sort Volosinov called "abstract objectivist" has been critiqued in this respect. Following Bourdieu's (1982, 1991) invocation of "practice," language has been considered – referentially (Hanks 1990), communicatively (Hanks 1996), conversationally (e.g., Hanks 1996; Ochs 1992) – through the emergent, multiply indexical significances which accrue to talk but often become residual under reified, detemporalizing, binarist code/use distinctions.

Chapters 8, 9, and 10 described and illustrated "speech modeling" as a Javanese conversational practice: recurring manifestations of the tacit, shared "knowing how" which enables shifting indexical relations between talk and its situat-ion. This knowledge can be called practical, as opposed to structural, insofar as it is linked to occasion, and irreducible to a description of grammar and lexicon. At the same time, the opacity of modelings for non-native speakers who may otherwise (think they) "know" Javanese shows that this knowledge is language- and culture-specific. In this respect it is collective, and allied to tacit, shared knowledge of sound/meaning relations which are describable under the rubric of code (and likewise acquired in processes of socialization).

Modelings, as instances of a recurring practice, are intrinsically and distinctively indexical; they derive significance from shifts in footings which they create and presuppose within contexts and acts of "direct" speech. Referential moments in such shifted part/whole relations have been particularly useful here as evidence of their existence and significances. Modeled pronominal usage in particular provided clear, referential "hooks" into the broader, shifted grounds for reference (cf. Hanks 1990, 1996; Haviland 1996b). But modelings do not obligatorily include such pronominal acts of reference, nor can they be reduced to them. And if speech modelings subsist on particular uses of particular contextualization cues (in Gumperz's sense), like those described in chapter 8, they cannot by that token be reduced to any such repertoire.

As an aspect of collective cultural knowledge, speech modeling can be seen as underlying not just ordinary talk but also the aesthetics of verbal art – recall shadow play performances mentioned in relation to text 8.1 – and the rhetoric of authority (discussed in chapter 5). In this respect, conversational speech modelings seem to be mundane, intimate refractions of more broadly salient assumptions about speech and its agents. Speech modeling appears to be the interactional refraction of one "horizon of the taken-for-granted, what the world is and how it works" (Comaroff and Comaroff 1991:18).

So too modeling seems distinctively Javanese, insofar as it does not carry over, as practice, into Javanese ways of monolingually speaking Indonesian. Viewed contrastively, a general absence of modeling in monolingual Indonesian interaction suggests different practical understandings of that language's metalinguistic capacities. Indonesian appears (like English and other languages) more an instrumentality for reporting talk, that is, for conferring on it the status of a referential object like others, rather than re-voicable conduct or thought process. Such metapragmatic framings are grounded in stable "first-person" stances *vis-à-vis* interactional others (addressees) on one hand, and utterances' "sources," objectified in the "third person," on the other.

This suggests a broader difference between modes of Javanese and Indonesian speakership, which emerge not from talk's structure *per se*, but from interactional experience; it is thus a difference which, to use Habermas' phrase, stands "behind the back of language" (encoded lexicon and grammar) as a broader difference in ways to "interpret the world" (1988:174). Such difference might be seen as an unobvious reshaping of interactional experience, and relations to speech, through the ideology or "imaginary" of national (language) development.

Another practical difference between Javanese and Indonesian, discussed in chapter 6, was the relative "flattening" of Indonesian personal pronoun repertoires. This interactionally grounded contrast between the languages may have clearer (because transcribable) correlates in use, but is not by that token simply a structural phenomenon. It seems misleading to assert that Javanese dialects of Indonesian lack the first-person pronoun *aku*, and more revealing to say that the personal pronoun lacks fit with Indonesian interactional dynamics among Javanese. This observation foregrounds the distinct senses of consociateship which use of Javanese and Indonesian might be seen as presupposing more generally.

This point can be extended, in turn, to the expository analogy I drew between the interactional significances of the *ngoko/básá* opposition on one hand, and referential significances of "first-" and "second-person" pronouns on the other. These two inconspicuous phenomena of "non-use" in Indonesian – of conversational practice on one hand, and pronominal resources on the other – suggest the extension of that metaphor to Indonesian not as an alien language, but an un-native "third-" person resource deployable in otherwise Javanese interaction.

Between micro and macro

I have developed my own "third-person" report on these interactional dynamics with a working distinction between the institutional, macrosocial sphere of "large-scale" change, and the interactional or microsphere (what Jelin calls the "microclimactic") of "small-scale" face-to-face processes. Macro/micro distinctions have been easily and intuitively deployed in linguistic description – as, for instance, by Fishman 1972 and Schegloff 1987 – in part because they make it easy to assume a unitary object of description on which each perspective – "large" and "small," "broad" and "narrow" – can be adopted, and later interrelated on some scalar continuum.

The punnish version of this distinction introduced in the book's title draws attention, I hope, to the temporal dimension of any such micro/macro distinction, the juxtaposed sociohistorical and "real-time" dimensions which I have invoked in different places. On the macro side is the temporality of sociohistorical and institutional change, in which language shift is putatively occurring; on the micro side are "real-time" dynamics of interactional self/other relations mediated by the language use in which code switching can occur.

Macrosocial accounts foreground institutional and collective change, which is easily treated as autonomous with respect to microspheres of interaction. Most framings of "development," for instance – as historical shifting constellations of political, economic, and linguistic institutions (among others) – partake of this view. Framed as gradual and entropic (Gellner 1983:65), or rapid and punctual, they make it easy to center institutions as the primary, underlying impetus for micro changes which count as their epistemological and interactional consequences.

One way to resist this tendency is to attend to the saliences which "development" and "modernity," as parts of narratives of Indonesian nationalism, might have in everyday life, and the ways they might be figurable, through language use, in everyday versions of the Javanese Indonesian "project for the assumption of modernity." Nationalism, as Anderson suggests, derives compelling subjective power as means for inscribing narratives of everyday life into transcendent narratives of nationally imagined communities. Lifeworlds (and the talk constitutive of them) can then be construed as partaking of the historical biography of the national community. When such notions of community are inscribed with a secular teleology like development, a language like Indonesian can figure as more than an emblem of Indonesian-ness; it can tacitly refract aspects of the nationalist narrative in everyday life. Micro processes of speaking can thus come into touch with larger, diffuse narratives, by virtue of languages' institutionally informed ideological values.

Such sociosymbolic saliences may seem minor derivatives of massive social change, and the state's institutional presence; one might plausibly deny social efficacy to such language use. But it is instructive in this regard to compare the spread of Indonesian in Java with that of another un-native language, Tok Pisin, in communities of Indonesia's neighbor, Papua New Guinea. Don Kulick has eloquently demonstrated that Tok Pisin has not just rapidly entered the tiny, peripheral community of Gapun, but begun to displace its indigenous language, Taiap mer, even in the absence of such institutional, macrosocial pressures. To understand language shift there requires recourse to local terms: it must be relativized to antecedent practices of socialization, and local versions of the totalizing narratives – morally, politically, and economically relevant – which are serving to relocate peripheral Gapun in a newly enlarged social landscape.

Kulick recognizes how the absence of such large-scale macrosocial forces throws into relief the efficacy of local narratives of change for reshaping collective identity in and through language. He is able to mount a powerful argument by example that unilateral invocations of "macrosociological change as a 'cause' of shift" neglect "the step of explaining how such change has come to be interpreted in a way that dramatically affects everyday language use in a community" (Kulick 1992:9).

Sociolinguistic change on Java is surely grounded in such powerful state institutions, and Indonesian is being propagated through processes of "exo-socialization" (Gellner 1983:38) in standardized school systems. But macrosociolinguistic change there, as in Gapun, cannot be divorced from the ways it is construed as an aspect of "people's conception of themselves in relation to one another and to their changing social world" (Kulick 1992:9). Emergent, still fluid understandings of collective identities – (Javanese) "ethnicity" and (Indonesian) "nationality" – shape and are shaped by local versions of the narrative of development, in ways alluded to in chapters 2 and 5. Indonesian's un-nativeness, like that of Tok Pisin, throws into relief the ways that institutionally grounded Indonesian "otherness" must be encountered and reconstructed, through talk, in microdimensional, interactional contact with and between Javanese.

On the micro side of this divide, code switching offers itself for readings as what Susan Gal has called "symbolic creations concerned with the construction of 'self' and 'other' within a broader political and economic context" (1988:247). These are "real-time" transiencies of interactional process: short-term events, measurable in fractions of seconds, in which (bilingual) talk happens. In chapter 10 I worked toward a relativized, situated alternative to one influential strategy for abstracting away from talk's event-ual character, and arriving at a comparative profile of it as data. An abstract distinction between "we" and "they," I argued there, allows Gumperz to assume a common (macro) institutional grounding for bilingualism, and so for his readings of (micro) interactional functions out of bilingual usage. To correlate features of use and context, he also has recourse to comparably abstract notions of "strategy," which allow moments in verbal process to be explanatorily recaptured through *post hoc* review of talk's transcribable elements.

The de-temporalizing, nomothetic thrust of this comparative approach has been pursued much more vigorously by Carol Myers-Scotton (1993), whose universal approach models code switchers (and, implicitly, speakers) much more generally. Her broad, laws-and-cases approach has explanatory recourse to presumedly universal properties of speakership, which license a divorcing of microphenomena of talk even more radically from their temporal situat-ions. She eliminates even residual interpretive appeals of the sort to which Gumperz has recourse, because these fall outside the domain of what Jürgen Habermas calls analytic social science. Myers-Scotton's scheme falls under this rubric because it presupposes that uniform, "strategic-purposeful rationality" is universal among social actors, as are "normative rules of action" (Habermas 1988:47) shared within and across social groups. (For discussion of Myers-Scotton's notion of markedness, as universalist as the Gricean conversational maxims which inspired it, see Meeuwis and Blommaert 1994.)

This radically de-situated, analytic point of view mobilizes "norm" and "strategy" as explanatory devices which need not be judged in terms of any fit, good or bad, with native speakers' points of view (cf. Romaine 1995:175). This is because they are joined to a notion of "social motivation" which, as Habermas observes, is constructed analytically and independently of "communication with the acting subjects themselves or with the traditions in terms of which their actions become understandable" (1988:55). When notions of strategy and agency are divorced from cultural variability and historical process, they subserve explanations of "meanings" of conduct, including code switching, which are "monologically . . . [and] 'unambiguously' understandable, accessible without hermeneutic effort" (ibid.).

When data of talk (and code switching) are disjoined from interactional process, "agency" and "strategy" figure as explanatory, universal notions. Transiences of interactional awareness, biographies of social relations, originary circumstances of interaction, and so on are all residualized by this model's self-contained logic (its auto-nomy). This is a mode of microanalysis which divorces talk radically from interactional temporality, and from broader scenes of social change in which those processes occur. As a result, they offer no purchase on culturally variable understandings of language difference, or conversationally variable practices like speech modeling.

So this profile accomplishes a double conflation of talk's temporality. On one hand, its operational logic assumes effective co-incidence between originary event and analytic moment, admitting of no slippage between talk as event and data. From this perspective, interpretively grounded questions about the implicational reach (as Irvine calls it) which moments in talk might have – "forward" and "backward" in "real-time" dynamics – appear superfluous. On the other hand, strictly linear modelings of talk's sequencing abstract away from experiential consociateship, the "actual simultaneity with each other of two separate streams of consciousness" (Schutz 1967a:163). Simultaneities of streams of consciousness emerge in part from actual, existential groundings which give talk multiple indexical significances in context. When talk's data is abstracted away from those transient, processual linkages, it is likewise divorced absolutely from the immediate temporality of the "specious present" or "vivid 'Now'" (Schutz 1967b:173).

My own recurring discussions of focalization strategies in chapters 8, 9, and 10 were part of an effort to keep that interactional temporality in sight, albeit in mediated, provisional ways. I believe that some sense of situated temporal dynamic is needed if one is to develop any correlative sense of situated, contingent agency which might inform talk. Such linkage, less explanatory than interpretive, subsists on the bringing together of talk's transcribable traces with narratives of interactional dynamic, and consideration of the institutional *cum* ideological values of speech varieties. To read particular texts as relatively strongly agentive, I proposed that at particular interactional moments talk appeared relatively clearly to subserve extrinsic individual interests. Only by introducing such situated strategies, bound to particular social projects and understandings of social values, can one read conduct (and talk particularly) as informed by a "consciousness of . . . a time scale beyond the present" (Taylor 1985:258). Without incorporating a broader temporal sense, notions of interactional strategy, which Indonesian can subserve, must be linked to what Charles Taylor usefully calls "subpersonal agency."

I have tried to keep a double temporal perspective in play here. I have viewed some instances of talk as relatively weakly intentful, that is, as seemingly parts of the taken-for-granted cultural and ideological background of Javanese (and, increasingly, Indonesian) social life. But I have tried to be attentive to occasions when they come to the foreground in the service of interactional strategies, and as instrumental to adducible, extrinsic purposes. Contrastively based notions of strong intent make it possible to countenance "interest" and "strategy" as interpretive devices in relativized, mediated accounts of "culturally specific views on language, meaning and intention" (Stroud 1992:127).

The result, I hope, is a doubled sense of Javanese and Indonesian speech and speakers which usefully links the macro and micro of sociolinguistic change and variation. Efforts to gauge talk's intentfulness here – recovered provisionally and mediately, across languages, cultures, and time – are of a piece with efforts to sketch the social shape of language change. This bringing together of both micro and macro temporalities has made for the punnish tension I have tried to develop to describe Javanese Indonesians' shifting languages.

NOTES

1 Introduction

1 The 1971 national census shows that some 40 percent of the national population of 118 million then knew Indonesian; the 1981 census placed that number at almost half of 150 million Indonesians; projections by Abas (1987; from whom these figures are adapted) are that 60 percent of approximately 190 million people know Indonesian as of 1991. By 2001 it can be assumed that this percentage will rise to slightly less than 70 percent of a projected population of 240 million. At a recent international conference on the teaching of Indonesian, the Indonesian minister of education and culture asserted that, in 1990, 131 million (83 percent) of citizens over the age of five knew Indonesian, and that, by the year 2010, all of its 215 million citizens will be speakers of the national language.
2 See, among other sources, J. Errington 1985, 1988; Geertz 1960; Keeler 1984; Poedjosoedarmo 1968a, 1968b; Smith-Hefner 1988; Uhlenbeck 1978; Wolff and Poedjosoedarmo 1982.

2 A city, two hamlets, and the state

1 Endhang addresses Iman here in a relatively but not extremely polite style of Javanese I call low *básá* in chapter 3; Iman returns ordinary unpolished *ngoko* Javanese to her.
2 Ignoring considerable variability in household composition, it is fair to say that among the fifty-three young adult offspring I learned had been raised in these households – i.e., older than sixteen, an age at which few villagers are still in school – twenty-nine have moved out of the area. A few have transmigrated permanently off Java; more moved to lowland cities, mostly Solo, where some have found not just work but spouses, and have set up households. Some commute on a weekly basis (as did I) to work in factories around Solo, like those in the Palur area. Others lived elsewhere in Central Java, Jakarta, or as far away as Sumatra.
3 Transcribed and later published as *Sasangka Djati*, these supernatural utterances became the central text of Pangestu, the organization which has developed around this event, which has members in many parts of Indonesia. *Sasangka Djati* has been translated and published in English as *True Light*.

4 This word is pronounced in Balinese fashion, with final shwa, rather than as in Javanese with final low, back, semi-rounded /á/ or Indonesian with final central, low, unrounded /a/.
5 Original: "Umat Hindu tidak boleh ragu-ragu untuk cancut taliwondha (satu kata dan perbuatan) berpartisipasi aktif di medan yang lebih luas, yaitu pembangunan di segala bidang kehidupan."
6 In a longer, broader account, this new temple could be located in the far grander ethno-religious revival engineered by officials at the very apex of the New Order state apparatus. Soedjono Humardhani (1919–86), a confidant of President Suharto, had then overseen (through his son-in-law) the refurbishing of Candhi Cetha in accordance with a dream he had of that site. See in this regard John Pemberton's diagnosis (1994:305–06) of New Order efforts to revivify connections with powerful authochthonous forces in the Mt. Lawu area.

3 Speech styles, hierarchy, and community

1 I have discussed some of this material in J. Errington 1989 and 1991.
2 For more on such vertical modelings, see J. Errington 1985:103–13.
3 For more on socialization in use of Javanese speech styles, see Smith-Hefner 1988.
4 I ignore here deferential honorifics called in the literature *krámá inggil* and *krámá andhap*, which serve in use to mark speakers' evaluations of status relations involving a referent who may or may not be addressee. See Poedjosoedarmo 1968a and 1968b, J. Errington 1988, and sources cited therein.
5 For further discussion of the stereotypically rural, non- or substandard *básá* vocabularies, especially those called *krámá désá* in the literature, see J. Errington 1988:200–04 and sources cited there.

4 National development, national language

1 In this respect Indonesian has analogs in Tok Pisin (spoken in Papua New Guinea) and Bislama (spoken in Vanuatu).
2 For discussion of the politics and evolution of spelling reform, see Vikors 1992.
3 Original: "Basa kerdja ialah basa untuk kerdja, djadi basa praktis jang setiap waktu bisa digunakan. Berbeda dengan basa standard jang perkembangannja mendapat bantuan jang kuat, bahkan dikultifikasi oleh Hindia Belanda, basa Melaju-kerdja tumbuh sendiri, menempuh perkembangan jang mendatar, tapi praktis dan bisa muntjul pada setiap kali dibutuhkan . . . Basa kerdja berkembang lebih meluas dan lebih dinamis, karenanja mendjadi objek penting bagi sosio-linguistik. Dari segi sosio-linguistik, dapatlah ditemukan beberapa unsur jang membedakannja setjara struktural daripada tulisan2 jang menggunakan basa standard, seperti pada: irama kalimat, matjam kata2, perbendaharan, konstruksi kalimat dan ideolek masing2."

My thanks to James Siegel for providing me with photocopies of these texts.

4 Original: "Melaju sekolah atau Melaju standard sering djuga dikatakan basa-resmi. Basa ini merupakan perkembangan basa . . . jang terpelihara dan jang diidentifikasikan. Hidup subur dikalangan sekolahan. Kalau politik hal ini perlu dikerdjakan, mengingat basa adalah alat penghubung antara pemerintah kolonialisme dan rakjat, untuk menjampaikan segala perintah2, undang2 dan peraturan2 jang harus mereka taati. Oleh karena itulah basa-sekolah hanja berlaku bagi mereka jang dididik mendjadi hamba pemerintah atau kader2nya. Basa ini mengembang dikalangan hamba2 pemerintah, para amtenar, terutama para guru, pemupuk benih birokrat."

5 Original: "basa perhubungan jang meluas disepandjang pesisir Indonesia, dipelabuhan2, dipasar2 digalangan2 kapal, dikantor2, sehingga lama-kelamaan berkembang mendjadi basa untuk bekerdja."

6 Original: "Pers Melaju biasanja dipimpin oleh 'ahli2' basa Melaju artinja: guru atau bekas guru . . . Adanja perpisahan jang menentukan antara basa Melaju dari basa pra-Indonesia ditambah dengan pemihakan jang berkuasa pada basa Melaju untuk masa sepandjang pendjadjahan Belanda menimbulkan komplikasi dan pertentangan2 di dalam masarakjat hanja karena tjara menggunakan kedua matjam basa tsb."

7 Original: "Sedjak peraturan edjaan Bahasa Indonesia dengan huruf Latin ditetapkan pada tahun 1901 berdasarkan konsep Ch. A. van Ophuysen . . ."

8 Original: "Sejak peraturan ejaan bahasa Melayu dengan huruf Latin ditetapkan pada tahun 1901 berdasarkan rancangan Ch. A. van Ophuysen . . ."

9 License for this hybrid designation can be taken from the *Ensiklopedi Indonesia* 1980, which refers to the language as Indonesian/Malay (*bahasa Indonesia dan bahasa Melayu*), thus placing emphasis on political rather than historical priority.

10 Original: "Mungkin sekali, dalam babad-babad kuna Tionghoa telah terdapat bukti-bukti jang menundjukkan hal ini: orang-organ Tionghoa jang pada permulaan kurun Masehi datang ke Indonesia telah menemui sedjenis lingua franca Indonesia de kepulauan ini jang dinamakannja Kwenlun."

11 More detailed invocations of a proto-national past would unavoidably involve names of empires or monuments which now count as Javanese, and so could be perceived as precursors to the current, Javanese-dominated state apparatus.

12 For instance, in the newsletter *News and Views Indonesia*, published by the Directorate of Information, Department of Foreign Affairs, Republic of Indonesia.

13 Original: "Indonesia yang dicita-citakan oleh generasi baru bukan sambungan Mataram, bukan sambungan kerajaan Banten, bukan kerajaan Minangkabau atau Banjarmasin. Menurut susunan pikiran ini, maka kebudayaan Indonesia pun tiadalah mungkin sambungan kebudayaan Jawa, sambungan kebudayaan Melayu, sambungan kebudayaan Sunda atau kebudayaan yang lain."

14 Original: "Gagasan tentang masyarakjat bangsa tidak akan dipahami dengan baik oleh masyarakjat bila satu bahasa nasional . . . tidak ada. Negara yang mempunyai satu bahasa umum yang dikenal oleh seluruh

rakyatnya kan lebih maju dalam pembangunan, dan ideologi politiknya akan lebih aman dan stabil."
15 Original: "ibarat orang mendirikan gedung besar."
16 This does not mean that even the highest and most "modern" of Indonesia's predominantly Javanese political elite has left an ethnic politics of culture behind; for extensive discussion see Pemberton 1994 and, in its linguistic refraction, J. Errington 1986, Forthcoming A.
17 "Industrial society['s] . . . educational system is unquestionably the *least* specialized, the most universally standardized, that has ever existed . . . The kind of specialization found in industrial society rests precisely on a common foundation of unspecialized and standardized training" (Gellner 1983:27).
18 "Not only is our definition of nationalism parasitic on a prior and assumed definition of the state: . . . nationalism emerges only in milieux in which the existence of the state [and] politically centralized units . . . are taken for granted and are treated as normative" (Gellner 1983:4).

5 Public language and authority

1 I have also presented material discussed here in J. Errington 1998.
2 Personal communication from Umar Khayam, in Indonesian: "Semua peserta menangisi kehilangan básá."
3 Representative of these is *Upacara mantu jangkep gagrag Surakarta*, "The complete Solonese wedding ceremony," by Suyadi Respationo (1994), which has been in print for the remarkably long period of almost twenty years as of this time of writing. Some other such works, such as *Upacara perkawinan adat Jawa*, by Thomas Wiyasa Bratawidjaja (1985), are written in Indonesian and interspersed with quotations of appropriate high *básá* usage.
4 Exemplary speech may soon become entirely detached from sponsor–spokesperson relations mentioned above if, as Pemberton suggests, the urban elite sponsors of ritual events are beginning to assume the role of spokesperson who, speaking on his own behalf, shows guests "that he [has] assumed responsibility 'consistent' (*konsekwen*) with his position as ritual commander" (1994:222).
5 Further discussion of these issues is in J. Errington 1995.
6 These are opium smoking (*madat*), gambling (*main*), drinking alcohol (*minum*), womanizing (*madon*), and stealing (*maling*).
7 PKI is an acronym for Partai Komunis Indonesia, the Indonesian Communist Party eradicated by the Army in 1965.

6 Interactional and referential identities

1 An obvious difference between them is that *bapak*, unlike Mister, can be used politely without a following name or title.
2 (*Ba*)*pakné* and *mbokné*, discussed later, are idiomatic in that they involve use of the allomorph -*né* rather than the expected -*é*. The nasal segment in the former ordinarily appears only epenthetically in suffixation to vowel final forms.

3 Other markedly rural variants are *mbokmu*, illustrated in text 7.2, and *mboké*, included in text 6.1. More on dialectal variation in this and other kin term usage can be found in Nothofer 1981, plates 129–38.
4 Discussion of intrafamily status within traditional elite circles can be found in J. Errington 1988:56–77.
5 In usage of sixty or so years ago, *ibu* and *mbok* could together be contrasted geosocially with two other distinctly countrified, now almost extinct terms, *biyung* and *mak*. This is an aspect of complex patterns of dialectal variation which cannot be discussed at length here. Nowadays *biyung* is almost extinct – I heard it in use by just one older Mulih villager to a women of about seventy – and has been widely displaced in village use by *mbok*.
6 Já, short form of Téjá, represents a common pattern of name shortening in Javanese. *Lé*, short form of *tholé*, is now a markedly rural form of intimate address to a young male.
7 Both terms are likewise commonly used in some communities outside Central Java, including Jakarta. Suwarso (1990) provides evidence of such usage among students there, but does not indicate whether such usage correlates with ethnicity of speaker, addressee, or both.
8 Considerations of space lead me to forgo discussion of these distinctions in third-person pronominal paradigms, where they exist in both languages as well. I likewise leave undiscussed the increasing salience among Javanese of distinctly non-standard urban pronominal usage associated with Jakarta. See Wallace 1983.
9 The many complications involving other Javanese personal pronouns – most notably first-person *dalem* and second-person *nandalem* – need not be discussed here; for more on these paradigms see J. Errington 1988. For more on Indonesian pronouns, see Wallace 1983.
10 My thanks to Igor Kopytoff, who first used the phrase "it language" in discussion with me of Indonesian.

7 Language contact and language salad

1 See for instance McConvell on aboriginal Mix-im-up (1988), Amuda on Yoruba English "verbal salad" (*adalu ade*) (Amuda 1986, cited in Romaine 1995:6), as well as Hill and Hill on Mexicano (1986:98–99). Buchori's article mounts a strongly modernist, prescriptivist criticism of *bahasa gadho-gadho*.
2 See for instance Ikranegara 1975 on the Jakartanese dialect of Indonesian.
3 Some of these latter Javanese particles, e.g., *árák*, *njajal*, and *athik*, and *jé*, may be distinguished both by the kinds of expressive import they bear in use and the broadly geosocial significance which can accrue to their use as stereotypically rural, unrefined (*kasar*) urban usage. This last observation does not cover *dhing*, which signals that a remark just made by the speaker or someone else is to be disregarded as incorrect. Other syncretic particles not discussed here include *anu* and *wah*.
4 The digraph /lh/ serves here, as in standardized Javanese orthography, to

indicate breathy voicing of this particle. The same sound appears in *lha*, discussed later.
5 Other more fully textualized examples of *kok* can be found in text 7.1 at lines 1, 4, 5, 7, 75, 80, 89, 91, and 94.
6 *Rádá* is Javanese, which might be treated as appearing here in place of Indonesian *agak*, "rather." I have no guess or evidence as to why the Javanese word appears here.
7 This is evident in several Javanese examples in chapter 8. See text 8.1 at lines 17 and 22, text 8.2 at line 4, text 8.5 at line 13, and text 8.6 at line 19.
8 Further examples are in text 7.1 at lines 4, 5, and 17.
9 *Bukankah*, in which *bukan* is affixed with the polite question marker *kah*, can appear in the former but not latter of these environments; note that *kah* is an Indonesian interrogative particle for which I have no examples in otherwise Javanese usage.
10 See also use of *kan* in text 2.2, line 13; text 7.1 at lines 15, 16, 17, 20, 35, 45, 46, and 68.
11 *Lak* is a common dialectal variant of *rak*.

8   Speech modeling

1 I have presented and discussed material in this chapter in J. Errington Forthcoming B.
2 English provides a wide range of framing devices for direct reported speech. For an interesting discussion of colloquial English usage, go to http://www.beta-tech.com/linganth/vercec.html.
3 Rich sources for exploration of this general topic are Lucy 1993 and Irvine and Hill 1992.
4 Similar modes of reported speech seem to be in use in Eastern European Jewish communities (Kirshenblatt-Gimblett 1974), aboriginal Australian communities (Rumsey 1990), and in children's use of English (Hickmann 1987).
5 Easy evidence of their ubiquity in everyday interaction can be found in Robson 1985, which presents examples of modeling in everyday usage selected without any particular concern for the practice.

9   Shifting styles and modeling thought

1 I have adapted their orthographic representations to those used in the rest of this book.
2 The trope of directionality "direct and nondirectness" can likewise be taken as alluding to the relative efficiency of communicative means and ends; in this respect it follows a logic of efficiency of the sort made explicit in Brown and Levinson's (1978) account of politeness through mechanisms for redressing "face."
3 For more about Sumarah, see Howe 1980.

10 Javanese–Indonesian code switching

1 These count as borrowings; see chapter 7.
2 For reasons of space I forgo discussion here of Gumperz's appeal to conversational implicatures, or the relevance of Grice's universalist conversational maxims for the study of code switching under an abstract, pan-cultural model of interaction.

WORKS CITED

Abas, H. 1987. *Indonesian as a unifying language of wider communication: a historical and sociolinguistic perspective.* Canberra: Research School of Pacific Studies, Australia National University. Pacific Linguistics Series D, no. 73.
Abrams, P. 1988. Notes on the difficulty of studying the state. *Journal of Historical Sociology* [1977] 1(1):58–89.
Alisjahbana, S. T. 1956. *Sedjarah Bahasa Indonesia* [History of Indonesian]. Jakarta: P. T. Pustaka Rakjat.
   1961. *Indonesia in the modern world*, tr. B. Anderson. New Delhi: Office for Asian Affairs Congress for Cultural Freedom.
   1977. *Polemik kebudayaan* [Cultural polemic], ed. Achdiat Mihardja. Jakarta: P. T. Dunia Pustaka Jaya.
Amuda, A. A. 1986. Yoruba/English code-switching in Nigeria: aspects of its functions and form. Ph.D. dissertation. University of Reading.
Anderson, B. R. O'G. 1966. The languages of Indonesian politics. *Indonesia* 1:89–116. Reprinted in Anderson 1990:123–51.
   1972. The idea of power in Javanese culture. In *Culture and politics in Indonesia*, ed. C. Holt. Ithaca: Cornell University Press. 1–69. Reprinted in Anderson 1990:17–77.
   1990. *Language and power: exploring political cultures in Indonesia.* Ithaca: Cornell University Press.
   1991. *Imagined communities: reflections on the origin and spread of nationalism.* 2nd edn. New York: Verso.
   1996. "Bullshit!" S/he said: the happy, modern, sexy, Indonesian married woman as transsexual. In *Fantasizing the feminine in Indonesia*, ed. L. Sears. Durham, NC: Duke University Press. 272–94.
Auer, P. 1995. The pragmatics of code-switching: a sequential approach. In Milroy and Muysken, eds. 115–35.
Bakhtin, M. M. 1981. Discourse and the novel. In *The dialogic imagination – four essays*, ed. M. Holquist, tr. C. Emerson and M. Holquist. Austin: University of Texas Press. 259–422.
Barthes, R. 1989. The division of languages. In *The rustle of language*, tr. Richard Howard. Berkeley: University of California Press. 111–26.
Bernstein, B. 1971. *Class, codes, and control.* London: Routledge and Kegan Paul.
Bilmes, J. 1985. Why that now? Two kinds of conversational meaning. *Discourse Processes* 8:319–55.
Bourdieu, P. 1982. The economics of linguistic exchanges. *Social Science Information* 16(6):645–88.

1984. *Distinction – a social critique of the judgement of taste*, tr. R. Nice. Cambridge, MA: Harvard University Press.
1991. *Language and symbolic power*, tr. G. Raymond and M. Adamson. Cambridge, MA: Harvard University Press.
Bratawidjaja, Thomas Wiyasa. 1985. *Upacara perkawinan adat Jawa* [The traditional Javanese wedding ceremony]. Jakarta: P. T. Sinar Harapan.
Brown, P. and Levinson, S. 1978. Universals in language usage: politeness phenomena. In *Questions and politeness*, ed. E. Goody. Cambridge: Cambridge University Press. 56–310.
Brown, Roger and Gilman, Albert. 1960. The pronouns of power and solidarity. In *Style in language*, ed. T. Sebeok. Cambridge, MA: MIT Press. 253–76.
Buchori, M. 1994. "Hybrid language" as an obstacle towards cultural maturity. In *Sketches of Indonesian society – a look from within*. Jakarta: Jakarta Post and IKIP Muhammadiyah-Jakarta. 26–31.
Bühler, K. 1990. *Theory of language: the representational function of language*, tr. D. Gooding. Philadelphia: J. Benjamins.
"Bupati Karanganyar resmikan pura tunggal ika" [The Bupati of Karanganyar officializes the Tunggal Ika temple]. 1991. In *Warta Hindu Dharma* [News of Hindu Dharma]. Vol. 294 (November). 21–22.
Burhan, Jazir. 1989. Politik bahasa nasional dan pengajaran bahasa [Politics of the national language and language teaching]. In *Politik bahasa nasional* [Politics of the national language], ed. A. Halim. Jakarta: Balai Pustaka. 65–83.
Chatterjee, Partha. 1985. *Nationalist thought and the colonial world*. London: Zed Books.
Clyne, M. 1987. Constraints on code switching: how universal are they? *Linguistics* 25:739–64.
Cohn, B. and Dirks, N. 1988. Beyond the fringe: the nation-state, colonialism, and the technologies of power. *Journal of Historical Sociology* 1(2):224–29.
Comaroff, J. and Comaroff, J. 1991. *Of revelation and revolution*. Chicago: University of Chicago Press.
Departemen pendidikan dan kebudayaan. 1972. *Pedoman edjaan Bahasa Indonesia jang disempurnakan* [General guide to improved Indonesian spelling]. Jakarta: Pusat Pembinaan dan pengenbangan bahasa.
 1979. *Pedoman umum ejaan bahasa Indonesia yang disempurnakan* [General guide to improved Indonesian spelling]. Jakarta: Pusat Pembinaan dan pengenbangan bahasa.
DeVries, J. W. 1988. Dutch loanwords in Indonesian. *International Journal of the Sociology of Language* 73: 121–36.
Djajadiningrat-Nieuwenhuis, M. 1987. Ibuism and priyayization: path to power? In *Indonesian women in focus: past and present notions*, ed. Elsbeth Locher-Scholten and Anke Niehod. Dordrecht: Foris Publications. Verhandelingen van het Koninklijk instituut voor taal-, land-, en volkenkunde 127. 43–51.
Duranti, A. 1994. *From grammar to politics*. Berkeley: University of California Press.
Duranti, A. and Goodwin, C., eds. 1992. *Rethinking context: language as an interactive phenomenon*. Cambridge: Cambridge University Press.
Ensiklopedi Indonesia. 1980. Bahasa Indonesia/Malay, gen. editor, H. Shadily. Jakarta: Van Hoeve. Vol. I, 358–60.
Errington, J. Joseph. 1984. Self and self-conduct among the traditional Javanese. *American Ethnologist* 11:275–90.

1985. *Language and social change in Java: linguistic reflexes of modernization in a traditional royal polity.* Athens: Ohio University Press. Ohio University Monographs in International Studies, Southeast Asia Studies, no. 65.
1986. Continuity and discontinuity in Indonesian language development. *Journal of Asian Studies* 45(2):329–53.
1988. *Structure and style in Javanese: a semiotic view of linguistic etiquette.* Philadelphia: University of Pennsylvania Press.
1989. Exemplary centers, urban centers, and language change in Java. Chicago: Center for Psychosocial Studies. Working Papers and Proceedings of the Center for Psychosocial Studies, no. 30.
1991. A muddle for the model: diglossia and the case of Javanese. *Southwestern Journal of Linguistics* 10(1): 189–213.
1995. State speech for peripheral publics in Java. *Pragmatics* 5(2):213–24.
1998. Indonesian's development: on the state of a language of state. In *Language ideology*, ed. B. Schieffelin and K. Woolard. Oxford: Oxford University Press. 271–84.
Forthcoming A. Indonesian's authority. In *Regimes of language*, ed. P. Kroskrity. Santa Fe, NM: School of American Research.
Forthcoming B. Speech modelling and style shifting in Javanese. *Proceedings of the fifth annual meeting of the Southeast Asian Linguistics Society*, ed. W. J. deReuse and S. L. Chelliah. Tempe, AZ: Arizona State University, Program in Southeast Asian Studies, Southeast Asian Linguistics Society.
Errington, S. 1983. Embodied Sumange in Luwu. *Journal of Asian Studies* 43(3):545–70.
Escobar, A. 1992. Imagining a post-development era? Critical thought, development and social movements. *Social Text* 31/32: 20–56.
1995. *Encountering development: the making and unmaking of the Third World.* Princeton: Princeton University Press.
Ferguson, C. 1959. Diglossia. *Word* 15:325–40.
Fishman, Joshua. 1967. Bilingualism with and without diglossia; diglossia with and without bilingualism. *Journal of Social Issues* 20:29–38.
1972. Domains and the relationship between micro- and macrosociolinguistics. In *Directions in sociolinguistics: the ethnography of communication*, ed. J. J. Gumperz and D. Hymes. New York: Holt, Rinehart, and Winston. 437–53.
1978. The Indonesian language planning experience: what does it teach us? In *Spectrum: essays presented to Sutan Takdir Alisjahbana on his seventieth birthday*, ed. S. Udin. Jakarta: Dian Rakyat. 333–39.
Fishman, J., Ferguson, C. and DasGupta, J., eds. 1968. *Language problems of developing nations.* New York: Wiley and Sons.
Florida, N. 1987. Reading the unread in traditional Javanese literature. *Indonesia* 44:1–15.
Fokker, A. A. 1891. De waarde van het Maleish als beschavingsmedium. *Tijdschrift voor het binnenlandsch bestuur* 5:86–87.
Frake, C. 1980. Plying frames can be dangerous. In *Language and cultural description*, ed. Anwar S. Dil. Stanford: Stanford University Press. 46–59.
Gal, S. 1988. The political economy of code choice. In Heller, ed. 245–64.
Gal, S. and Irvine, J. 1995. The boundaries of languages and disciplines: how ideologies construct difference. *Social Research* 62 (4):967–1001.
Gardner-Chloros, P. 1995. Code-switching in community, regional and national repertoires: the myth of the discreteness of linguistic systems. In Milroy and Muysken, eds. 68–89.

Geertz, Clifford. 1960. *The religion of Java*. Chicago: University of Chicago Press.
  1973. The politics of meaning. In Geertz, *The interpretation of cultures*. New York: Basic Books. 311–26.
  1980. *Negara*. Princeton: Princeton University Press.
Gellner, Ernest. 1964. *Thought and change*. Chicago: University of Chicago Press.
  1983. *Nations and nationalism*. Ithaca: Cornell University Press.
  1994. Culture, constraint, and community. In Gellner, *Anthropology and politics*. London: Blackwell. 45–61.
Goffman, Erving. 1974. *Frame analysis: an essay on the organization of experience*. Cambridge, MA: Harvard University Press.
  1981. Footing. In Goffman, *Forms of talk*. Philadelphia: University of Pennsylvania Press. 124–59.
Gumperz, J. J. 1982. *Discourse strategies*. Cambridge: Cambridge University Press.
Gumperz, J. J. and Wilson, R. 1971. Convergence and creolization: a case from the Indo-Aryan/Dravidian Border. In *Pidginization and creolization of languages*, ed. D. Hymes. Cambridge: Cambridge University Press. 151–67.
Gupta, A. and Ferguson, J. 1992. Beyond "culture": space, identity, and the politics of difference. *Cultural Anthropology* 7(1):6–23.
Habermas, J. 1988. *On the logic of the social sciences*, tr. S. W. Nicholsen and J. A. Stark. Cambridge, MA: MIT Press.
  1989. *The structural transformation of the public sphere*, tr. T. Burger. Cambridge, MA: MIT Press.
Handler, R. 1988. *Nationalism and the politics of culture in Quebec*. Madison: University of Wisconsin Press.
Hanks, W. 1990. *Referential practice: language and lived space among the Maya*. Chicago: University of Chicago Press.
  1996. *Language and communicative practices*. Boulder: Westview Press.
Haviland, J. 1996a. Text from talk in Tzotzil. In Silverstein and Urban, eds. 45–78.
  1996b. Projections, transpositions, and relativity. In *Rethinking linguistic relativity*, ed. J. Gumperz and S. Levinson. Cambridge: Cambridge University Press. 271–323.
Heller, M., ed. 1988. *Codeswitching: anthropological and sociolinguistic perspectives*. Berlin: Mouton de Gruyter.
Heryanto, A. 1985. The language of development and the development of language, tr. N. Lutz. *Indonesia* 40:35–60.
  1988. *Language of development and development of language: the case of Indonesian*. Unpublished typescript.
Hickmann, M. 1987. The pragmatics of reference in child language. In *Social and functional approaches to language and thought*, ed. M. Hickmann. New York: Academic Press. 165–83.
Hill, J. and Hill, K. 1986. *Speaking Mexicano: dynamics of syncretic language in Central Mexico*. Tucson: University of Arizona Press.
Hoffman, J. 1973. The Malay language as a force for unity in the Indonesian archipelago 1815–1900. *Nusantara* 4:19–35.
  1979. A foreign investment. *Indonesia* 66:65–92.
Howe, D. 1980. Sumarah: a study of the art of living. Ph.D. dissertation. University of North Carolina.
Ikranegara, K. 1975. Lexical particles in Betawi. *Linguistics* 165:93–108.

Irvine, J. T. 1979. Formality and informality in communicative events. *American Anthropologist* 81:773–90.
  1989. When talk isn't cheap: language and political economy. *American Ethnologist* 16(2): 248–67.
  1996. Shadow conversations: the indeterminacy of participant roles. In Silverstein and Urban, eds. 131–59.
Irvine, J. and Hill, J., eds. 1992. *Responsibility and evidence in oral discourse.* Cambridge: Cambridge University Press.
Jakobson, Roman. 1960. Closing statement: linguistics and poetics. In *Style in language*, ed. T. Sebeok. Cambridge, MA: MIT Press. 350–77.
  1971 [1957]. Shifters, verbal categories, and the Russian verb. *Selected Writings* II, 130–47. The Hague: Mouton.
Jelin, Elizabeth. 1987. *Movimentos sociales y democracia emergente.* Buenos Aires: Centro Editor de América Latina.
Keeler, W. 1984. *Javanese: a cultural approach.* Athens: Ohio University Press. Ohio University Monographs in International Studies, Southeast Asia Studies, no. 69.
  1987. *Javanese shadow plays, Javanese selves.* Princeton: Princeton University Press.
Kirshenblatt-Gimblett, B. 1974. The concept and varieties of narrative performance in East European Jewish culture. In *Explorations in the ethnography of speaking*, ed. R. Bauman and J. Sherzer. New York: Cambridge University Press. 283–308.
Koentjaraningrat. 1957. *A preliminary description of the Javanese kinship system.* New Haven: Yale University Southeast Asia Studies Cultural Report Series.
Kompas Online. 1996. "Pasar 'Prit' Sumber Solo" [The whistle market in Solo]. February 10. http://kompas.com.
Kulick, D. 1992. *Language shift and cultural reproduction: socialization, self, and syncretism in a Papua New Guinean village.* Cambridge: Cambridge University Press.
Kurylowicz, J. 1964. *The inflectional categories of Indo-European.* Heidelberg: Carl Winter Universitatsverlag.
Labov, W. 1971. Some principles of linguistic methodology. *Language in Society* 1:97–120.
Liddle, W. 1988. *Politics and culture in Indonesia.* Ann Arbor: University of Michigan Press.
Lucy, J., ed. 1993. *Reflexive language: reported speech and metapragmatics.* Cambridge: Cambridge University Press.
McConvell, P. 1988. MIX-IM-UP: aboriginal codeswitching, old and new. In Heller, ed. 97–151.
Maier, H. M. J. 1993. From heteroglossia to polyglossia: the creation of Malay and Dutch in the Indies. *Indonesia* 56:37–65.
Meeuwis, M. and Blommaert, J. 1994. The "markedness model" and the absence of society: remarks on codeswitching. *Multilingua* 13/14:387–423.
Milroy, L. and Muysken, P. eds. 1995. *One speaker, two languages: cross-disciplinary perspectives on code-switching.* Cambridge: Cambridge University Press.
Moeliono, A. M. 1993. The first efforts to promote and develop Indonesian. In *The earliest stage of language planning: the "First Congress" phenomenon*, ed. J. Fishman. Berlin: Mouton de Gruyter. 129–42.
  1994. Contact-induced language change in present-day Indonesian. In

Language contact and change in the Austronesian world, ed. T. Dutton and D. Tryon. The Hague: Mouton de Gruyter. 377–88.

Mulder, N. 1978. *Mysticism and everyday life in contemporary Java*. Singapore: Singapore University Press.

Myers-Scotton, C. 1992. Codeswitching as a mechanism of deep borrowing. In *Language death: factual and theoretical explorations with special reference to East Africa*, ed. M. Brenzinger. New York: Mouton de Gruyter. 31–58.

   1993. *Social motivations for codeswitching*. Oxford: Clarendon Press.

Nagel, Thomas. 1986. *The view from nowhere*. New York: Oxford University Press.

Neustepny, J. 1974. Basic types of treatment of language problems. In *Advances in language planning*, ed. J. Fishman. The Hague: Mouton de Gruyter. 37–48.

Nothofer, Bernd. 1981. *Dialektatlas von Zentral-Java*. Weissbaden: Otto Harrassowitz.

Ochs, Elinor. 1979. Transcription as theory. In *Developmental pragmatics*, ed. E. Ochs and B. Schieffelin. New York: Academic Press. 43–72.

   1992. Indexing gender. In Duranti and Goodwin, eds. 335–58.

Peet, R. and Thrift, N. 1989. Political economy and human geography. *New models in geography*, vol. I, ed. R. Peet and N. Thrift. London: Unwin Hyman. 3–29.

Pemberton, John. 1994. *On the subject of "Java."* Ithaca: Cornell University Press.

Poedjosoedarmo, Soepomo. 1968a. Javanese speech levels. *Indonesia* 6:54–81.

   1968b. Wordlist of non-ngoko vocabularies. *Indonesia* 7:165–90.

Poplack, S. 1980. Sometimes I'll start a sentence in Spanish Y TERMINO EN ESPAÑOL: toward a typology of code-switching. *Linguistics* 18:581–618.

Pramoedya Ananta Toer. 1963. Setengah abad setelah Abdullah Munsji – beberapa aspek historik yang digelapkan [Half a century after Abdullah Munsji – a few historic aspects which have been hidden]. 25 August, 22 September, and 20 October. *Minggu Bintang Timur: Lentera – Lembaran kedudajaan Bintang Timur* [Sunday edition of the Eastern Star, Lantern (culture section)].

Priyono. 1964. *Glimpses of Indonesian education and culture*. Jakarta: P. N. Balai Pustaka.

Respationo, Suyadi. 1994. *Upacara mantu jangkep gagrag Surakarta* [The complete Solonese wedding ceremony]. Semarang: Dahara Prize.

Ricoeur, Paul. 1981. The model of the text: meaningful action considered as a text. In *Hermeneutics and the human sciences*, ed. and tr. J. B. Thompson. Cambridge: Cambridge University Press, Paris: Editions de la Maison des Sciences de l'Homme. 197–221.

Robson, S. 1985. Spoken Javanese in the countryside. *Review of Indonesian and Malay Affairs* 19:106–73.

Romaine, Suzanne. 1995. *Bilingualism*. Oxford: Blackwell.

Rumsey, A. 1990. Wording, meaning, and linguistic ideology. *American Anthropologist* 92(2):346–61.

Sack, R. 1986. *Human territoriality: its theory and history*. Cambridge: Cambridge University Press.

Schegloff, E. 1987. Between micro and macro: contexts and other connections. In *The macro–micro link*, ed. J. Alexander, B. Geissen, R. Munch, and M. Smelser. Berkeley: University of California Press. 207–34.

Schiffrin, D. 1987. *Discourse markers*. Cambridge: Cambridge University Press.

Schutz, A. 1967a. *The phenomenology of the social world*, tr. G. Walsh and F. Lehnert. Evanston: Northwestern University Press.

1967b. Scheler's theory of intersubjectivity and the general thesis of the alter ego. In *Collected papers I: the problem of social reality*, ed. M. Natanson. The Hague: Martinus Nijhoff. 150–79.

Shiraishi, S. 1992. *Young heroes: the family and school in New Order Indonesia*. Ph.D. dissertation. Cornell University.

Siegel, James T. 1986. *Solo in the new order: language and hierarchy in an Indonesian city*. Princeton: Princeton University Press.

Silverstein, Michael. 1976. Shifters, linguistic categories, and cultural description. In *Meaning in anthropology*, ed. K. H. Basso and H. A. Selby. Albuquerque: University of New Mexico. 11–56.

1981. *The limits of awareness*. Austin: Southwest Educational Development Laboratory. Sociolinguistic Working Papers, no. 84.

1993. Metapragmatic discourse and metapragmatic function. In Lucy, ed. 33–58.

1995. Indexical order and the dialectics of sociolinguistic life. *Proceedings of SALSA III*. Austin: Texas Linguistic Forum. 266–95.

1996. Monoglot "standard" in America: standardization and metaphors of linguistic hegemony. In *The matrix of language: contemporary linguistic anthropology*, ed. D. Brenneis and R. Macaulay. Boulder: Westview Press. 284–306.

Silverstein, M. and Urban, G., eds. 1996. *Natural histories of discourse*. Chicago: University of Chicago Press.

Smith-Hefner, N. 1988. The linguistic socialization of Javanese children in two communities. *Anthropological Linguistics* 30(2):166–98.

1989. A social history of language change in mountain East Java. *Journal of Asian Studies* 48:258–71.

Someya, Yoshimichi. 1992. Linguistic development in Java. In *Japanese civilization in the modern world VII*, ed. Umesao Tadao, J. Unger, and Sakiyama Osamu. Osaka: National Museum of Ethnology. Senri Ethnological Studies, no. 34. 49–64.

Steinhauer, H. 1994. The Indonesian language situation and linguistics: problems and possibilities. *Bijdragen tot de taal-, land-, en volkenkunde* 150(4):755–84.

Stroud, C. 1992. The problem of intention and meaning in code-switching. *Text* 12(1):127–55.

Subalidinata, R. S. and Nartoatmojo, Marsono. 1975. *Sejarah ejaan bahasa Jawa dengan huruf Latin – dan ejaan yang disesuaikan dengan ejaan bahasa Indonesia yang disempurnakan* [History of the spelling of Javanese in Latin characters – and its spelling in accordance with improved Indonesian spelling]. Yogyakarta: Balai Penelitian Bahasa. Widyaparwa, no. 12.

Suharto. 1971. *Kumpulan Kata-kata Presiden Soeharto 1967–1971* [Words of President Suharto, 1967–1971]. Jakarta: Sekretariat Kabinet R. I.

Suryakusuma, J. 1996. The state and sexuality in New Order Indonesia. In *Fantasizing the feminine in Indonesia*, ed. L. Sears. Durham, NC: Duke University Press. 92–119.

Suwarso, Suyati. 1990. Kata sapaan di kalangan mahasiswa Universitas Indonesia [Terms of address among students at the University of Indonesia]. *Lembaran Sastra* 11:155–63. Special number: *Bilingualisme dan variasi bahasa*, ed. Muhadjir and Basuki Suhardi. Depok: Fakultas Sastra Universitas Indonesia.

Tambiah, Stanley, J. 1976. *World conqueror and world renouncer*. Cambridge: Cambridge University Press.
Tannen, D. 1994. *Gender and discourse*. Oxford: Oxford University Press.
Taylor, C. 1985. The person. In *The category of the person: anthropology, philosophy, history*, ed. M. Carrithers, S. Collins, and S. Lukes. Cambridge: Cambridge University Press. 257–81.
Teeuw, A. 1971. Foreword. In H. N. van der Tuuk. *A grammar of Toba Batak*. The Hague: Martinus Nijhoff. KITLV translation series 13. Original *Tobasche Spraakunst*. 1864. xiii–xxxix.
   1973. *Pegawai bahasa dan ilmu bahasa* [Language officers and Indonesian linguistics], tr. of *Taalambtenaren en Indonesische taalwetenschap*, tr. J. Mayor Polak. Jakarta: Bhratara Publishers.
Thomason, S. G. and Kaufman, T. 1988. *Language contact, creolization, and genetic linguistics*. Berkeley: University of California Press.
Tsing, A. L. 1993. *In the realm of the diamond queen*. Princeton: Princeton University Press.
Uhlenbeck, E. M. 1978. *Studies in Javanese morphology*. The Hague: Koninklijk instituut voor taal-, land-, en volkenkunde. Translation series, no. 19.
Urban, G. 1996. Entextualization, replication, and power. In Silverstein and Urban, eds. 21–44.
Urciuoli, B. 1985. Bilingualism as code and bilingualism as practice. *Anthropological Linguistics* 27(4):363–86.
Valentijn, François. 1726. Omstandig verhaal van de geschiedenissen en zaaken het kerkelyke ofte den godsdienst betreffende, zoo in Amboina, als in allie de eylanden, daar onder behoorende. In *Oud en Nieuw Oost-Indien*. Dordrecht and Amsterdam: n.p.
Vikors, L. 1992. *Spelling discussions and reforms in Indonesian and Malaysian, 1900–1972*. Dordrecht: Foris. Verhandelingen de Koninklijk instituut voor de taal-, land-, en volkenkunde, no. 133.
Volosinov, V. N. 1986. *Marxism and the philosophy of language*, tr. L. Matejka and I. R. Titunik. Cambridge, MA: Harvard University Press.
Wallace, S. 1983. Pronouns in contact. In *Essays in honor of Charles F. Hockett*, ed. F. van Coetsen and L. Waugh. Leiden: E. J. Brill. 573–89.
Weinreich, U. 1953. *Languages in contact*. New York: Columbia University Press.
Wolff, John U. and Poedjosoedarmo, S. 1982. *Communicative codes in central Java*. Ithaca: Cornell University Press. Southeast Asia Program, Department of Asian Studies, Linguistics Series VIII, data paper no. 116.
Woolard, K. 1985. Language variation and cultural hegemony: toward an integration of sociolinguistic and social theory. *American Ethnologist* 12:738–47.
   1988. Codeswitching and comedy in Catalonia. In Heller, ed. 53–76.
Woolard, K. and Schieffelin, B. 1994. Language ideology. *Annual Review of Anthropology* 23:55–82.

INDEX OF JAVANESE AND INDONESIAN WORDS

This list mentions only those forms in conversational texts which are directly discussed.

-á, 125
adat, 65
adhiluhung, 67
agak, 200
ájá, 142, 147
aku, 92–95, 177, 178, 189
ampun, 142
-an, 106
anda, 92, 94–96, 174
anu, 163
arisan, 130
arti, 129
awis, 39, 40

bahasa, 67
bahasa Belanda, 54
bahasa campuran, 98
bahasa gadho-gadho, 98–99, 107–08, 113, 116, 187
bahasa iklan, 96
bahasa Indonesia, *see General index*
bahasa kerdja, 55
bahasa Melayu, 52, 54–56
bahasa pasar, 52
bahasa pra-Indonesia, 55
bakso, 136
bánggá, 109
bangkang, 109
bangsa, 3
bapak, 29, 78, 83–85, 86, 87–88
bapakism, 88
bapakné, 198
basa, *see* bahasa
básá, *see General index*
básá Mlayu, 28, 52
batin, 30
berdiri, 26
biyung, 90, 199
bu, *see* ibu
budaya, 67

bukan, 104–05, 200
bupati, 34
buta huruf, 27

cárá, 36, 50
contoh, 109

dados, 78
daerah, 28, 109
dalem, 92, 148, 199
darah, 112
definisi, 173, 175
desa, 23, 78
désá, 21, 35, 36
dhagelan, 119
dhalang, 119
dhing, 199
dhukun, 141

-é, 85, 89–90, 108, 112, 198
engkau, 92

gadho-gadho, 98
gasir, 124, 125
getih, 112
gubris, 108

ha, 121
halal, 164
hánácáráká, 67
haram, 164

ibu, 83, 85–89
iki, 40, 163, 177, 178
iklan, 96
iman, 175
-ipun, 78
iyá, 125

janggal, 173

Index of Javanese and Indonesian words

kagèt, 152
kakang, 89–90, 121
kamu, 93–96, 174
kan, 104–06, 109, 163
kang, see kakang
karep, 129, 131
kasar, 21, 37
kawi, 33, 68, 109
kawulá, 74
-ké, 109
kebatinan, 30, 145
kelingan, 177
kelurahan, 31
kembang, 59
keuangan desa, 78
ki, see iki
kiblat, 33
KKN (kuliah kerja nyata), 28
kok, 101–03, 106
komunikasi, 58
konangan, 151
kowé, 92, 94–96, 123, 149, 164
krámá, 37–39
krámá andhap, 196
krámá désá, 196
krámá inggil, 196
kraton, 17
kulá, 74, 79, 92, 182
kulá nuwun, 128
kuwi, 180

lah, 104
lak, 200
larang, 39–40, 101
lha, 102–04, 121, 200
lho, 101–02, 106
lik, 90, 133
lomba desa, 23
loro, 101
lurah, 31, 78, 131
luwes, 41

má limá, 74
macak, 74
mak, 86
makna, 129
maksud, 129
mami, 86, 91
manak, 74
mas, 88–90, 135, 141–42
masak, 74
masih bodoh, 22, 27
masih terbelakang, 22
mbak, 89–90
mbakyu, 88, 89
mbasakaké, 124
mbok, 85–86, 199

mbokdhé, 135–36
mboké, 199
mbokgedhé, 135–36
mboklik, 133
mbokmu, 199
mbokné, 198
mboten, 144
mbuh, 145
menápá, 39
meniká, 39, 40
menilai, 180
menteri dalam negeri, 77
mikir, 143
Mlayu, 28
-mu, 90
muatan lokal, 68

nagari, 17, 35
nandalem, 199
nápá, 39, 40
nasional, 28
ndhuk, 124, 141, 142
ndhuwé gawé, 68
ndiká, 48
-né, see -é
negárá, 35, 59
nèk, 163, 177
ngabéhi, 29
ngadi sarira, 74
ngelu, 109
ngetrapaken busáná, 74
ngéyèl, 164
nggih, 125
ngono, 96, 125
ngudarásá, 139
ngulah-ulah, 74
ngunandiká, 139–40, 142–43, 146–47
niki, 39, 40
niku, 182
niru, 143
njutan, 135
nuwun inggih, 128
-nya, 112

om, 91
ong, see wong
ora, 144
Orde Baru, 57
Orde Lama, 57

pak, 85
  see also bapak
pak béhi, 29
pak dhé, 85, 135
pak lurah, 31, 80
pak pálá, 31
pakéwuh, 42

paman, 90
pamong, 150
panjenengan, 49, 92–94, 96, 128
papi, 91
pembangunan, 22, 31, 34, 59, 61
   see also development *in General index*
pemborosan, 101
perkembangan, 59, 60
polos, 92
pranátácárá, 69
protokol, 69
puhung, 21
pura, 33

rádá, 200
rak, 105–06, 163
rakan, 106
rapat desa, 77
rásá, 108
ratu, 16
resmi, 109
rukun tetangga, 75
runding, 108

saiki, 123
sampéyan, 48, 49, 92, 94–96, 148, 149
sampun, 142
sarjana, 95
saudara, 182
saya, 92, 94–95, 182

sederhana, 92
sedhèrèk-sedhèrèk, 77
segá, 21
segá jagung, 21
segárá gunung, 18
sosiolinguistik, 55

tá, 101, 104, 106
tahun anggaran, 78
tak-, 108, 123
tante, 91
tátá, 35, 50
tawar, 92
teges, 129
telur, 112
tersesat, 163
tholé, 199
tradisi Jawa, 67

underpol, 77
upámá, 121

wá, 90
wah, 177
wayang, 148
wayang kulit, 119
wong, 102, 103
wong désá, 21
wong gunung, 21, 22

yu, 89–90

GENERAL INDEX

Abas, H., 195
Abrams, P., 4, 51
accent, 98
addressee/audience relations, 71, 75–77, 117, 122–25, 137, 140–43
agency, 132, 146–47, 149, 152, 192–93
agriculture, 20–23, 53
Alisjahbana, S. T., 56, 58, 60, 66, 95
Amuda, A. A., 199
Anderson, B., 2–3, 7–8, 26, 47, 65, 70–71, 81, 88, 184, 190
Asia Pacific Economic Conference (APEC), 1
Auer, P., 158, 172, 185
author/animator relations, 124–25, 131

Bakhtin, M. M., 54, 72, 77
Balai Pustaka, 54
Bali, 33
Barthes, R., 4
básá, 30–31, 35, 36–50, 64–66, 69, 71, 92, 94, 97, 124, 131, 139–40, 189
 see also high *básá*, low *básá*, *ngoko*
Batavia, 52, 55
Bernstein, B., 62, 157, 162
bilingual usage, 66, 70, 72, 75–78, 80–81, 97–98, 104–16
Bilmes, J., 126
Blommaert, J., 192
Bopp, F., 53
borrowing, 10, 98–100, 106–14, 162, 185, 187, 201
bound morpheme constraint, 108–09
Bourdieu, P., 41–42, 47, 49, 92, 188
Brantas River, 19
Bratawidjaja, T. W., 198
Brown, P., 200
Brown, R., 36, 40, 45, 82, 92, 158
Buchori, M., 98, 185
Bühler, K., 38, 64, 97, 100–01, 139, 180
Burhan, J., 59

Candhi Cetha, 19, 33

Castilian language, 162
Catalan language, 162
Chatterjee, P., 184
Chinese language, 54, 56
Clyne, M., 162
code switching, 5, 10–12, 14, 66, 98, 108, 139, 154–78, 181, 185, 187, 192
Cohn, B., 7
Comaroff, J., and Comaroff, J., 4, 189
conative function, 97, 100, 101, 104, 139, 158, 180
consociateship, 8, 71, 78, 188, 189, 193
contextualization cues, 100, 188
conversational intent, 15, 128, 129, 130, 132, 160, 194
conversational practice, 10, 12, 60, 83, 97, 118, 132, 137–38, 140–41, 153, 155, 156, 174, 178, 188, 189
conversational sequencing, 102–03, 121, 172
conversational strategy, 118, 127–33, 147, 153, 192
conversational texts, 14–15, 117, 126–38, 140, 146, 149, 152–53, 173, 185, 193

deictic transposition, 126, 188
demonstrative pronouns, 39
development, 2, 5, 7, 22, 34, 51, 57, 58–65, 68, 80–81, 95, 184–85, 186, 190, 191
DeVries, J. W., 3, 99
Dewantoro, 88, 91
diglossia, 46, 54–5, 185
Dirks, N., 7
discourse particles, 10, 100–06, 110, 115, 116, 121, 178, 186–87
Djajadiningrat-Nieuwenhuis, M., 2, 88
duplex structures, 118
Duranti, A., 126
Durkheim, E., 61
Dutch colonialism, 52–57
Dutch East Indies, 2, 52–55
Dutch language, 53, 91, 163
Dutch language scholarship, 53–56

213

educational institutions, 20, 24, 26–27, 33, 48, 54, 59–61, 67–68, 191
elaborated code, 63
electronic media, 24–26
epochalism, 6, 8, 10, 185
erasure, 40
Errington, J., 2, 17, 30, 35, 37, 41, 43, 46, 49, 89, 100, 142, 145, 185, 196
Errington, S., 69
Escobar, A., 4, 184
ethnicity, 1, 68, 54–59, 65–70, 72, 75, 80, 83, 91–92, 98, 106–07, 113–15, 162, 185, 187–88, 191
exemplary center, 7, 17, 30–31, 35–36, 44–48, 83, 90
exemplary speech, 29–31, 68–76

Ferguson, C., 46, 185
Ferguson, J., 34
Fishman, J., 5, 185, 190
Florida, N., 2, 67
focalizing operations, 126–27, 132, 146, 161, 193
Fokker, A. A., 54
footing, 11, 130, 141, 146, 174, 177, 188
Frake, C., 160

Gal, S., 11, 40, 42, 191
Gardner-Chloros, P., 188
Geertz, C., 3, 7, 8, 195
Gellner, E., 7, 47, 51, 59–64, 68, 77, 91, 157, 176, 185–86, 190–91, 198
GESTAPU (Gerakan September Tiga Puluh), 57
Gilman, A., 36, 40, 45, 82, 92, 158
Goffman, E., 11, 12, 71, 72, 123–24, 130, 139, 152, 154, 158
Goodwin, C., 126
Grice, H. P., 192, 201
Grimm, J., 53
group style, 36, 45, 158
Gudhangan, 20–36, 44–46, 76, 89
Gumperz, J. J., 28, 100, 115, 126, 129, 155–61, 164, 188, 192, 201
Gupta, A., 34

Habermas, J., 70, 189, 192
Handler, R., 186
Hanks, W., 10, 123, 188
Haviland, J., 14, 188
Heryanto, A., 59, 60
Hickmann, M., 200
high *básá*, 30–32, 34, 42–46, 65–70, 72–81, 109, 128, 185
Hill, J., and Hill, K., 9, 108
Hindu Dharma, 32–33, 45, 68, 70, 76
Hobsbawm, E., 184

Hoffman, J., 53, 54
Howe, D., 12, 150, 200
Humardhani, 196

Ikranegara, K., 199
imagined communities, 7
implicational reach, 132, 134, 148–49, 193
indexicality, 39, 41–42, 82, 87, 101, 116, 121, 123, 126, 130, 132, 147, 156, 158, 161, 187–88, 193
indirect discourse, 117
see also speech modeling
Indonesia, Department of Religion, 33
Indonesian language, 2–5, 8–12, 28, 30, 51–60, 66–70, 72, 75, 80–83, 92–99, 101, 104–14, 137, 155–58, 175–81, 187, 190–91
interactional self/other relations, 4, 5, 9, 11–12, 38, 82, 92–97, 99, 100–15, 117, 119, 121, 123, 139–40, 144, 146, 153–54, 177, 180–83, 186–89, 191
interference, 98, 99, 106, 185
interjections, 145
Irvine, J. T., 40, 42, 72, 132, 143, 200
Islam, 32, 33, 34, 54

Jakarta, 1, 17, 23, 26, 91, 92
Jakobson, R., 101, 118, 157, 159
Japan, 52
Javanese culture, 6–10, 80, 95, 101–04
Javanese language, 8–9, 23–24
see also ngoko, *básá*, high *básá*, low *básá*, exemplary speech
Javanese Language Congress (Kongres Bahasa Java), 66, 67, 68, 80
Jelin, E., 4, 81
Jogjakarta, 2, 7, 13, 17, 19, 74, 88

Kannada language, 115
Karang Anyar, 19
Karang Pandan, 19, 23, 32
Kartasura, 18
Kaufman, T., 99, 106, 107, 113, 115
Keeler, W., 31, 68–71, 117, 119, 133, 136–37, 153, 195
Kelompencapir, 75–76
Keluarga Berencana (Ka Bé), 74
Khayam, U., 198
kin terms, 9, 29, 82–92, 96, 100, 110, 124–35, 186, 187
Kirshenblatt-Gimblett, B., 200
Koentjaraningrat, 124
Kopytoff, I., 199
Kulick, D., 191
Kurylowicz, J., 9

Labov, W., 13

lagging emulation, 49
language acquisition, 42, 98, 99
language contact, 4, 10, 98–99, 113–15, 185, 191
language development, 2, 5, 24, 51, 59, 66
language ideology, 6–7, 9–10, 12, 51, 62–64, 83, 93, 96, 155–58, 175, 186–89, 193
language salad, 10, 98–100, 113–15, 185, 187
language shift, 48, 10, 66, 78, 99, 113–15, 185, 191
language standardization, 61
Levinson, S., 200
lexical borrowing, 100, 106, 112–13, 115
Liddle, W., 4
lingua franca, 52, 56
literacy, 26–27, 61, 67
low *básá*, 40–46, 74, 86, 109, 112, 136, 144, 146
   see also *básá*, high *básá*
Lowenberg, P., 3
Lucy, J., 200

McConvell, P., 199
Madagascar, 52
madyá, 37, 39, 146
   see also low *básá*
Maier, H., 54
Malacca, Straits of, 52
Malay language, 2, 28, 53–57
Malukus, 52
Mangkunegara, 29, 30, 31
Marathi language, 115
Meeuwis, M., 192
metalanguage, 14, 175, 189
metapragmatic usage, 118, 120, 126, 164, 189
micro/macro, 5, 10–11, 66, 190, 194
migration, 19–20
mixed usage, 98, 100, 110
modeled thought, 140, 143–44, 177, 181–82
modernity, 3, 97, 190
Moeliono, A., 52, 54
motivational understanding, 127, 129
Mt. Lawu, 18, 19, 33
Mulder, N., 8
Mulih, 20–36, 44–46, 52, 68, 89–90
Myers-Scotton, C., 106, 192

Nagel, T., 62
Nartoatmojo, M., xiv
nationalism, 1, 4, 7, 51, 56, 61, 65–68, 91–92, 184, 187, 190–91
negative optative, 142
Neustepny, J., 51
New Order, 1–7, 16–18, 24, 29, 50–51, 57–63, 66, 68–69, 72, 75, 80, 184

ngoko, 30–31, 37–47, 64, 92, 94–97, 139–40, 144–54, 189
non-directed speech, 146
   see also speech modeling
Nothofer, B., 191

Oath of the Youth, 52, 56
objectivization, 173–78
observer's paradox, 13
Ochs, E., 14, 188
Old Javanese language, 2, 33
   see also kawi *in Javanese and Indonesian words index*
orthography, 14, 56, 66

Pakubuwana X, 16
Palur, 18, 19
Panca Sila, 57, 58, 61
Pangestu, 30, 31, 45, 70, 71, 76, 150
Parisadha Hindu Dharma, 33
participant roles, 125, 130, 133, 137, 139–41, 148–49, 153, 158, 172
   see also footing
Peacock, J., 150
Peet, R., 6
Pemberton, J., 2, 67, 69, 71, 196, 198
Pendidikan Kesejahteraan Keluarga (Pé Ka Ka), 73, 75
personal pronouns, 9, 40, 48–49, 82–83, 92–97, 100, 124, 155, 156, 174, 179, 186, 188, 189
personalization, 173–78
Philippines, 52
Poedjosoedarmo, S., 139–40, 143, 146–47, 149, 195–96
Poplack, S., 108
potency, 69, 80
pragmatic markedness, 38–39, 97, 139
pragmatic salience, 49, 186
Pramoedya Ananta Toer, 55–57
priyayi, 2, 29–30, 32, 35–37, 40–48, 67–69
Priyono, 8
proper names, 135
psychoostensives, 100
   see also discourse particles
public speech, 8, 30, 46, 66, 71–80
Purwareja, 74

referential meaning, 62, 82, 97
replaying, 123, 143, 147
reported speech, 118–21
Respationo, S., 198
restricted code, 63
Riau Islands, 52
Ricoeur, P., 133, 152
ritual speech, 68–72, 74–75
Robson, S., 200

Romaine, S., 11, 14, 107–08, 139, 161–62, 192
Rumsey, A., 200

Sack, H., 6
Sang Guru Sajati, 31
Sang Hyang Sejati, 71
Sartre, J.-P., 63
Sasangka Jati, 71
Schegloff, E., 190
Schieffelin, B., 10, 97
Schiffrin, D., 101, 103
Schutz, A., 8, 71, 127, 147, 152, 193
Semarang, 17, 66
shadow play, 117, 119, 121
Shiraishi, S., 88
Siegel, J., 38, 39, 65, 117, 119, 129, 133, 137–38, 172, 196
Silverstein, M., 10, 41, 42, 62, 100, 106, 118, 126, 186
Smith-Hefner, N., 48, 195, 196
social identities, 187
socioeconomic class, 92
Solo, *see* Surakarta
Someya, Y., 5–8, 51, 58, 60, 63, 185
south-central Java, 3, 7, 31, 53
speech modeling, 1112, 14, 96, 117–20, 128, 133–38, 140–42, 145–46, 155, 159–60, 173–78, 186, 188–89, 193
speech styles, 7, 11, 35–38, 40–41, 47, 49, 82, 96–97, 100, 158
standardism, 51, 83, 86
Steinhauer, H., 3
Stroud, B., 194
style shifting, 11–12, 14, 117, 137–38, 140–43, 147, 150–53, 155, 173, 174, 186
Subalidinata, R. S., xiv
Suharto, 2, 57–60, 66, 196
Sukarno, 3, 57–58
Sumarah, 145, 150
Sumpah Pemuda, 52
Surakarta, 2, 7, 12, 16–20, 26–30, 35–37, 42–43, 46–48, 69–70, 91
Suryakusuma, J., 88
Suwarso, S., 199
syncretism, 8, 9, 83, 90–91, 96, 100, 104, 106–08, 110, 112–15, 116, 155, 159, 162, 178, 183, 185, 187–88

Taiap mer, 191
Taman Siswa, 88
Tambiah, S., 7
Tannen, D., 123
Tawamangun, 19
Taylor, C., 193
Teeuw, A., 53, 54
temporality, 4–5, 127, 190, 192–94
territoriality, 6–9, 16–17, 24, 33–34, 36, 47–49, 65, 68, 72, 81, 91–92, 158, 187
"they" code, 28
third-person perspective, 15, 97
Thomason, S. G., 99, 106, 107, 113–15
Thrift, N., 6
title inflation, 49
titles, 83
Tok Pisin, 191
topic/comment relations, 160, 163
transcriptions, 12–15
Tsing, A. L., 2

Uhlenbeck, E. M., 39, 195
Urban, G., 14, 126
urban center, 17, 27, 43, 70
urban usage, 91, 92
Urciuoli, B., 116
Urdu language, 115

Valentijn, F., 53
van der Tuuk, H. N., 53
van Ophuysen, C., 54, 56
Vikors, L., 196
Volosinov, V. N., 118, 124, 188

Wallace, S., 199
"we/they," 155–58, 161, 178, 192
Weber, M., 61
wedding ceremonies, 69
Weinreich, M., 98, 107
Wilson, R., 115
Wolff, J., 139–40, 143, 146–47, 149, 195
Woolard, K., 10, 48, 97, 162

STUDIES IN THE SOCIAL AND CULTURAL FOUNDATIONS
OF LANGUAGE

1. Charles L. Briggs *Learning How to Ask* 0 521 31113 6
2. Tamar Katriel *Talking Straight* 0 521 32630 3
3. Bambi B. Schieffelin and Elinor Ochs (eds.) *Language Socialization Across Cultures* 0 521 33919 7
4. Suzanne U. Philips, Susan Steele and Christine Tanz *Language, Gender and Sexual Perspectives* 0 521 339800 7
5. Jeff Siegel *Language Contact in a Plantation Environment* 0 521 32577 3
6. Elinor Ochs *Culture and Language Development* 0 521 34894 3
7. Nancy C. Dorian (ed.) *Investigating Obsolescence* 0 521 43757 1
8. Richard Bauman and Joel Sherzer (eds.) *Explorations in the Ethnography of Speaking* 2nd edn 0 521 37933 4
9. Bambi B. Schieffelin *The Give and Take of Everyday Life* 0 521 38654 3
11. Alessandro Duranti and Charles Goodwin (eds.) *Rethinking Context* 0 521 42288 4
12. John A. Lucy *Language Diversity and Thought* 0 521 38797 3
13. John A. Lucy *Grammatical Categories and Cognition* 0 521 56620 7
14. Don Kulick *Language Shift and Cultural Reproduction* 0 521 59926 1
15. Jane Hill and Judith T. Irvine (eds.) *Responsibility and Evidence in Oral Discourse* 0 521 42529 8
16. Niko Besnier *Emotion and Authority in a Polynesian Atoll* 0 521 48087 6 hardback 0 521 48593 8 paperback
17. John J. Gumperz and Stephen C. Levinson *Rethinking Linguistic Relativity* 0 521 48087 6 hardback 0 521 48539 8 paperback
18. Joel C. Kuipers *Language, Identity and Marginality in Indonesia* 0 521 62408 8 hardback 0 521 62495 9 paperback
19. J. Joseph Errington *Shifting Languages* 0 521 63267 6 hardback 0 521 63448 2 paperback